LOOKING INWARD AND REACHING OUTWARD
WHEN YOU'RE FAR FROM HOME

ANGIE BUSCH ALSTON

© 2021 Angie Busch Alston All Rights Reserved

No part of this publication may be reproduced, distributed, or transmitted in any form or by any means, including photocopying, recording, or other electronic or mechanical methods, without the prior written permission of the publisher, except in the case of brief quotations embodied in reviews and certain other non-commercial uses permitted by copyright law.

ISBN Paperback 978-1-7355943-1-6
ISBN E-book 978-1-7355943-0-9

West Tanglewood Press
Brevig Mission, Alaska

Cover design by Ana Grigoriu-Voicu

Formatting by Polgarus Studio

To the people of Shishmaref and Brevig Mission. Thank you for letting this nalaagmui teacher into your hearts. You'll always be in mine.

Contents

Introduction 1

PART I: Preparing the Soil 17
   1. Transplant Challenge: Getting past assumptions 23
   2. Transplant Challenge: Adequately Prepare. 37
   3. Bonus Challenge: Bringing Kids 48
   Soil Health Checklist 55

Part II: Nurturing the Seedling 57
   4. Transplant Challenge: Environment is Different 62
   5. Transplant Challenge: School Environment is Different. .. 67
   6. Transplant Challenge: Social Norms are Different 79
   7. Social Norms: Try Things and Stay Positive 82
   8. Social Norms: Mind Your Manners and Mind Their
       Manners 91
   9. Social Norms: Community Gatherings 99
   10. Social Norms: You're Gonna Need Some Allies 110
   11. Social Norms: Communication or What you think
       you said and heard may not exactly be what you said
       and heard 123
   12. Transplant Challenge: Logistical Systems are Different . 131
   13. Logistics: Food and Supplies 134
   14. Logistics: Transportation 145

15. Logistics: Law Enforcement, Government, and
    Health Care 150
16. Bonus Challenge: Nurturing Kids 156
Plant Health Checklist 163

Part III: Nurturing the Seedling in the Classroom 171
17. Getting to Know Each Other 175
18. There Are Things You Can Control and Things
    You Can't 182
19. Feedback from Students 201
20. Classroom, Community, and Connections 207
Plant Health Checklist 215

Part IV: Putting Down Deep Roots 219
21. Deeper Understanding 224
22. Removing the Weeds of Negativity 239
23. Meeting Your Needs 261
Plant Health Checklist 274

Part V: How To Know If It's Time To Go? 279

Conclusion 297
Acknowledgements 313
About the Author 315

Introduction

In 2005 I flew into an Inupiaq Eskimo village on a tiny island twenty miles south of the Arctic Circle in Alaska, new husband in tow, ready to take on the world as a first-year teacher. I had no trouble leaving the world of Idaho behind in a quest for a larger paycheck and an extraordinary life.

My student teaching mentors referred to me as "the student teacher who's been doing this for twenty years," I was an oft-requested substitute teacher, and I expected to sail through my first year of teaching with the same ease and success.

Instead, I ended up crying on my couch alone every night the first three months we were in Shishmaref. My students hated my lessons. I couldn't get them to behave, and I felt useless as a teacher. I wondered what happened to the teaching skills I thought I had. My husband wondered what happened to the happy girl he thought he married.

Fast forward twelve years to a nearby village where I've lived and taught for eight years. I'm still crying, but this time it's because of the news of the death of a dear friend. And this time I'm not alone. I'm surrounded by my eighth and ninth grade students in a spontaneous group hug because I heard the news in their fifth hour class.

I went from being a frustrated outsider to a supported member of the community. It wasn't that the environment changed. It wasn't that my students suddenly became perfectly behaved. A wealthy benefactor didn't outfit my classroom with cutting edge technology and resources. What changed was me.

I'm Angie, the Transplant Teacher. I left everything familiar behind when I started my teaching career in the Alaska Bush. For months I was miserable as I resisted change. I blamed my unhappiness on everything wrong with the school, the community, and the administration. The schedule was too erratic. The materials were out of date. People didn't care enough about education. Policies were inconsistent. But I stayed. And I learned.

I'm in my fifteenth year now. Our one-year adventure turned into real life. I love my life in the village and my job at the school. I still have days when I want to give up and run away, but I think that's normal for all teachers (at least, I hope it is…).

I'm a different person than the one who set foot in Alaska for the first time in 2005. The key to my happiness and success has been turning inward to change my expectations and reaching outward to connect with my communities. I believe all teachers have the same opportunity, no matter where they land on their Transplant Journey.

A Transplant Teacher is a teacher who relocates to teach in an unfamiliar environment. The environment might be across the country, across the world, or in a different part of their city or state. You might move into a new climate, a new language, a new population density, or all of the above. No matter where you choose to transplant, it's going to be different. But no matter the differences, successful Transplant Teachers simultaneously look inward to change themselves and outward to connect with their new communities to thrive in the classroom and beyond. In this book, I'll show you what worked for me.

This book primarily tells the story of my journey of looking inward and reaching outward to put down roots, but there are some important supporting characters. Steve is my husband. He's my college sweetheart and an elementary teacher who's been by my side through this whole crazy experience. Our oldest daughter is Kaitlyn. She's currently nine and in third grade. Our son is Levi. He's seven and in first grade. Ella is our baby. By the time this book is published, the ages and grades will be different. I trust you'll be able to do the math to get a rough idea of our family makeup.

Some people dream of teaching in Alaska. That wasn't us. Steve and I didn't even give Alaska a thought until one of our friends from college went out to teach in an Inupiaq Eskimo village. We thought she was crazy. Alaska seemed far away and foreign, and we wondered why she would even bother going up there when there were perfectly good teaching jobs in the Lower 48. We said goodbye and heard nothing else from her, about her experience or how she was surviving for the first semester, until one day in February when she instant messaged Steve (remember those days?). Her school had two openings for the upcoming year. One elementary and one secondary position. Steve and I were engaged and looking for jobs for the upcoming school year, and we happened to be an elementary and secondary teaching couple.

That message initiated obsessive Internet searches and relentless e-mail exchanges. I researched (what I thought was) every possibility of shipping food twenty miles south of the Arctic Circle and calculated food prices. I priced plane tickets. I compared it all to the district salary scale and calculated the amount we could save in one year.

The more we looked into it, the less crazy it seemed (except for the almost-non-existent plumbing—more on that later). Adventure! High salaries! No commute! One cold call to the principal and one phone interview with the assistant superintendent later, and we were in. Without ever setting foot in Shishmaref, or even Alaska, we committed to spending almost an entire year there as teachers.

With contracts signed, a teacher housing unit waiting for us, and a plan to order food, I assumed the most difficult part of the experience was behind us. I confidently headed into the adventure of a lifetime.

My confidence lasted until the first day of school. I expected the kids to be attracted to me like magnets. I was young! I was fun! The students during my student teaching adored me! But the kids in Shishmaref only stared at me while I outlined my classroom expectations. I tried using fun facial expressions. Nothing. I tried to connect to a middle school student with the same name as my favorite college roommate, but the attempt only embarrassed her. There was no instant respect. I couldn't even instantly get their attention.

Things got worse from there. The most used word in my class was "boring." The students said it to my face. They wrote it on their papers, the tables, the classroom posters, the furniture, and the outside of my portable. I wondered if maybe it was true.

Even when I prepared what I thought was a really cool lesson or project, they hated it. I had dreamed of having a first amendment wall ever since my education classes in college. I envisioned students writing things on the wall and holding lively debates about whether they qualified as free speech based on Supreme Court precedent. The discussion would continue over the course of the year and inspire my students to think critically and vigorously defend their points of view.

When the opportunity arose, I proudly introduced the wall and invited the students to write anything they wanted on it. They wrote nothing. I reminded them they could write anything. Anything at all. This was their constitutional right to free speech! They still wrote nothing. Finally, I required them to write something on the wall before they left the classroom. They each slapped something up on the way out the door and forgot about the wall, never to touch it again. All the preparation resulted in nothing but forced compliance and a lackluster result. I convinced myself that my teaching dreams would never be realized in Shishmaref and seriously doubted whether there was anything I could do to spark my students' interest.

Their disengagement reached the point that in the middle of class the particularly squirrely junior high kids ran out of my portable to the slide of the nearby playground. I hollered consequences at them from the window, but they didn't care.

And that's what led to the months of crying alone on the couch. Everything was wrong. Nobody liked me. Nobody in my classes was learning. My high school students still couldn't name the continents. I couldn't find a topic that my composition class had any interest in writing about. My assignment to write a descriptive paragraph about their bedrooms bombed because none of them had their own rooms. I brought a collection of items for them to use as clues to write about the person who might have these items in their bathroom. That assignment made no sense to them either. My students used honey buckets, and nobody kept similar items in their bathrooms because they didn't spend extended time in there. (For those of you unfamiliar with honey buckets, allow me to explain. Imagine a five-gallon bucket lined with a garbage bag and covered by a plywood box with a toilet seat on top. When the bucket is full the bag has to be dumped in a metal container outside. City employees get rid of the waste in full outside containers with a giant vacuum-like contraption.)

I didn't have students who loved me. I wasn't receiving constant external validation of my lesson-planning or classroom management skills. I didn't enjoy teaching.

The bottom line was, I didn't enjoy anything. It was cold. I was tired of eating the same things over and over (turns out the five recipes I'd bookmarked in my *101 Things to Do With a Crockpot* cookbook weren't all that satisfying). The Internet was so slow at home that I could barely upload pictures. The orange water that came out of the faucet had to be distilled for five hours to yield one gallon of semi-drinkable water. We were losing daylight at a rate of about seven minutes a day. I woke up in the dark and walked home in the dark.

To top it all off, Shishmaref had no central sewer system. The school had flush toilets and running water, and we were lucky enough that our little house was close enough to the school that our sink and shower hooked into the pipes. Our toilet, however, was not.

Instead, we had an Incinolet. It was a toilet with a little oven at the bottom. We lined the top compartment with a paper liner. After doing our business, we would step on the little black foot pedal to drop the liner, and any accompanying waste, into the oven where it would burn to ashes. Besides creating a nasty smoke that left our bathroom via a chimney and alerted the entire village we had just used the restroom, the ashes had to be cleaned out once a week.

Once we got a phone line installed we described the conditions to our families. They were incredulous that such a place existed. During one of our weekly phone calls, my mother-in-law even told us to just leave and come home.

It was an interesting proposition. We'd only been in Shishmaref for a few months. We didn't have a lot of possessions there. I was miserable. I slept and read young adult fiction to escape from the realities of my life. My abilities weren't being appreciated, and I was sure I could go somewhere else, anywhere else, where the students would adore me.

The problem was, we had signed contracts for a year. Breaking a contract is bad news in the teaching world, and I was afraid we'd never get hired anywhere with the black mark of fulfilling only three months of a year-long contract. We decided to stay to preserve our professional reputations.

In November, I was still referring to our time in Shishmaref as "this Alaska thing" in e-mails to family and friends and admitting I wasn't sure how long it would last.

And then something unexpected happened. I got a taste of what it was like to have an authentic connection with my students and change my expectations. It was the last day of school before Christmas Break 2005. I had spent all of December trying to introduce my students to winter holiday traditions around the world. We spun dreidels, we made paper Diwali lanterns, and we delivered Swedish St. Lucia Day *Lussebullar* to Elders around town. But, I still didn't know what an Inupiaq Christmas was like (I was however, wearing a pair of beaded Santa Claus earrings made by a woman from the village).

The thought of trying to corral my students into more learning activities made me want to curl up in a ball and cry, so I didn't. I asked them what they did for Christmas. When they raved about the Inupiaq games they play during the week between Christmas Day and New Year's Day, I asked if they wanted to show me. They jumped at the chance.

We shoved the tables and chairs aside, and my students showed me how to play a series of games. I tried them all. I shocked the class when I beat some of the boys at leg wrestling. Lying down side by side with my students and locking legs in an attempt to flip each other over is not a technique I ever heard about in my teacher preparation courses, but it's a technique I tried that day. We used a broom to play Inupiaq stick pull. We laughed and cheered. Together.

The highlight of the class was when we tried to use the broom to play wrist carry. Two of the boys held the two ends of the broom. I sat underneath and reached up over the broom with one wrist. The broom holders lifted me off the floor so that I was suspended by my wrist. The idea was that they would walk forward and see how long I could last. It didn't take long for the handle to crack in half, prompting more laughter, jokes about my weight, and even some literal rolling on the floor from the sheer hilarity of seeing their white teacher break a broom during an Inupiaq game.

It was fun! I enjoyed my students. They enjoyed me. The class period didn't go at all like I imagined it should, but it was still a great experience. And most importantly, my mind started to open.

The magical day of Inupiaq games was followed by an equally magical Christmas break. Instead of going to the Lower 48 like most teachers do every year, we decided to stay in Shishmaref (primarily to save money, but it worked in our favor in other ways too). When people in town found out we were staying, they were surprised and delighted.

We attended the local Lutheran Christmas Eve Service. The church was packed full of almost everyone in town. I don't know for a fact that all seven hundred people were in the pews, but it felt like it! Piles of presents hauled in on sleds towered over the Christmas tree at the front of the church. All the elementary kids had a part in the program, and they were adorable as they passed the microphone between themselves to say their little parts. Dressed in their Sunday best under shepherd and angel costumes, they shyly mumbled short snippets of verses from the Christmas story. It felt vaguely familiar to church Christmas programs of my childhood. I smiled and laughed at how cute they were. After the service the young people passed out the big piles of presents, and Steve and I sat and soaked in the happiness.

We went to the Christmas Day Feast and ate caribou stew in the school gym, surrounded by hundreds of community members. We watched the men and boys compete in Inupiaq games there every night. And every night we had kids all over our laps, our backs, and sitting right next to us.

We ran in the annual Christmas footraces and took part in the awards ceremony and gift-giving later that night. They called each heat of racers up in front of the crowd. The significant other (or "honey" in local lingo) of each racer pinned a ribbon on the racer's chest (mine was blue for first place, in case there was any doubt). The racers exchanged presents with each other, and we put the presents in big black garbage bags. One of the community leaders led the crowd in a "hip, hip hooray!" Each heat of racers was similarly celebrated.

I stood in the gym after the cheering holding a black garbage bag, and community members approached and put presents in my bag. The gifts leaned toward the practical side: shampoo, lotion, and paper towels, but one woman put in a pair of earrings she made. I think a few of my students snuck in a few items too. As I watched my garbage bag fill up with presents, my heart filled too. It was as if I finally felt noticed and appreciated. Not how I expected to, but in a very Shishmaref way.

In that moment, I made a mental note to purchase a collection of presents for next year's races, so I would be prepared to return the generosity the community showed me. And I found myself shocked to think I was planning for another year.

Christmas week was fun. I had connected with the community as a person, not just as a teacher. And I understood my students' lives a little better. I saw Shishmaref at its best.

Life after Christmas was far from perfect, but things had shifted. The first evidence that a little extra life had been breathed into me was my first effort at proactively doing something extra outside of school. For months I had tossed around the idea of hosting an event that would give little girls a chance to dress up and do something fancy. Shortly after school started in January, I had the energy to make it happen. Twelve elementary school girls descended on our house wearing dresses underneath their snow clothes. We painted nails, curled hair, and ate fancy desserts (including mini cheesecakes). None of the girls were my students. They were all in elementary school, but it still felt like a valuable contribution. I was sharing a little piece of me in a way that felt appropriate to my environment.

By mid-January, I was emailing family and friends that Steve and I were thinking about coming back to Shishmaref for the next school year. Here's an actual quote from an email to my best friend from high school: "We're starting to know the people and students well enough to be more effective, and it's good to feel like we're making a difference somewhere." I was just starting to sense the possibilities that come with reaching outward.

I played on a team for the local Spring Carnival Basketball Tournament. I played basketball in high school, but I wasn't very good, despite trying really hard. When some ladies invited me to play on their team, I was flattered to be included, but terrified that they would regret it after watching me play. The Spring Carnival Tournament is one of the main events of the year in Shishmaref, and the gym is always full of spectators. Spectators that might witness me embarrassing myself.

I worried for nothing. The crowd cheered for me, and I scored twenty-three points in one game (which happens to be my lifetime record since I topped out at ten points per game during my short and less than illustrious high school basketball career). Basketball was and is hugely popular and important in Shishmaref, and I tapped into the local pulse.

I served on a committee that founded Inupiaq Days at Shishmaref School. We invited local and regional cultural experts into the school for a week of cultural activities during the Spring Carnival tournament.

During one activity I watched fascinated as one of my classroom aides butchered a seal. I saw walrus meat with my very own eyes. I discovered I love maktak (little slices of whale blubber and skin). I almost froze my legs off on a frigid walk with elementary students to the Shishmaref Tannery. I saw more of the cultural side of Shishmaref. I was wide-eyed and fascinated. I was also exhausted after helping coordinate everything, but it was worth it.

When contracts for the next year came out, I stood in the principal's office while he said, "we'd love to have you back next year," and replied, "I could probably just sign this right now."

I didn't sign that instant in reality. Steve and I took almost the full allotted thirty days to decide what to do. On one hand, teaching in Shishmaref was the hardest thing I'd ever done. There were still lots of bad days. I spent hours online searching for lesson ideas to compensate for the lack of materials in my classroom. We were far away from our families. We missed the birth of a nephew and my sister's engagement because it was too expensive to fly down to be a part of either event. We had a nephew that wouldn't know us or even get a chance to meet us until he was almost a year old. I felt cheated not being able to celebrate with my sister except over the phone. Picking out bridesmaid dresses and invitations was fun online, but it wasn't a substitute for being there and giving her a real hug.

On the other hand, life was getting better. The students started connecting with me (they even laughed with me occasionally). They talked to me about things happening outside of school. The junior high kids and I created a homemade episode of Law and Order to illustrate the judicial process. Almost every student in the junior high and high school took part, and the principal let us show it at a schoolwide assembly. The kids laughed hysterically at themselves and each other (it was a pretty good video), and everybody else got to see that there was something good going on in my classroom. I was having more fun and feeling more effective. I didn't come home and cry every day. I laughed more, both in and out of the classroom.

We were making more money than we would in Idaho. We had

a contract in hand in Shishmaref, and there was no guarantee of a job anywhere else. But, the money didn't seem worth it if we would not be happy.

My dad says I'm not afraid of hard things, and that's both my gift and my curse. That's what led me to Shishmaref in the first place. I knew it would be hard. I knew going in that I would have to live without a flush toilet and my own washer and dryer. Yet, I came anyway. The curse part comes when I take on more than I can handle. Even if a task seems daunting, I take it on and add it to everything else I'm doing.

But I didn't want to give up. I believed I could get better as a teacher in Shishmaref. I wanted to get better, and that was what made the difference.

I didn't want to change Shishmaref any more. I wanted to change myself. Looking inward in this way allowed me to better look outward and connect with my new community to put down roots. They were baby roots, but they were there.

We ultimately signed on for another year. And another year after that. And… well, you get the idea. That's what eventually launched me to a neighboring village, happily teaching composition to a class of slightly naughty eighth and ninth graders.

I try not to check my email during class, but an e-mail notification popped up from the superintendent while I took attendance online, and I had to open it. I rationalized that since the eighth and ninth graders in my composition class were busy typing the fifteen sentences required for their daily journal entry, it wouldn't hurt. I opened the email and read it.

A colleague and friend from our district had died unexpectedly that morning. I had to read the e-mail two or three times to grasp what it meant, not because my reading comprehension is poor, but because I was in shock. Once I fully understood that our friend had passed, I threw my glasses on the table, put my hands on my head, and whimpered "no" over and over.

Memories of this friend throughout our years in the Alaska Bush flashed through my mind, and I realized I had to call Steve.

By the time I had tracked him down on his prep period and sobbed the news to him, each and every one of my students surrounded me in a tearful group hug. I knew those students (mostly) liked me, but I was surprised every single one of them joined the group hug. I was grateful not to be alone. A beautiful moment born out of the years of cultivating a Transplant Life. I wasn't just one of the countless teachers that comes and goes. I wasn't an outsider walled off from their community. I was one of them. My pain was their pain, and we sat in it together. There were still tears, but they weren't miserable, lonely tears. There were still hard things, but I was weathering them surrounded by support and love.

I was wholly unprepared for my time in Alaska, but I not only learned to survive, I thrived. I learned to love my students, my community, and my environment. And you can, too. What follows is a set of principles I learned (mostly the hard way) to make that transition. Transplant Teachers can look inward to change themselves and outward to connect to the people and places around them.

Digging up a plant's roots and removing it from its familiar surroundings can be jolting. Transplant Teachers go through a similar process when they leave behind the familiar for something new. They might have been comfortable in their original environment. They might have been effective teachers. They might have flourished. The adjustments to their Transplant Home might be a little (or a lot) shocking. Transplant Teachers might doubt themselves or question the wisdom of relocating at all. But, it is possible to push through the difficulties and get to the rich reward of thriving.

Thriving isn't about finding the perfect location. It isn't about finding the nicest classroom facilities or the shortest contract day or the best-behaved students. It isn't about working for the perfect principal or operating only in efficient and logical systems. Transplant teachers can thrive in imperfect places!

That's good news because you can't always control your environment, but your attitude, expectations, and reactions are under your control. You can use humility to acknowledge other perspectives and be open to learning. The strength to thrive comes from within the Transplant Teacher as they take the time to look inward.

The inward work creates space for Transplant Teachers to gain more strength by reaching outward. Connections with the community, students, and colleagues provide support and joy. Besides being more effective in the classroom, connected Transplant Teachers can learn and grow and enjoy themselves inside and outside of school. Outward solutions involve reaching out to colleagues and community members, participating in community events, and actively seeking out information.

Looking inward and outward throughout the Transplant Journey is a way for Transplant Teachers to thrive.

The journey to thrive begins before the Transplant Teacher changes location. Preparing the soil gives the transplant the greatest chance to survive and flourish. Logistical and mental preparations present plenty of opportunities for the Transplant Teacher to look inward. Examining expectations and checking for stereotypes, arrogance, and assumptions prepare the soil for growth, as do gathering information and making connections across distances.

When Transplant Teachers first arrive in their new location, they nurture the transplant seedling with gentle care. They acknowledge that culture shock is a natural reaction to new surroundings and social norms. They look inward to decide how to remain flexible and adapt to a potentially new way of life. They build connections with their students and community while looking outward and learning as much as possible about the people and culture around them.

As Transplant Teachers settle into their new homes and routines, they put down deeper roots. They look inward to deal with difficulties and conflicts in a healthy way. They examine their own reactions to decide how to cope with situations that may not be in their control. Transplant Teachers also use this time to connect with the community on a deeper level and explore cultural and historical contexts and their implications.

Thriving doesn't mean you're perfect. Thriving doesn't mean there's no room for improvement. Progressing can be part of thriving. Thriving means pushing past merely surviving or being okay. Getting to okay is a good start (and sometimes a victory in and of itself), but there's much more to life as a Transplant Teacher. Beyond okay is enjoying your life and your work. Beyond okay is feeling effective and satisfied. Beyond okay is fulfillment. Beyond okay is connection and joy.

Each phase of the journey is full of challenges. I don't just mean challenges as in a difficult situation or trial, although there will probably be plenty of those. I mean challenges as something to accomplish and push yourself toward. Kind of like a No-Spend Challenge or Whole 30 Challenge or Couch to 5K Challenge. These challenges are hard, but they're not something miserable to simply be endured. They're something to reach for and stretch you beyond your current abilities. Something you work for because you know the reward will enrich your life in ways you can't yet imagine.

Transplant Challenges are like that. They're an ideal, a goal you work toward. Transplant Challenges can be hard. They can stretch you. But the reward is worth the effort.

While looking back on my time as a Transplant Teacher, I've identified some Transplant Challenges I've encountered since I arrived in the Alaska Bush, and I talk about them in the coming chapters. I also talk about how I've learned to look inward and outward to meet the Transplant Challenges and move toward thriving. I share strategies that can propel Transplant Teachers through meeting the challenges. Some strategies involve looking inward to examine and change yourself. Others involve reaching outward to connect and learn.

Thriving plants flourish. They're green and strong. They blossom—if that's what they're meant to do. They reach for greater heights and push outward and upward. That's what this book is about. It's about growing yourself and reaching those greater heights and beyond. It's about thriving.

Part I

Preparing the Soil

Before Steve and I flew to Shishmaref, this is what I knew about Alaska: it's cold, it's dark in the winter, there's not many people there, and there are polar bears. That's it. I think I would have admitted that I didn't know very much about Alaska, but I still made assumptions. Things that seemed like such a given they weren't even on my radar.

I assumed my classroom and school would be pretty much the same as others I'd worked in, just smaller and colder. I assumed I would be able to drink the water out of the kitchen faucet. I assumed mail would come regularly. I assumed flights would run on the day and time scheduled. I assumed I would be able to quickly learn my students' names.

I was wrong. My classroom was missing any kind of current curriculum, the water came out of the faucet orange, mail and planes came whenever the weather allowed, and all the boys wore similar dark sweatshirts and short haircuts, so I couldn't tell who was who.

I made a mistake by assuming. I knew enough to avoid the stereotypes of igloos and spears and Eskimo kisses, but, looking back, I had no basis for my other assumptions other than my own life experiences. I based my expectations on my assumptions, which caused problems later on as I tried in vain to insist that things should be done my way.

If I'd humbly realized my expectations weren't universal before we left for Shishmaref, I might have been better prepared to handle hordes of kids showing up at my door wanting to visit, birthday party invitations that came as the party was happening, community events that changed dates and times at a moment's notice, and seemingly endless classroom interruptions that included a marine mammal in a plastic tub (more on those stories later).

Thriving as a Transplant Teacher begins with the actions you take before you even set foot in your Transplant Home. This is like preparing the soil before transplanting a tree or a tomato plant or a raspberry bush. The idea is to create an environment where the plant will have the best shot at nourishment in order to thrive. The steps a Transplant Teacher takes before arriving in their Transplant Home is "preparing the soil." Doing this work in advance won't guarantee that all will go well, but it provides a better chance at flourishing.

Preparing the soil in a garden can involve removing items that will get in the way of the plant's growth. As a Transplant Teacher getting ready to relocate, you might carry attitudes, expectations, and assumptions that keep you from seeking relevant information or adequately preparing.

It takes effort to remove rocks or sticks or whatever's in the way. Sometimes the soil needs to be loosened. You might need to find a tool like a hoe, a spade, or some water. You might have to dig or pry or struggle. A Transplant Teacher might need to spend time and effort to replace stereotypes with open-mindedness… Or replace assumptions with researched facts… Or replace arrogance and with humility… you get the idea.

Another part of preparing the soil involves enriching it. Enriching the soil is about adding positive things. A gardener might add compost or fertilizer to the soil to offer nutrients and promote growth. A Transplant Teacher uses background information, stories, context, and communication from people on site. Enriching the soil begins with the Transplant Teacher seeking information about their future home.

As the Transplant Teacher reads, studies, and looks at images, they prepare their mind and adjust expectations. The information and context might prompt curiosity and wonder. It might prompt the imagining of possibilities. It might generate excitement and anticipation. It might raise fears and concerns, but those can be useful too. This preparation helps give the plant the best start possible and prepares the roots to take hold.

The biggest Transplant Challenges while preparing the soil are getting past assumptions and adequately preparing. The challenges are (obviously) related in that if you have incorrect assumptions, your preparations will be based on faulty information. If you blast through your preparations on the way to your next great adventure, you might miss the fact that you have any assumptions at all. Then you risk ending up in an Alaskan winter with a cute beanie with a fur ball on top that does nothing to keep your face warm. Examining your assumptions so that your preparation is better informed is the goal at this stage in your Transplant Journey.

The most important strategy you can use at this stage of the game is *Humility*. Admitting you don't know everything about your Transplant Home is the start of being open to learning more.

When you're humble, you're in a better place to use the next strategy: *Managing Expectations*. Expectations can be the source of a lot of disappointment. If I'm expecting a surprise party on my birthday, and I don't get one, disappointment will follow. There's nothing wrong with not having a surprise party. It doesn't mean that my friends and family are slackers or don't care about me. The disappointment is a direct result of my expectation—which can be reasonable or not. The cool thing about expectations is that they're under your control. Trouble comes when we clasp onto our expectations as if they're the only way things should be.

Research and Reaching Out to People On Site helps Transplant Teachers get relevant information. One option for a Transplant Teacher is to drop into their Transplant home with no idea of the context or reality on the ground. Another option is to take advantage of resources that will help with both inward and outward preparation. You choose. (Spoiler alert: the second option is better.)

Through all the preparation, *Open Your Mind to Possibilities*. The possibility that you have a lot to learn. The possibility that you will find lots of new things to do. The possibility of trying new foods and activities and liking them. The possibility of meeting and connecting with interesting people. Don't limit yourself by thinking you already know what your Transplant Home will be like and how you'll respond to it. Be open and ready to embrace whatever opportunities come.

CHAPTER 1

Transplant Challenge: Getting past assumptions

You might assume that you know all about the place you're going. Maybe you've been on a couple of Alaskan cruises and flown in and out of Anchorage, so you think you know all about Alaska and what Brevig Mission will be like. Maybe you've stayed at a hotel in the Bahamas, so you're sure you know what teaching there entails. Maybe your friend/uncle/neighbor/hairdresser has been to or even taught in your future home and told you all about it. Maybe you read an issue of National Geographic that featured your future home. Maybe you did a report in fifth grade about the country/city/state as part of Geography Night.

There are many sources of assumptions, some more reliable than others. It's important to remember that the assumptions you carry block you from seeking more information. This is where the strategy *Humility* is useful. Instead of assuming that you already know what your Transplant Home will be like, consider that you have a lot to learn and a lot to find out. Then you're set up to seek after information.

There's more than the tip-top of the iceberg

Start by realizing that your Transplant Home will be different from where you've been. That might be the most obvious sentence ever written. The differences might be what attracted you to the opportunity in the first place, you adventurous spirit, you! In fact, your Transplant Home might not just be tip-of-the-iceberg different, it might be all-the-way-down different. Imagine an iceberg in the water. The tip of the iceberg is visible above the water, and a much larger part is below the water.

The Lower Kuskokwim School District in Alaska developed a graphic called the "Iceberg Analogy."[1] The tip of the iceberg is labeled "Folk Culture" and includes things like dress, fine arts, dancing, and cooking. Those are the things you can see. They're visible. They take place in public places. They're relatively obvious. You might see them on a postcard or in a textbook.

The part of the iceberg hidden underneath the water is labeled "Deep Culture" and lists things less visible. They may reflect deeply ingrained beliefs. They may only manifest in private places. They might be so deeply embedded that members of a culture don't even realize they are there. The deep culture examples of the iceberg graphic are primarily knowledge and skills related to survival and hunting, and the bottom of the iceberg says "and much, much more…" I'd like to suggest some things that fall into the "much, much more" category: beliefs about justice, honor, familial obligations, deference, gratitude, and conflict resolution (see the chapter on Putting Down Deep Roots for a deeper look at these ideas).

You may not even realize that you have assumptions about deep culture. Your assumptions might be so ingrained in your worldview you don't notice them. They might have gone unquestioned your entire life, so you don't realize those views are not universal.

Keep this in mind if you're convinced your Transplant Home

---

[1] (2006) Iceberg Analogy. Retrieved from
http://www.ankn.uaf.edu/IKS/iceberg.html

won't be that different or that you already know all about it. You might not even be aware of all that could possibly be different. Use *Humility* to admit you might not know everything and approach your Transplant Home with an attitude of curiosity.

What exactly are your expectations?

Preparing the soil is a great time to take a look at your expectations. Taking time to intentionally do this will help you use the strategy *Manage Your Expectations*.

I want you to actually write your expectations down somewhere that will be easy to find later because you'll want to revisit the list after you arrive. A notebook or journal might work (loose-leaf paper is less advantageous for obvious reasons). You could also record your expectations in an app or online in a Google Doc if you know you'll have reliable Internet access in your Transplant Home.

Open your journal/notebook/Google Doc and answer the question: Why are you transplanting and what are your goals? The answers could range from wanting to travel, hoping for adventure, looking for professional experience, wanting to help people, hoping to save money, etc.

For me, I didn't want to be boring. I don't mean boring personality-wise. I mean boring by following a predictable and expected pattern in life. I graduated from high school and college in Idaho, and I didn't want to immediately settle down permanently in the same state (as lovely a state as it might be). Moving to Alaska to teach in an Inupiaq village was different! It was new! It was exciting!

I also wanted money. Not so much money that becoming a teacher was a poor life choice, but enough to save for a house and pay off Steve's student loans. Teacher pay in Idaho was dismally low in 2005, and even with the lower cost of living, I didn't like the idea of adding to our savings only a pittance at a time.

My list of specific reasons/goals for going to Shishmaref had three items on it:

- have an interesting life
- make more money than in Idaho
- help Steve pay off his student loans

That's it. I'm not even kidding. Looking back, I could have added some other goals related to having an interesting life. Maybe: try cross-country skiing, sew a parka, learn to Inupiaq dance, or eat traditional foods. The truth is, I didn't know enough about where I was going to even come up with a list like that. *Opening My Mind to the Possibilities* that awaited me might have allowed me to reach out for more information.

With your reasons for going and goals in mind, make a list of the expectations that go along with them. What are you assuming will be true about your Transplant Home and Experience? Here were my expectations:

- Shishmaref will be full of interesting and different experiences
- I will be able to participate in the experiences
- We will save lots of money
- I will teach high school level classes
- The classes will be similar to classes I've taught elsewhere
- The students will love me
- I will have up-to-date textbooks and materials to support my teaching
- I will have supplies in my classroom to do projects
- My students will listen to me
- I will have Internet to email friends and family and surf the Web

If you're having trouble coming up with specific expectations, it might help to ask yourself the questions, "What will my job be like?" "What will my life be like outside of school?" and "What will my living conditions be like?" See what kind of expectations stem from those answers.

Of course, I have the benefit of making these lists with hindsight. Some items on my list would have seemed so obvious to me (such as my students will listen to me) that I probably wouldn't have added them to the list. That's the problem with expectations; they can be so implicit and based on deep assumptions that we don't even know we have them.

The process of identifying your expectations and where they come from can help prepare the soil. You may realize that your expectations are based only on your own experience or stereotypes. What you expect your job and life to look like might be completely different from what the people in your Transplant Home expect your job and life to look like. What seems unthinkable in one context is normal in another.

It's tempting to consider the expectations and norms we grew up with as "the right way" and everything else as wrong. That is simply not true. As my high school government teacher used to say, "there are things upon which reasonable minds can differ." There are an infinite number of ways to do many things, and the more you prepare your brain to accept that, the easier your transition will be.

Take the lists and clearly label them "My Expectations." Pack them with your belongings that will be transplanted with you. They'll come in handy when you arrive in your Transplant Home and experience frustrations. You can look at the lists and see if the source of your frustration is that your expectations aren't being met in some way. Recognizing your expectations as the root will help you decide if the expectations are what need to change. It's easier to change your expectations than to change the people and places around you.

Identifying my original expectations might not have relieved the culture shock, but at least I might have been able to realize sooner that my expectations weren't being met and shift from "Something's wrong with this place?" to "This is not what I expected."

You don't have to necessarily abandon all of your expectations. It's more like holding them lightly so you can be flexible. Without rigid expectations, you can adapt your life and teaching to the conditions of your Transplant Home and needs of your students instead of dogmatically adhering to what you think you should be doing and teaching.

Goals can be flexible too. If you realize your initial expectations aren't being met, you may also realize that your goals need to change. You may realize that you want to change your goals. That's okay. Goals are living, breathing things, and their fluidity is a natural part of life. My goals for life aren't the same as they were when I was twelve. I've grown and matured and experienced more, so my goals now reflect that perspective. The same might be true of you as you experience life as a Transplant Teacher.

I shifted my goals during my first year in Shishmaref. I was making plenty of money, and paid-off student loans were in sight, but that wasn't enough anymore. I wanted to be more than another teacher on a temporary adventure. I wanted to know I was making a difference in my classroom by making things engaging and relevant. I had a sense I could do it if I dug deeper into my role as a teacher and community member. I wanted to stretch my branches and deepen my roots. I wanted to thrive.

How not to be humble

One overarching expectation I had was that I would be the one teaching because I assumed I was the one with knowledge and wisdom to offer. There's a video interview with Steve and me in Seattle before we headed up to Shishmaref. I'm wearing this cantaloupe-colored skirt suit and nylons. My hair is dyed and curled and volumized. I'm wearing makeup. Steve is wearing a white dress shirt and a tie. We're uptight and formal and absolutely clueless about what we're doing. In the video, I wax philosophical about how we're heading to Shishmaref to do good and serve all of God's children.

What's noticeably missing from my comments is any sense of what Shishmaref will offer us. I saw myself as the one with something to offer. In my defense, I probably didn't know enough about Shishmaref to have an idea about what I might gain from going there (besides a large paycheck). It was good to feel a sense of purpose. That's what got me on the plane, but I wish I could tell the twenty-two-year-old me with eyeliner and coiffed hair that I wasn't the only one who would do the teaching. Shishmaref would teach me too.

Approaching Shishmaref as a savior set me up as a judge and critic. Time spent identifying and labeling things as wrong or inferior was less time getting to know and understand the place and people.

Similarly, some unhelpful thoughts might include that you are saving the students in your new community by coming to teach them or that you have a wealth of knowledge to offer them if they will only listen to you. The truth is that you may have a lot to offer, but so does your Transplant Home. Transplant Teachers have a lot to learn. Transplant Teachers can benefit from their communities and neighbors. Transplant Teaching is about your growth as much as it's about generating fruit for the surrounding environment.

The strategy to deal with self-importance is, you guessed it,

Humility. It's realizing that your way may not be the best way. It's realizing that you can still learn and grow. It's realizing that all people, places, and situations can teach you something. *Humility* fertilizes the soil. It makes growth easier. It's possible for plants to grow in barren soil, but they thrive in rich soil full of nutrients. An openness to learning and growth will nourish the Transplant Teacher from the beginning. It's always possible to add the openness later on, but you might as well give yourself the advantage right away.

An attitude of *Humility* would have been the perfect replacement for the "I'm Saving This Place" attitude I had before I arrived in Shishmaref. It might have set me up to learn and adapt from the beginning. You don't have to make the same mistakes. Prepare yourself to use the strategy of *Humility*.

Humility checks keep you in check

It's not always easy to shift your mindset to one of openness and humility. There's not exactly a switch in your brain you can toggle between arrogance and humility (though wouldn't that be nice!). There aren't brain yoga poses you can do to stretch your mind open. There's no quantifiable way to measure your place on the arrogance-humility spectrum to see if you're making progress. Instead, it takes time and focus to look inward and contemplate what you think and why. It takes stepping back and trying to more objectively see if you're making assumptions.

It might have helped if I'd taken the time to craft statements that acknowledged my way isn't necessarily the best way, I still have things to learn, and that everyone and everything can teach me something. The process of creating such a statement is what I call a humility check. Humility checks are a reminder to check yourself (get it? check? get it?) against arrogance, assumptions, thinking you're all that—basically any attitude that provokes judgment and closes you off to learning. A big part of thriving as a Transplant Teacher is being receptive to new ideas from a variety of places. It's being open to growth. It's letting go of the idea that what you know is superior to everything else.

One possible statement is "how will this new school help sharpen my teaching skills?" The humility check here is that a Transplant Teacher is aware that they are not the definitive master teacher that has no need to change or improve. It suggests that their way is not necessarily the only or best way.

Each teaching experience is an opportunity to become a better teacher. Teaching a class with little curriculum guidance can allow you to experiment with routines, methods, and skills that are your priorities. Creating your own curriculum also offers insight into the process of sifting through infinite possibilities and thoughtfully considering each element. A scripted curriculum that isn't suited to your students can give you experience in considering your students' needs and adapting to meet them. It can also develop your skills in finding relevant examples and making connections to the students' daily lives.

An especially chatty class can prompt you to reevaluate your attention signal and consistency using it. Students that argue and fight can prompt you to experiment with conflict resolution formats. Students that insult each other and make fun of each other's answers give you a chance to consider how you're modeling respect and how you can explicitly teach and expect it. Classes with microscopic attention spans can prompt you to use multiple forms of instruction and activities to keep the students engaged.

Even well-behaved students can facilitate teaching growth. Curious students can prompt you to provide opportunities for students to follow their personal interests and personalize their learning. Students that regularly finish their work quickly and accurately can prompt you to develop new academic challenges.

Approaching your teaching with a "how will this sharpen my teaching skills?" will help you focus on growth and development. Rather than blaming something you can't control, you'll be changing something about yourself or your teaching. You won't let external circumstances be an excuse for not adapting or improving. As you look for ways to improve, you'll shift away from thinking you already know everything.

Another example of a humility check is "what can I learn from my new community?" Each community has its own customs and traditions. Transplant Teachers have an opportunity to go beyond participating and learning the mechanics of each custom. You can consider the beliefs and intentions of each custom. You can incorporate some customs into your own life. You can adapt them and make them your own. You can enjoy taking part and trying on new behaviors.

Communities also have their own unofficial personalities and vibes. A community might be generous. A community might be forward and transparent with a low expectation of privacy. A community might value humor and wit. A community might be formal and reserved. A community's personality grows up out of the environment. In the Alaska Bush, survival has traditionally depended on people working together and taking care of each other. The interconnected natures of Brevig Mission and Shishmaref reflect that.

Being a part of different communities can prompt a Transplant Teacher to consider their own default settings. A Transplant Teacher might realize that people don't have to be light-hearted and upbeat all the time. A Transplant Teacher might realize that all things don't have to be approached with seriousness. Transplant Teachers can decide what elements of their new community's personality they want to weave into their own lives.

Think of the phrases that result from humility checks ("this school will help sharpen my teaching skills" or "I can learn from my community") as being like mantras. Not that you'd necessarily repeat them while meditating (although I guess you could if you wanted to), they're more like mottos you will return to as you prepare to be transplanted.

Humility checks prepare the soil by removing unhelpful thoughts and attitudes and replacing them with an openness to new experiences and knowledge. They set you up to thrive. Consider writing your mindset shifting statements (aka humility checks) down. The very act of writing in a journal helps me process things more completely as I try to write things clearly and succinctly. It might be enough for you to think about these questions and ideas, but you might benefit from writing them down too. You can even add them after your expectations list from earlier in the chapter. When you pull out your expectations after you arrive in your home you'll be reminded of the importance of keeping an open mind and preparing to learn.

You may not physically see the effects of humility checks, but the inward work is as important as any you'll do before you arrive in your Transplant Home.

Learning from things that are dumb, frustrating, ridiculous or just plain difficult

While you're humility checking, keep in mind that even negative and incompetent people and systems can prompt growth. You may consider the people and systems worthless. You may disagree with everything they do and stand for, but you can still learn from them. Even poop can fertilize a plant, and it's, well, poop. If the process for making staff decisions is inefficient and takes hours longer than it should, if your department is run by grumpy old men (or women!), if your coworkers criticize your classroom management because it's different from theirs, you can still learn patience, diplomacy, or how to develop the courage of your own convictions.

I'm not suggesting that you approach your Transplant Home expecting negative situations and people. I'm just reminding that even when things seem bad, there's still an opportunity to learn. Transplant Teachers can learn from any situation and in any circumstances. You can turn the bad stuff into fertilizer.

Transplant Teachers that rush into new locations thinking they know all there is to know may miss opportunities to learn and improve. Remind yourself that you don't know everything. Remind yourself that every place and person has something to offer, even if the lessons are born out of your frustration with them.

Do: Research, Don't: Expect it to be all you need to know

Fighting assumptions and maintaining *Humility* is a mental workout, but there are also things you can do outwardly that will help you temper assumptions. One strategy is finding accurate information to fill in your knowledge gaps. The information you find will both enrich the soil and help you get past assumptions and stereotypes.

I did not take the time to enrich the soil before I flew up to Shishmaref. I wish I had made an effort to research Inupiaq culture, traditions, and history. I'm embarrassed to admit that I didn't even know the people of Shishmaref were Inupiaq. I'd heard Shishmaref described as an Eskimo village, but I didn't know what that meant or the differences between the peoples referred to as Eskimos across the world.

(Note to readers: Some people consider Eskimo an offensive

word. In Brevig Mission, people use it all the time as an adjective to describe Indigenous things. "What's your Eskimo name?" "I'll bring some Eskimo food." "I can't wait for Eskimo dance practice," so I feel okay about using it here. However, I firmly believe in everybody's right to decide what they want to be called. If an individual or group does not want to be referred to as Eskimo, I respect that.)

I assumed that Inupiaq culture (even though I didn't know that's what it was called) wouldn't be that different. I knew my physical surroundings would be different and colder, but I wasn't expecting the differences in worldview.

It's a good idea to do some research about the place you will start your new adventure. Research can be a way to connect to your future home. Your curiosity will (hopefully) be piqued, and you'll be primed to find out more. Research is nowhere close to being the same level of connection as being on the ground, but it's a beginning.

It can start with a simple Google search. Your search might lead you to books about the history, people, and customs of your new home. You might find pictures or a blog of someone who's visited or even taught there. An online version of a regional newspaper might offer some insight into local happenings. Nothing can substitute for your own experience actually in the location, and sources are always biased in one way or another, but they can offer you something to think about as you get ready to go.

In your quest for information, remember that general information may be readily available, but local information is infinitely more valuable. General information is good. It can give you an idea of what to expect, but each individual community has its own personality and nuances that can't be captured in general sources. I could have read countless books on Alaska without even touching the values and customs of Shishmaref. Alaska is a big place. It's impossible for a book about the state to include the differences of each community. This will probably be true of any other location. Unless you find a blog written by somebody from the exact same school in the exact same community, you're only getting background information.

Research with as much gusto as you want, but realize it's impossible to find all the information you need from afar. It's impossible to verify that all the information you do find is accurate. Seeking after information will help, but don't kid yourself into thinking it will be enough all by itself.

Try to assume as little as possible about your future home, but be aware that you will still be assuming. All the research (outward) and reflection (inward) in the world won't unearth and dislodge every one of your assumptions, but the process can still get you off to a good start. Prepare the soil knowing that you will need to reevaluate and give the plant what it needs as it starts to grow. Expect things to be different in ways you can't imagine. Then enjoy the journey of discovering those differences.

CHAPTER 2

Transplant Challenge: Adequately Prepare.

A major challenge while preparing the soil is to adequately prepare for your Transplant Home. It's impossible to prepare perfectly and completely, but there are likely things you can do to make the transition smoother.

Before we moved to Shishmaref, I owned dozens of shoes. Realizing I was moving to a place where fuschia flowered stilettos would be impractical, the only pairs I packed were dress loafers for teaching and white Nike tennis shoes. I congratulated myself on my foresight and practicality. It turns out neither of those pairs were especially well-suited for walking around in the sand in Shishmaref. I managed as best I could until I bought a pair of used half rubber/half hiking boots from another teacher at a rummage sale. I started wearing them, and the kids around town kept asking me why I was wearing Spring boots. Apparently, in Shishmaref you only wear rubber boots in the Spring when the snow and ice are melting. Sigh… I could have arrived better prepared in the shoe department. Luckily, having the wrong shoes didn't put me in any serious danger or discomfort, but it did make me self-conscious when I went outside.

Inadequate preparation can inhibit growth. If you arrive in your Transplant Home worried about how to secure food or basic supplies, you'll have less energy for exploring and observing the details and patterns of your new home. If you don't have the right shoes or outerwear or transportation, getting around will be difficult and might prevent you from experiencing events outside of school.

Another thing that can get in the way of adequate preparation is the assumption that things won't be that different from where you are now. Maybe it will be very similar, maybe you will slip right into the rhythm of the place, but maybe you won't. If you prepare yourself for things to be different and they're not, you're just pleasantly surprised. If you don't prepare yourself for things to be different, you might be unnerved.

My mistakes

I thought I had done a great job preparing to relocate to Shishmaref. I expected Steve and I would survive using five different recipes from my 101 Ways to Use a Crockpot recipe book, so I didn't bother to buy food items outside of those ingredients lists. We ended up loathing the endless cycle of five recipes and had nowhere to conveniently buy new supplies. We were stuck enduring food monotony until our online orders came in.

I also wasn't prepared to buy the correct quantities of non-perishable items we'd need throughout the school year. Some things we bought in Anchorage on our way up lasted three weeks. On the other hand, most of the jugs of lotion I bought on that same shopping trip had to be thrown away unopened when we moved to Brevig Mission five years later. (I had a similar experience with a stash of shredded coconut that lasted for over ten years, but that's a different story…)

Then there were the assumptions about our teacher housing. The district office told us our house was fully furnished. We arrived to no TV and no microwave. One could reasonably argue that microwaves and televisions are not part of a furnished apartment, but to our twenty-something minds, they were anything but optional. We didn't think about considering alternate definitions of "fully furnished," let alone taking the time to ask.

We had to make do without a microwave and a TV. I realize that sounds like the epitome of first-world problems. And it was. But the transition was hard enough without dealing with inconveniences that could have easily been prevented.

My assumptions got in the way of my preparation. The *Humility* strategy would have helped. I would have benefited from a little *Humility* that acknowledged I didn't know exactly what I would need (inward). Then I might have sought after more information and been more prepared (outward).

Don't convince yourself that you know how you will feel and react to everything. You might have done some research and discovered some potential challenges. It's a mistake to think you can predict exactly how they will play out. When you assume things won't affect you, you do yourself the disservice of not preparing.

Possible Mistake: It really is freezing up here!

A new teacher researching Brevig Mission could easily find out that Brevig Mission is dark a lot in the winter, gets very cold, and is isolated. A Transplant Teacher enriches the soil with that information and at least starts thinking about it. But, a new teacher would be foolish to assume to know how these factors will affect them.

"The cold won't bother me. I'll wear a coat." Okay, but have you ever gone outside and had your nose hairs freeze instantly? Have your eyelashes ever frozen to your face so you couldn't shut your eyes?

Not being prepared for the freezing cold would be physically uncomfortable and possibly painful. It's hard to concentrate on anything else when you're cold. Knowing it's going to hurt when you go outside will likely keep you holed up in your house, preventing you from going places and meeting people. Without those opportunities to build relationships and experience local places, you deny yourself connections and understanding.

A better approach is to acknowledge the conditions and temper your predictions with the idea that you might not know exactly how you will react to the conditions. When you find out how cold Brevig Mission is, you might say, "I've been in cold places before, but I better research what kind of cold weather gear they wear up there just in case." If you find out you need more intense winter gear later on, you'll at least have an idea of what's available, how much it costs, and where you might get it.

Possible Mistake: Darkness. A lot of darkness.

"The darkness won't be a big deal. I like night." Okay, but have you ever lived anywhere for an extended period of time where you only get two hours of daylight every day? Have you ever walked to work in the dark and walked home in the dark every day for months?

The long stretches of darkness are challenging enough even when you're prepared. The darkness can contribute to depression and Seasonal Affect Disorder. Losing motivation and desire to work, socialize, and even get out of bed will cripple your efforts to interact with people and places. Feeling constantly lethargic does the same thing. Your reaction to the darkness might be, "I don't think I'll get depressed from a lack of daylight, but I better find out how people deal with that." Then if you feel yourself getting tired and depressed, you will have some strategies in mind to cope.

Possible Mistake: Isolation is not an overstatement.

"I won't mind the isolation, I don't like crowds." Okay, but do you know that there are literally no restaurants, coffee shops, movie theaters, or bars? Do you know that you're moving to a place with a network of extended families that might take a while to break into as an outsider? Do you know that the Internet is way slower than many other places and at times works intermittently? Do you know that mail can take weeks to arrive, so games or books or diversions you order may not be there for a long time?

Isolation can be a challenge. Without a variety of entertainment and social stimulation, you may end up with time you're unsure of what to do with. Even if you fill that time with books, TV, or surfing the Internet, you may not be satisfied. The challenge is compounded if you're not prepared to deal with it. Expecting a hopping social scene or countless entertainment options when there are limited resources might prompt disappointment. If you know you're headed to a tiny village twenty miles south of the Arctic Circle (like me!), you can mentally prepare to find something to do that isn't going to the movies or eating at a restaurant.

If you don't prepare, or brush the isolation off as something that won't be a big deal, you risk ending up bored and frustrated. A more helpful reaction to the isolation might be, "That is far away from a lot of things. What can I do to keep myself busy without my usual nights at the movies/bars/restaurants?"

Every location will have its own flavor of challenges.

A Transplant Teacher heading to Quito, Ecuador will have to worry less about their eyelids freezing to their face. A Transplant Teacher heading to Beijing, China will have to worry less about a lack of restaurants and entertainment options. Wherever you're headed, the inward work remains the same. Identify your expectations and assumptions and open your mind to rearranging them.

As I mentioned above, locally specific information is way more helpful than general information. Recent information is also a good idea. Airlines that flew into Shishmaref in 2005 no longer exist. Postal and freight prices are not the same. If we'd tried to book a ticket with the now-defunct Cape Smythe Airline and budgeted a certain amount of money for shipping supplies, we would have been toast. So, just as you would with any Internet information, check the date and verify.

Making first contact

One way to get locally specific information is to get in contact with someone on site in your future home. Depending on your Transplant Home, you may need to figure out how to get food, supplies, gear, and all sorts of things. Before we moved to Shishmaref, we knew there would be no Wal-Mart or Target, but we weren't aware of specific alternatives in the Norton Sound region. Before you arrive is a great time to use the strategy of *Reaching Out to People On Site* in your Transplant Home.

After we signed our first contract, we received a letter from a veteran teacher in Shishmaref. She welcomed us to the staff and explained some logistics of getting food and supplies into the village. She included a map of Anchorage and marked helpful locations on it. That letter was invaluable. It was specific to our location and full of current information.

You may not be lucky enough to have someone from your future staff reach out to you, but that's okay because you can do the reaching! After you sign a contract, ask your administrator if there's someone on staff you can reach out to with questions. Or ask the administrator to pass on your contact information to anyone that might be willing to correspond with you.

If you end up getting in touch with some future colleagues, consider that contacting them will be their first impression of you, so make it a good one. Try not to be obnoxious and contact people too frequently or with overly lengthy communications. They're working and likely have lives and responsibilities outside of school. Also, do a bit of research first so your questions can sound semi-intelligent. We once had a future co-worker email our staff and ask if he should get a post office box in a village about two hundred miles away. If he had looked at a map, he could have answered his own question and raised fewer eyebrows.

Some suggested questions are:

- What should I bring with me instead of trying to find/buy it?
- What are the minimum supplies I should bring to get started?
- How easy is it to get medication/specialty items/anything you just have to have?

You may have to alter the questions to fit your situation. The question about minimum supplies will be less relevant if your new location is a city with lots of shopping options.

As far as specialty gear, some of the best advice we got about Alaska was to wait and see what cold weather gear people were using in our community and buy that. We arrived in Shishmaref in August. There was no snow then, so we had a chance to look and ask around before we purchased our snowsuits, boots, etc. Waiting also gave us the chance to buy locally. We purchased sealskin and beaver gloves and beaver hats from local seamstresses. Not only were we supporting local people with our purchases, but those items wouldn't have been available on Amazon.com.

If we had arrived in Alaska in January, waiting to get cold weather gear would not have been an option. We probably would have had to use our future colleague contact time to ask about boots, hats, and gloves.

Another area to consider is the clothes you'll be teaching in. Get this information from someone who teaches at your specific location rather than a district or central office because you want local and current information. Ask about a dress code. Is there an official one? Is there an unofficial one?

Before Alaska, I taught wearing blazers, skirts, and nylons. If I did that now it would be confusing to people in Brevig Mission, not because they don't know what blazers and nylons are, but because they would wonder if I thought I worked for the President of the United States or something. Now I wear dress slacks and blouses, sometimes even dark jeans. On Fridays I wear jeans and a school shirt.

That kind of information is generally only available from people who live and work in your new location. Reaching out to them almost guarantees that the information will be accurate and relevant. (Of course, you may end up in contact with the one staff member who thinks that elastic waist pleated pants and plastic hair clips from the 1980s are acceptable attire. In that case, good luck.)

Nice-to-have items

Removing the assumption that you'll be fine and replacing it with "what can I do to prepare?" opens up the possibilities for how to prepare for must-have items and nice-to-have items. Start by thinking about what kind of hobby or entertainment supplies to bring with you and work the strategy *Open Your Mind to Possibilities.*

Your Transplant Home will likely be filled with new and interesting things, even if you're not exactly sure what they are yet. You might bring things that will help you document all of the interestingness. Photography is fun. Some of the best photos I've ever taken were of hunting and fishing activities in Shishmaref. A video camera or cell phone can capture fascinating moments. Editing the footage can provide hours of satisfaction as you document your adventures. Sketching and painting can take on a new life in a new location. Whatever you do, or want to learn to do, can feature your new surroundings. You can share the pictures and videos with friends and family via letters or emails or with the world on a blog or YouTube channel.

When considering what to bring, keep in mind that it might be nice to bring things that will help you get to know other people. Reading a book is awesome. I'm a total bookworm and have been known to read a book for twelve hours straight until I finish it. But, it doesn't provide me with the same social stimulation that a gathering does. You may not need that social stimulation, but if you do, think of how you can turn hobbies and interests into opportunities to interact with others. Book reading can turn into book clubs. Board games with your spouse can turn into game night with members of the community. Interesting food items can make it fun to invite people over for lunch or dinner.

A new location can also offer the possibilities to learn new skills or crafts. In Shishmaref and Brevig Mission I was (and am!) surrounded by things I once didn't know how to do:

- prepare or eat local game (now I know how to make heart and tongue soup)
- make Shishmaref style doughnuts or blueberry delight (I can make both thanks to some generous ladies)

- pick berries or make them into Eskimo ice cream (now I can pick but leave the ice cream making to the experts and just do the eating)
- cut fish (now I theoretically know how but am still pretty bad at it)
- use a sewing machine to make traditional clothes (now I've sewed a doll kaspaq (Inupiaq shirt/dress). Full disclosure: it was an excruciating experience, and now I just buy them)
- Inupiaq dance (now I know one dance really well and kind of just follow during the others)
- carve (I still don't know how to do it myself, but I know enough about the process to better appreciate carvings I buy and give as gifts)
- speak any Inupiaq words or phrases or read written Inupiaq text (now I can read, write, and say lots of things, even though I'm nowhere near proficient and have tons to learn)

There were and are so many things to learn in my Transplant Home. I didn't even touch on the outdoorsy things. Hunting, fishing, butchering, drying fish and meat, driving a four-wheeler, driving a snowmachine (that's what we call snowmobiles up here). I've probably left out some things that will be embarrassingly pointed out to me later on, but the point is that there are countless opportunities to try new activities and learn new skills. The options in Shishmaref and Brevig Mission are clearly not going to be the same as what's available in other places, but I feel good about saying every place has a variety of skills, crafts, and potential adventures.

Now, you might not be able to arrive prepared with all of the supplies to jump right in and start participating. I might have decided before I came to Shishmaref that I wanted to learn skin sewing, but I wouldn't have known what kind of needles or thread to buy, what size of beads work the best, etc. Giving it some thought in advance would have still been helpful because it would have heightened my awareness of possible opportunities to learn to sew once I arrived. It also would have provided a conversation starter or extender. As I got to know people, I could have asked them about skin sewing. "What kind of needles do you use?" "Where do you get the Tuscan lamb fur?" "Do people always use the same size beads?"

I could have even asked about chances to learn. "Is there someone in town that would let me watch them sew?" "Could I watch you sew sometime?" "Do ladies ever get together to sew?" "If I bought you some supplies, would you show me how to use them?"

The above example is about skin sewing, but you could replace that with any other local craft: carving, sled-making, etc. If you don't know what specific crafts are available in your future home, you can still arrive interested in learning a craft and watch out for what that might be. Keep yourself open to possibilities so you can seize opportunities as they come.

There's a lot to think about when you're preparing the soil for the move to your Transplant Home. Being overwhelmed is normal, especially in the face of so much unknown. Let the overwhelm nudge you to take action rather than make you throw your hands up in the air and do nothing. You can adequately prepare even if you can't perfectly prepare, so make a reasonable effort and be ready to adapt to the unexpected.

CHAPTER 3

Bonus Challenge: Bringing Kids

We grew our family while in Alaska, but some readers may have ready-made families to start their new lives! Bringing kids along is a Bonus Transplant Challenge. And it's not just physically bringing kids with you, it's bringing them along on the inward journey as well.

Preparing kids for what will be different is essential. It's also tricky because you won't be able to tell them exactly what will be different. Kids will have their own set of expectations about your Transplant Home. You might assume you know what they expect, but you might be wrong.

Ask your kids about their expectations. What do you think it will be like? What are you looking forward to? What makes you nervous? What do you think school will be like? What do you think your new bedroom will be like? You might be able to help them adjust their expectations, and they might bring up issues you haven't even thought about.

These discussions could be a good starting point for you to share some of your research. You may have a few things to offer them from things you've found online or correspondence you've had with your future colleagues. The new information can help your kids *Examine Their Expectations*. They might see that their expectations don't match what they see from your research. They might start to wrap their heads around what they'll have to adjust to. Just looking inward to think about the differences ahead of time will make them more ready to explore and accept/examine/adjust to their Transplant Reality.

An important message to get across is that different isn't necessarily better or worse. This is the same *Humility* strategy you used earlier in the chapter. Think of it the same way you would explain differences in your former home. If your child saw a family with different skin color, it wouldn't be "bad" or "good," it would just be different. The same would be true for a child dressed differently, of a different religion, etc.

Here's a little Alston Family Example. Our faith prohibits drinking coffee. Coffee is ubiquitous in our region. When our kids ask why Daddy and I don't drink coffee or why so-and-so does, we just explain that we believe coffee isn't good for our bodies, so we don't drink it. So-and-so doesn't believe that, so she drinks coffee. We're all doing what we think is right.

That explanation has worked so far. The kids are satisfied with the answer, and we haven't vilified anyone who does something different from us. (We'll see how it works when they get older.)

Another way to help your kids prepare mentally is to help them *Open Their Minds to Possibilities*. I wouldn't frame it in those exact words because it might sound kind of lame, but you might be able to come up with something catchy and fun.

- What new things will we discover?
- What will we add to our Cool Things List?
- What will we add to our New Foods List?

Maybe frame the activity as going on a mission (not the church kind) to find out as much as possible about your Transplant Home. The YouTube videos you watch and images you search online can be intel that prepares you for the mission. Or, you can be explorers getting ready to go on an adventure to experience all they can in the Transplant Home.

Those ideas are definitely more suited to elementary school-aged kids, but you could come up with something for older kids too. Maybe get ready to make a list of one hundred things different about your new home. Or one hundred new foods to try. Or a mini bucket list of experiences with room to add more items once you're on location. You could even do a reverse bucket list and keep track of all the bucket list-worthy experiences you have once you arrive.

Whatever you do, set the experience up as one full of opportunities and wonder. *Open Your Kids' Minds to Possibilities*, just as you're opening your own. It won't completely protect them from culture shock and homesickness, but it can set them up internally to better deal with those challenges.

Reaching Out to Someone On Site can make a big difference in outward preparation. For example, if you're corresponding with someone from your future home, it would be helpful to ask what kids do for fun, so your kids can arrive prepared. Almost every kid in Brevig Mission has a bike, and kids spend every moment during nice weather on their bikes. If I was advising new teachers with children on what to bring up or have shipped in, I would definitely put bikes on the list. Then the kids could hit the ground pedaling with all the other kids in town. Do kids kick soccer balls all around town? Are they nuts about collecting friendship bracelets? Marbles? Cards? Do they play basketball? Arriving prepared with the right toys/equipment can give your kids an easy way to interact immediately.

Take the time to feel out what your kids are worried about. They might be less concerned with how many Ziploc bags to bring or whether you'll be able to buy flavored toothpaste, but they'll have their own concerns. Find out what your kids need to feel safe and happy. Our daughter wouldn't even think about going anywhere without her purple unicorn. Other things might be important to your kids. Favorite books, toys, breakfast cereal. Whatever it is, find out how to get it or bring some along to preserve at least a little of the familiar.

Whatever you're doing to prepare for the move to your Transplant Home, involve your kids. They don't have to stand by your side as you box up your household goods or sell your house (unless they're really helpful at those things), but they need the soil prepared for them just as you do. The inward preparation you do together will help them sort through expectations and prepare for all the differences. The outward preparation will give them a foothold to make connections. You want your kids to thrive too, and the work you do ahead of time can help set them up for that.

Transplant Teacher Bulletin: Don't forget inward preparation!!!

This break in our regularly scheduled programming is to emphasize (and re-emphasize) the importance of inwardly preparing for a new place with new cultural and institutional norms.

Don't assume the only thing you'll need help with is logistics. Teachers can arrive in Shishmaref and Brevig Mission with top-notch winter gear and a solid supply of food and household goods and still be miserable. The logistics of food and gear is important, but it's not the only aspect of Transplant Teacher life that requires preparation. An attitude of *Humility* and a realization that expectations are not universal will be extremely valuable as a Transplant Teacher.

As Steve and I prepared to head up to Shishmaref, I was in regular contact with our friend from college and the veteran teacher who reached out to us after we signed contracts and sent us the map. They both graciously answered our questions and provided us with guidance. The questions I asked were primarily about logistics. I wanted to know how to get food and supplies. I wanted to know the cost and availability of local goods. I wanted to know about teacher housing and what household supplies to bring.

All of that information was great! We arrived in Shishmaref with a stock of food and supplies, and we weren't surprised by what our house looked like (although I was surprised that we had an incinolet toilet instead of a honey bucket).

Never once did I ask about the teaching. I wish I had asked at least one question: What should I do to prepare myself for the teaching? I could have asked other questions about my responsibilities: What are the students like? How do they react to new teachers? What materials are in my classroom? Are computers and internet access available for student use? But, that one question about preparing myself for the teaching would have gone a long way to help me begin to shift my mindset.

I've communicated with new teachers before they've come up to Brevig Mission. I usually tell my principal to offer new hires my email address if they have questions. I'm grateful to the Shishmaref teachers who patiently gave me advice for my journey up to Alaska, and I want to do the same thing for others. Our conversations usually center on logistics. I explain their options for shopping and how to get food and supplies sent to Brevig Mission. I tell them the baggage and weight limits on the different airlines. I recommend which items to bring from the Lower 48 and which to buy in Anchorage.

I think I will start offering a piece of advice about the teaching. It's a statement I wish I had pondered before I moved up to the Alaska Bush to begin my career:

Be ready to adapt your teaching to the needs of the students. Be ready to make local connections to the content so it's relevant to the kids and their lives.

We'll talk more about that concept later, but for now, just know that it would have helped me transition to a new teaching life. It might help you too.

If you have an opportunity to visit with any of the teachers in your future Transplant Home, here's a list of sample questions you might ask that will help you move beyond logistics:

- What do adults do for fun?
- What do kids do for fun?
- What do adults talk about when they're not talking about school or work?
- What do kids talk about when they're not talking about school?
- How do people use their spare time?
- Where does the community gather?
- What kind of school events are available and best attended?
- What kinds of skills are passed from parents to children?
- What does the community celebrate (formally and informally)?
- What is the composition of households?
- What kinds of things do people laugh at?
- How connected does the community feel to surrounding communities/villages/cities/etc?

Give yourself the benefit of inward preparation. In the frenzy to pack and plan, take some time to ponder. Warm gloves and peanut butter may be important, but taking stock of your perceptions and expectations will help you approach your planning and arrival with greater awareness.

Soil Health Checklist

Parts I, II, III, and IV have checklists at the end for a Transplant Teacher to use to gauge how things are going. The checklists aren't the only gospel-truth way to know if things are going well or not, but they're at least a start. The following checklist is about taking stock of the soil.

Signs of Health

- ☐ I research and seek more information. I don't try to know everything (it's impossible to anyway), but I look for multiple sources and perspectives to prepare my brain for the transplant.

- ☐ I do some cursory research about food, supplies, and transportation (so I don't look like an idiot when I ask a real human being questions).

- ☐ I ask questions beyond how to get pop-tarts and garbage bags because food and logistics are important, but they're only part of the preparation a Transplant Teacher needs to make.

- ☐ I list my expectations about my job and life, even things as basic as "I will have a working copier" and "potable water will come out of my faucet."

- ☐ I conduct humility checks against arrogance and assumptions and know I have lots to learn and lots of people and places to learn from. I avoid thinking of myself as a superhero swooping down to save the people in my Transplant Home (no matter how good I look in tights and a cape).

Warning Signs:

- ☐ I don't even do a google search of my Transplant Home. "How different could it be?"

- ☐ I assume I already know what to expect about life in my Transplant Home. "I saw a show once on National Geographic."

- ☐ I assume everyone will share my expectations. "My worldview is right, obviously."

- ☐ I assume I am the one that will do all the teaching/saving/insert any patronizing verb here. "This place is so lucky to have me."

- ☐ I only ask questions related to food or plane tickets. "There's nothing else I really need to know."

Part II

Nurturing the Seedling

Three days before the start of New Teacher Orientation, Steve and I flew up to Alaska out of Seattle. We took Alaska Airlines to Anchorage, picked up our rental car, and headed straight to Wal-Mart and Sam's Club to buy as many supplies as we could.

After a night of packing boxes in the post office parking lot until two or three in the morning, Steve and I woke up exhausted to catch our plane to Nome. We landed in Nome to grey skies and rain. Amidst the flurry of passengers surrounding the baggage claim, we somehow ended up in a Bering Air van with our suitcases. I honestly don't remember how we got there or how we knew we were supposed to be there. It just happened.

We tripped up to the check-in desk and handed over our bags. A while later the pilot called out, "Shishmaref," and we followed him outside to the plane.

The flight took about an hour. All I could see out of the window was tundra. Steve didn't really see anything out of his window because he had a splitting headache and kept his eyes closed most of the time while holding a pillow.

I think I was expecting someone to meet us at the airport, greet us by name, and welcome us to Shishmaref. That didn't happen.

Instead, we stepped off the plane to no one. The pilot tossed our suitcases onto the ground as he unloaded the rest of the freight. Then he got back in the plane, taxied down the runway, and took off.

I looked around. Did they forget we were coming? Did they even know we were coming? Were we supposed to know what to do? We had a plan for getting to Alaska and shopping in Anchorage on our way, but our plan ended there. We had assumed someone would take over once we landed in Shishmaref.

We picked up our bags and started walking toward town. We were eventually met by one of the school maintenance workers who put our bags on his four-wheeler and drove us the rest of the way. I spent the short ride to town trying to hang on. We weren't going very fast, but I had limited experience riding four-wheelers in the first place and had never ridden on the back of one.

By the time we stopped near the school I had mostly gotten over the fact that on one had been there to meet us at the airport. I chalked it up to some miscommunication and was just grateful we were no longer standing at the airport alone.

Then they didn't know what house we would be in. Apparently, the apartment we were supposed to move into didn't get remodeled over the summer, so they were scrambling to shift things around so we had a place to live. The administrators unlocked a house near the school and told us, "Just put your bags here for now."

I wanted to unpack. I wanted to get settled, but for a few hours I didn't even get that. I was tired. I was hungry. And I was temporarily homeless.

I had a choice in those moments. Was I going to be offended? Was I going to write off my Transplant Home and my new colleagues as disorganized and incompetent? Was I going to start life in my Transplant Home with a metaphorical sour taste in my mouth? Or was I going to find out more about what Shishmaref offered and nurture curiosity and positivity.

Setting foot in your new location is an important moment. It's the moment you're set in the soil of your new home. It's the moment when preparation is past. It's the beginning of putting down roots.

The differences in your Transplant Home might be obvious from the second you step off the plane (or train or boat or bus…). Or, they might be less obvious, but there will certainly be things to discover. When you first arrive is a great time to start soaking in all the differences and features that make your Transplant Home unique.

I call the time when the Transplant Teacher arrives the Nurture the Seedling phase. This is when the teacher is placed into the (hopefully prepared) soil and begins to grow. As a seedling, a plant needs care and protection. It needs to be nourished and treated gently. So it is with a Transplant Teacher. Dropping into a new place can be traumatic or overwhelming, but with the proper care, the Transplant Teacher can begin to thrive.

The primary challenge during the Nurturing the Seedling phase is that things are different, really different. The specifics of this different-ness will vary based on where you transplant. The food might be different. The language might be different. Gender roles might be different. Transportation might be different. All of the above might be different!

There are a variety of solutions to this challenge. The chapters that follow will dive into a different one and offer ideas that will help you nourish your seedling and weather the challenges of everything (or most things or some things) being different.

Remember that different isn't necessarily better or worse. Sometimes it's just different. Different can be overwhelming, but it can also be exciting and fun. The next pages aren't exactly a comprehensive field guide, but they might help you navigate the different in a positive way.

CHAPTER 4

Transplant Challenge: Environment is Different

One of the most obvious things about Brevig Mission and Shishmaref is that there are no roads in and out. Both villages can only be reached by plane or boat. Regional airlines fly to the villages multiple times a day bringing passengers, mail, and freight. (Fun fact: the first time we flew into the Shishmaref, the entire left side of the plane was filled with Top Ramen and soda pop for the store.) You'll be flying over vast stretches of tundra and, boom, a village will pop up, seemingly out of nowhere. Brevig Mission has a neighboring village about six miles away, but Shishmaref is on its own coastal island many miles from any other community.

When you land at the "airport" in Brevig Mission or Shishmaref, you're greeted by a tall garage for the snowplow. I put airport in quotation marks because the garage is the only thing there. There are no chairs to sit in while you wait for your flight, no screen telling you if the flight is on time or delayed, and no place to put your baggage other than the ground. This would be quite a shock to a Transplant Teacher who had only experienced airports that provide a place to buy a latte and a magazine before sitting down and charging their phone.

Most flights are greeted by agents that work with the airline, family members picking up arriving passengers, and people waiting to get on the return flight. Baggage gets unloaded from the cargo holds and tossed on the ground. Arriving passengers pick up their luggage and toss it on the back of four-wheelers or in sleds behind snowmobiles before heading home.

Most of the airline agents give rides to people without one, and a Transplant Teacher could likely get a ride into town. Heading through town the Transplant Teacher would notice no street signs, no stoplights (although Brevig Mission does have a few stop signs!), and almost no cars (there are three trucks in town. One belongs to the school).

Like me, you probably realize the environment in your Transplant Home will be different. When I say *environment* I mean the surroundings, including the weather and nature, but also the buildings and traffic. Basically, what you see when you walk around.

You'll need to figure out how to deal with these differences. When faced with the cold in Shishmaref and Brevig Mission, it would be futile to say "it shouldn't be this cold" or "I need it to be warmer." That wouldn't change anything. You don't have control over the weather. Your energy would be better spent finding out what kind of gear protects against the cold and borrowing or ordering some. Likewise, when observing how neighborhoods are organized, streets are named, or materials are stored. It doesn't do any good to insist it should be different. Just figure out how to deal with the way things are.

The most important strategy to use with environmental differences (and any differences, really) is to *Withhold Judgment*. My favorite phrase about withholding judgment is "just because you grew up that way doesn't mean it's the right way." Sometimes we think our traditions, habits, etc. are normal and everything else is strange. Sometimes we label the different things as wrong or bad. It doesn't actually work that way. What's outrageous and shocking in one place might be mainstream in another. What is ho-hum hum-drum in your hometown might be unheard of somewhere else.

If Transplant Teachers judge everything based solely on their own backgrounds and worldviews, they'll miss out on understanding and risk functioning awkwardly in their Transplant Home. This strategy is about resisting the urge to issue knee-jerk judgments and instead learn and understand.

Which leads to another important outward strategy: *Explore and Find Out More*. Your Transplant Home will be bursting with things to discover. Taking the time to do that can inform your understanding and lead to opportunities to do and experience more. Taking the time to explore on a deeper level will enhance and multiply those opportunities.

Transplant Teachers can also *Focus on What You Can Control*. This is another all-purpose strategy that fits countless circumstances. There are things you can control and things you can't. Figuring out the difference can save you from uselessly butting your head against something that's not going to change. Save that energy for things you can control.

Some environmental features of your Transplant Home will seem curious and interesting, but others might provoke knee-jerk judgment. It's in these instances that the strategies will be most useful.

For example, one notable feature of the environment in Brevig Mission and Shishmaref is that kids are everywhere outside. Even two-year-olds wander the dirt roads in little clusters, playing together. At first it horrified me to see children so young playing outside unsupervised.

This was an opportunity to *Withhold Judgment*. Seeing the little kids outside instantly made me think adults were being negligent and irresponsible. I saw a situation different from how I grew up, and I labeled it negatively.

Eventually I realized the less obvious truth that community members possess an inherent trust in the environment and community that allows kids to play outside by themselves. Everything will be okay because there's always an adult or teenager nearby to help out. Almost everybody in the village is connected by blood or friendship, and they watch out for each other's kids. If I can't find Levi when he is supposed to play close to the house, I just stick my head out the door and ask the nearest person if they've seen him. Usually it only takes one or two people before I can find out exactly where he is and which buddies he is with.

Another obvious feature of both Shishmaref and Brevig Mission is broken-down vehicles around town. Old snow machines (snowmobiles) and four-wheelers are scattered between houses in various states of disrepair. My initial judgmental thought was, "Gross! Why don't they throw those away?" According to my expectations, the vehicles belonged in the dump. This would have been a great opportunity to *Find Out More*. I eventually learned that old vehicles are important sources of replacement parts, so they're kept close to the house for needed repairs. In a place without a parts replacement store down the street, that makes sense.

A walking tour of Brevig Mission would make obvious the lack of any place to order coffee or prepared food. This could easily be seen as a downside to living in Brevig Mission. But, as a Transplant Teacher took the time to *Explore and Find Out More*, they would realize the less obvious up side is the fact that you could walk into anybody's house and be offered coffee (and food if it's meal time!).

(Note to readers: I'm not advocating you use the generosity of others as a restaurant replacement. Visiting people purposely at mealtime so you can get free food seems rude, unless you're really hard up for food and have no way of feeding yourself. I am just using this as an example of something that's not apparent until you *Explore and Find Out More*.)

One possible reaction to environmental differences is to insist things should be different. This is useless. A Transplant Teacher's time and energy is better spent *Focusing on Things They Can Control*, like how to respond to the differences. Find ways to function in the environment without declaring how it *should* be.

Environmental differences aren't something for a Transplant Teacher to judge or change. Many of them, like the weather, can't be changed, anyway. The differences are something to discover and learn about. A Transplant Teacher exploring and learning is a Transplant Teacher on the way to thriving.

CHAPTER 5

Transplant Challenge: School Environment is Different.

The school environment in your Transplant Home might be different than you're used to. Before I moved to rural Alaska I never would have imagined scheduling Spring Break around a basketball tournament and dogsled race, but that's what happens every year around here. I guess I assumed that all schools follow some predetermined dates set by a central office somewhere. In Brevig Mission there's a raging annual debate about whether Spring Break should coincide with the regional basketball tournament in Nome in March or the Spring Carnival tournament in Shishmaref in April. It's serious stuff.

Here's another example of a difference in the larger school environment (we'll talk about classroom specifics in a later chapter). I grew up with separate elementary, middle, and high schools each housed in their own building. My high school was the only one in town, but there were multiple elementary and middle schools. That is not how the school system in Brevig Mission is set up.

The only school in town houses kindergarten through twelfth grade. This year we have five seniors in high school, but there are twenty-two second graders! Younger classes are generally bigger than older classes, as Brevig Mission is experiencing a population explosion. About eighteen babies were born last year, and the trend looks as if it will continue. Five teachers teach eighth through twelfth grade. Two teachers teach sixth and seventh grade. The younger grades have one teacher per grade, and we have two Special Education teachers. Our principal covers the entire school of 160 students, and we have a counselor that splits time between our site and another in a neighboring village.

The school is housed in one building, and all thirteen grades share the same lunchroom and gym. This causes some scheduling conundrums as we try to accommodate lunch time, recess, and PE for all the students. Planning school-wide events requires thinking about five year-olds all the way to eighteen year-olds.

Some problems in our K-12 school would be unfamiliar in the schools I went to growing up, where elementary students, middle school students, and high school students were all separated. Sometimes the high school students use the elementary bathrooms during lunch because they're closer. Sometimes middle school bathroom breaks end up happening during high school passing periods. Sometimes kindergarteners are leaving the gym as high schoolers are entering, and the high schoolers don't understand why they can't hug and play with their little cousins while the teacher is trying to get them to line up and exit in an orderly fashion.

During staff meetings all the teachers meet together, and inevitably some topics relate more to one age group than another. High school teachers have to sit through conversations about scheduling class bathroom breaks, and elementary teachers wait while the high school teachers discuss supervision during passing periods. Our principal does a pretty good job of splitting us up into age-level groups for discussion on relevant topics, but there's no avoiding the difficulty entirely. A separate elementary school would probably not spend time determining how to calculate mid-quarter GPAs for sports eligibility, and a separate high school would not have to create a policy for using stuffed animals as attendance incentives.

One of the biggest challenges is helping elementary and secondary teachers understand each other's needs. Timing and routine are critical to elementary classroom success, but secondary teachers sometimes view that as inflexible. On the secondary side, four to five grades at a time need to operate in synchrony because the students change classes, and elementary teachers can resent the "preference" the secondary schedule is given during scheduling. It's a lot of coordination to keep everything flowing smoothly.

These annoyances are a perfect place to use the strategy *Consider Different Perspectives*. I might roll my eyes at the idea of creating a seating chart for school-wide assemblies, but I need to consider how important that is when teaching little kids. Realizing that different things are priorities at different levels of teaching can give me patience during those discussions at staff meetings.

These situations are also a good place for a Transplant Teacher to *Focus on What You Can Control*. I can't change the importance of bathroom schedules and preserving small group time. I can moan and groan that I shouldn't have to sit through those discussions, but that likely won't change anything.

Instead, I can find a way to make that time useful to me. I can write down ways the principles of the discussion can apply to my classroom. I can observe the dynamic between staff members to use as an example or non-example when discussing my own issues later on. I can make a to-do list of things I need to get ready for the week. I can sketch out a draft of a graphic organizer. I can control how I use my time, even when the main discussion is out of my control.

Another way teaching in Brevig Mission differs from the schooling system that I went through is that I have the same students year after year. I can't use the same activities year after year. I can't play the same games or simulations. The kids have already done those.

In fifteen years of teaching, I've taught: Alaska History, US History, World History, Government, Entrepreneurship, World Literature, Developmental Writing, Composition, Reading, Corrective Reading, Leadership, Photography, Video Production, Art, PE, Technology, Academic Decathlon, and facilitated Inupiaq language classes. I'm not sure what the typical range of subjects is for teachers in other places, but I think my range is on the broad side.

Teachers in Brevig Mission are also dealing with the many roles they play in the school setting. Because of our small staff, teachers take on added responsibilities. We coach sports, advise activities, coordinate state testing and academic interventions…the list goes on and on.

With a larger staff, those positions can get spread around, but there is only us. It doesn't work to say, "Somebody will do it." We are the somebodies, and if we want something to happen for our student body, we have to make it happen.

As much as I am challenged by the range of classes and responsibilities and a lack of adequate prep time, it's a reality. It's a great opportunity to practice *Focusing on What I Can Control*. I can't control the number of minutes in a day or the number of minutes allotted for prepping for my classes. I can control how I use my time and what I prioritize. I can control the time I put in outside of the contract day and set boundaries for myself and my family. I can choose to point out the time discrepancies to my supervisors and make suggestions about how to get more prep time, but that's about the extent of my control. *Focusing on What I Can Control* helps prevent needlessly wasting energy on complaining.

You may or may not end up in a K-12 school, but there will almost certainly be competing needs and preferences no matter where you teach. Things you've taken for granted at other schools may not be business as usual for your new school. A good practice is to

Consider Different Perspectives around scheduling and other needs. Your classroom is not an island, and it's important to think of the greater good of the school in addition to advocating for your individual classroom.

Shift your focus from "this should be different" to "how can I deal with this." When you focus on what you can do, your time and energy go to things that are in your control.

Positive solutions

Even on the best of journeys to stay positive and find the good where you are, conflicts will inevitably arise. The teacher across the hall from you might regularly let their students out five minutes early for lunch, causing your students to go into five minutes of solid begging to leave early too. A paraprofessional might show up late and leave early almost every day, leaving you without help for part of the day. When dealing with these unpleasant situations, remember to *Focus on What You Can Control.*

It's helpful to go straight to the source. If a coworker or community member is doing something that bothers you or that you find inappropriate, go speak directly to them. If you hear rumors that a coworker or community member is criticizing you or doing something that affects you negatively, go speak directly to them! Talking to other people or bringing it straight to your supervisor will just create more bad feelings.

Sometimes students from a particular teacher's class will wander into my classroom during the day. When reminding the student where they're supposed to be and why doesn't correct the habitual behavior, the next logical step is for me to talk to that teacher. I could start the conversation off with, "Does so-and-so tell you they're going to the bathroom during sixth hour? Because he/she is actually coming into my classroom." Going straight to the teacher gives him/her a chance to know what's going on and to fix it. Going straight to our principal about the problem feels like tattling and could embarrass the other teacher.

It's also important to make a few attempts when trying to correct things. You may not be communicating as well as you think you are. Generational, language, and cultural gaps can all contribute to misunderstandings, even during attempted resolutions. Several times I've talked to a coworker about something, felt really good about the conversation, mistakenly believed that everyone agreed, and then watched as the unwanted situation continued.

This still happens when I make sub plans. I think I'm being crystal clear about what I want the class and the sub to do, and I come back to an assignment completed with a different interpretation or an assignment abandoned in favor of something else. I do my best to be clear, but I'm not always successful. I don't always know how the disconnect happens. It doesn't happen every day (thank goodness), but it does still happen.

At Brevig Mission School, we apply the general rule of speaking directly with a coworker at least three times to work things out. It's even written into our staff handbook. This guideline gives us a chance to communicate in different ways to be understood and offers grace to people who are trying to change and just forget or slip back into old habits.

If I ask one of my coworkers to not use their cell phone while they're helping students in my class, he/she will probably agree. I might see that cell phone out again. It doesn't mean that the coworker is defying me; it just might be a habit he/she is trying to break. I can remind them again in a good-natured way and extend that courtesy to them at least three times. After that, it's appropriate to reach out to our principal for problem-solving support.

This method strengthens relationships and trust among colleagues instead of setting up a system where we all look for ways to tattle on each other to the principal. The principal has better things to do than settle challenges we can handle ourselves, and strengthening respect and trust among coworkers is always a good thing.

It's also important to direct others to the source. Coworkers and community members may complain to you about other teachers or staff members. Unless I have personally witnessed whatever they are talking about, I try to point them in the direction of the source. For example, if a parent is complaining about their child's low grade in another class that they think is unfair, I might say, "Go talk to the Social Studies teacher. Find out what she thinks. I'm sure she'll work something out."

Or, if a parent had heard that another teacher yelled inappropriately or threw something in class, I might say, "You know, I'm not sure exactly what happened with that, but I'm sure if you go talk to him, he'll tell you what happened from his perspective." This encourages people to get first-hand information instead of relying on rumors. It helps them and you *Consider Different Perspectives* as you sort through all the factors that may be in play in these types of situations. It also builds trust among staff members as they come to believe they won't be trash-talked by their colleagues.

Professionalism is possible

Above all, remember that you can treat colleagues, parents, students, and community members professionally because you are a professional, not because they deserve it. You can be professional while you disagree. You can be professional when institutional priorities are out of whack. You can be professional when things are unfair. You can be professional when you're un- or underappreciated.

Sometimes being professional means keeping your mouth shut. Sometimes it means speaking up in a diplomatic and non-threatening way. Sometimes it means giving people the opportunity to do the right thing and be professionals themselves, even if you're pretty sure they won't take it.

Being a professional is not about the other person, it's about you. Our actions reflect who we are. Decide who you want to be. Then, no matter what kind of ridiculousness happens around you, you can feel good about how you respond.

The danger of should

In situations around school (and everywhere else, really), I recommend avoiding *should* as often as possible. I don't mean every sense of the word. The one that the *New Oxford American Dictionary* describes as "indicating a desirable state" is fine. As in "I should stop by the store after school" or "I should call my grandma for her birthday." I suggest avoiding the word when "used to indicate obligation, duty, or correctness."

The danger of the second kind of *should* is that it often operates on judgment and indignation. The *should* sets up a right and a wrong, and you can get so angry over a perceived (or actual) injustice that it saps your energy. Being judgmental, indignant, and angry probably won't help the situation, and it will likely leave you exhausted and unhappy. Avoiding *should* is kind of a variation on the strategy *Stay Positive*. Staying positive is not always about sunshine and rainbows. Sometimes it's about avoiding the negative. Limiting your use of the word *should* and the "idea of should" is one way to avoid the negative so you don't stunt your positive growth.

Consider this example:

> They should give us more notice about schedule changes.

"They" might refer to the school office, the administration, or the guidance counselor(s). It might very well be the office/admin/counselor's responsibility to handle schedule changes. It might be their responsibility to notify teachers of the changes. The notification may not happen immediately. Unexpected schedule changes absolutely might be an inconvenience, even be a major inconvenience.

But, as I mentioned above, using a *should* statement creates a situation in which someone is right and someone is wrong. It fosters judgment and righteous indignation, which may not be helpful. You may end up getting worked up and needlessly angry, especially if the factors contributing to the situation are out of your control. The office/admin/counselor may disagree with your *should* statement, and insisting on its inherent rightness may shore up resistance. Consider the following revised statement:

> It would help us plan in advance if the administration gave us more notice about schedule changes.

This statement acknowledges the inconvenience of the situation. It acknowledges that the responsibility of the notification rests with someone else, but, it is less adversarial. It's not about making someone "right" or "wrong." Revising the statement doesn't let the admin off the hook or relieve them of their responsibility. It acknowledges the situation and what a change in behavior or policy could mean. It also leaves room for the possibilities that the situation is not intentionally inconvenient or that more information might change your view of the whole thing.

Here's another example. Say you've noticed that some of your colleagues have extended periods of prep time while you're scrambling around trying to find enough time to go to the bathroom once a day. You might think:

> We should all have the same amount of prep time.

Again, there might be a measurable difference in the amount of preparation time teachers are given, but the *should* is unhelpful. A revised statement could look like this:

> It's inequitable that we have different amounts of prep time.

The revised statement acknowledges the problem, and although "inequitable" has a negative connotation, it seems softer than the should statement. It shifts the focus from blame to identifying the problem. Reframing the thought doesn't make the situation go away. It doesn't take away the burden of not enough prep time, but it does change how you think about and approach the situation, and that can make a big difference in how you feel and function.

Try this one:

> They should fix my SmartBoard (or window or bookshelf or doorknob or...).

The responsibility to install SmartBoards (or windows or bookshelves or doorknobs) may very well rest with someone else. The repairs may have been waiting for months. The problem may cause serious inconvenience, but the *should* sets you up to focus on the negative with a dash of self-righteous that the repair *should* have taken place months ago. This negative thinking can drain your energy. You might be better off reframing the thought, so it's less likely to interfere with your efforts at *Staying Positive*.

Revised statement:

> A working SmartBoard will give me more options and make teaching easier.

The revision acknowledges the problem without blaming anyone and focuses on the positive effect the change would have.

Other examples:

> The school should have a working copy machine → A working copy machine is essential to preparing for my classes.

> Everyone should help fundraise → More help with fundraising would lighten the load for everybody.

> We should only have to go to training relevant to our jobs → Time spent in irrelevant training could be better used to prepare for classes.

Revising *should* statements may seem like a minor thing that doesn't actually solve the problems that arise, but it creates an important inward shift. The revision may not fix your SmartBoard or change a policy, but it can change how you think about the unfair/inconvenient/irritating situations. Removing overt blame simmers the situation down. Being in a highly combative mode is exhausting. The problem may never be solved. The situation may never change, and if you've worked yourself into a frenzy, you'll use up valuable energy. Energy you could put into something you can control.

Considering Other Perspectives can help you at least understand the other people's decisions (even if you think they're unwise). When you know that maintenance is working on frozen pipes in teacher housing or that the fuel tanks won't stop leaking, you might better understand why the maintenance crew considers a SmartBoard to be a lower priority. When you know that your colleague has additional responsibilities, you might better understand the decision to allot them additional prep time.

Remember, the only thing you really have control over is yourself. As you deal with these inevitable situations, you monitor how you're framing the situation and what effect that's having on you. Nobody wants to be angry all the time. Nobody wants to feel mistreated all the time. Shifting your thinking is something you can control that can help you move away from less desirable states. When you work to adjust your inward reaction to issues in school, your outward reactions will be more in control and effective.

CHAPTER 6

Transplant Challenge: Social Norms are Different

Being a Transplant Teacher can mean being dropped into a whole new world of social norms. Consider my failed experience with thank-you notes. I was raised that thank-you notes are the preferred way of expressing gratitude, and my mom always insisted we write them. At the time I responded with the requisite whining, but the expectation stayed with me. A paraprofessional once subbed for me for a couple of days in a row on short notice. I wrote a nice thank-you note expressing my appreciation and left it in my classroom for her. When I came back to my room, the note was in the trash can.

I was hurt. I couldn't believe my expression of thanks had been tossed so quickly. I had assumed she would consider the note a meaningful expression of gratitude. Rather than desperately cling to the expectation I had been raised with, I looked for other ways of saying thank you. The next time she subbed for me I brought her back some food from Anchorage. That was just right.

I could have wasted my time and energy assuring myself that thank-you notes were the "right" way to express gratitude. Instead I made a small change to my behavior to be more in line with local norms. Again, it's not a matter of right and wrong, it's a matter of operating under the social norms of your new home.

A big part of your journey to deal with different will be navigating social norms. Trying to connect with people (outward) and getting to know them amidst a sea of protocols, manners, and new expectations can be challenging. Even more challenging is the fact that the protocols, manners, and expectations are often unspoken. There's probably not going to be a guidebook in your school outlining definitive steps for community participation and making friends. You'll have to figure it out.

Looking inward will help you examine your reactions to the social norms in your Transplant Home. The strategy *Withhold Judgment* is back. Interacting with people will throw you into all sorts of situations where behavior might surprise you. Don't immediately label those behaviors as wrong or bad. Reserving judgment will help you *Stay Positive* (both in your thoughts and in what you share with others).

Looking outward will help you connect to your Transplant Home and the people there. The most important strategy here is to *Get Involved! Try Things! and Participate!* Notice all of the exclamation points? That's because this part is supposed to be fun! You'll likely have to deal with some nervousness and awkwardness as you put yourself out there, but push yourself through that so you can *Make Connections a Little at a Time*. Transplant Teachers can't expect a grandiose transformational event that propels them into the social network of their Transplant Home. Instead, small individual efforts add up to build stronger connections.

Through this whole process Transplant Teachers will need to *Accept Feedback*. Feedback comes in all sorts of forms. It might be as overt as someone saying "You're doing it wrong" or it might be as subtle as a raised eyebrow. Transplant Teachers can examine the feedback (inward) to see what they can learn from it. Then they can respond to feedback in a gracious way and act on it (outward).

Transplant Teachers also need to be willing to *Ask for Help*.

Asking for help signals humility and a desire to know more. You don't have to figure out everything alone. People in your Transplant Home can offer know-how and advice if you're wise enough to ask for it.

Facing unfamiliar social territory can be scary, but there's more to the experience than just fear and anxiety. Getting to know people and building relationships can be fun, even when you have to deal with new social norms. Use the strategies to help you enjoy the process.

CHAPTER 7

Social Norms: Try Things and Stay Positive

So, you're ready to step into the social landscape of your Transplant Home. ™What do you do with all the newness? You jump in to try new things, learn from your mistakes, and stay positive!

Trying new things puts you at risk for making mistakes. That's okay! You can learn from those mistakes. You might come across things that seem strange or uncomfortable. That's also okay! You can learn from those too. Through it all, staying positive will help you appreciate the interesting things around you and carry you through the things that are not so pleasant.

Things are new. Try them anyway.

One way to *Participate and Try Things* is to do things you might not normally do. If hobbies and recreation are different in your Transplant Home, you may not have the skills or inclination to participate. Get over that!

I am not a sewer (as in one who sews, not a system for dealing with water and waste). The one sewing project I embarked upon with my mom led to fights and tears and was never finished. But, women in Shishmaref sew. A lot. So, I gave it a try. Several kind women helped me complete a doll-sized kaspak (traditional Inupiaq dress). It was not easy. My work was not perfect. I had to *Ask for a Lot of Help*, but I did it anyway and was rewarded with the communion of the women around me in addition to an actually finished product.

I've already discussed my less-than-illustrious basketball career in high school, and there's little need to bring up my pathetic attempts to play or the time someone in the crowd yelled, "Pass it to number ten! She can't dribble!" (I was number ten). But, young people in Shishmaref play basketball. A lot. It was the primary social activity. So I put my running shoes on and played again. I was nervous that I would make embarrassing mistakes, and I did. My team instructed me not to try to take the ball down the court on my own, but people were super supportive, and the memory of the students chanting my name while I was at the free throw line is one I treasure. I was trying. I was interacting, and it was received warmly.

I'm not a runner, but I run in Christmas foot races every year. I've never been one to work out, but when a group of ladies invited me to do aerobics with them, I accepted. I've never regretted stepping out of my comfort zone to do something new with my community and friends. I've had my fair share of awkward moments, and I'm not going to win any awards for my fishing or dancing skills any time soon, but the discomfort paid off in the form of connections and relationships. Even the reputation that develops as someone willing to try is worth it.

How do you ask to join in if you're not invited? A good method is to ask if you can help next time someone sews, hunts, carves, builds a boat, etc. In my communities this is often perceived as a kind offer of assistance rather than inviting myself to come along. People are busy and don't always have time to slow down their work to teach, but they usually will accept any offers of free help. Even if you're just handing over tools or cleaning up scraps, there will be opportunities for conversation and relationship-building. You'll establish yourself as someone with a genuine interest in their skills, and more opportunities to observe or participate will flow.

One of my teacher friends in Shishmaref tried sewing a bunch of local crafts. She got really into it, and would visit ladies while they sewed. She even started making her own parka.

Another teacher friend in Brevig Mission got involved with Inupiaq Dancing. He started going to weekly dance practice. He learned some of the songs and dances and now drums with the dance group.

Another Brevig Mission teacher likes to go camping in the country. A local family unofficially adopted her, and she goes with them when they camp and fish.

While I've tried lots of different activities, I don't do them all regularly. Part of the growing process includes thinning out your crop. When growing vegetables, you plant a bunch of seeds, see what sprouts, and then thin out the carrots so they're not competing for nutrients in the soil. When growing fruit trees, you prune the tree so that the energy and nutrients go into producing fewer fruit of better quality rather than lots of substandard fruit.

You will find the need to do this as a Transplant Teacher. You try a bunch of new experiences and meet a bunch of new people, but you don't have to do everything. That would be overwhelming, and you wouldn't have the time and energy to make the interactions meaningful and high quality. It's okay to scale back and focus on the relationships and activities that you truly enjoy and that benefit you. Remember, the strategy is *Get Involved! Try Things! Participate!* Not Get Involved and Participate in Everything all the time (I stand firm on *Try Things* because I think it's okay to try everything, even if it's only a little bit).

Mistakes happen

There will be times when you make mistakes. The first time I tried Inupiaq dancing was during the Inupiaq Days celebration in Shishmaref. The drummers were drumming and singing a song while the third and fourth grade students danced. The students all seemed to know exactly what to do, so I stood behind some students and copied their posture: feet apart and hands moving with the beat of the drums. They just so happened to be boys. One of the Shishmaref women ran up to me and told me I needed to stand with my feet together because I am a woman.

I hadn't noticed that the boys and girls stood differently. I had just copied the kids right in front of me. Some little kids laughed as I shifted my feet together. It was embarrassing, but I *Accepted the Feedback*. I wanted to protest, "But I didn't know!" to defend myself, but I fought the urge. My face probably turned red, but I sucked it up and kept dancing, making a mental note that Inupiaq women dance with their legs together. I've never made the same mistake again!

During my first year in Brevig Mission I sang in a young adult church choir, and we were practicing for an upcoming church conference. There was just a few weeks before the conference, and we were singing songs that weren't in the traditional Lutheran hymnal. The choir consisted of young adults from Brevig Mission and me and one other teacher new to the village. The other teacher and I had only been to a few other practices. Someone suggested we practice singing in formation like we would during the conference. We all stood up in front of the keyboard. The other teacher, who happened to be a man, stood in front, and the local ladies laughed and told him to move to the back because men always stand in the back. There's no way he could have known that, but he simply moved to the back.

The laughing could have felt hurtful if he had chosen to be offended. He didn't show any outward signs of embarrassment, but I would have been humiliated. In situations like this, it would be easy to let the offense and embarrassment get in the way of trying again. It would be easy to become defensive and ask "who says that's a rule?" or "what kind of rule is that?" Accept correction and learn. "That's how they do things here" is a good mantra.

Chances are, if you listen and correct your behavior, the community members will appreciate the effort. Just like I had to suffer the embarrassment of standing the wrong way during my first attempt at Inupiaq dancing to continue, you may have to suffer some embarrassment. Keep going! Now community members like it when I dance, and I enjoy it too. I would have missed out if I'd given up after being corrected.

The strategy for dealing with mistakes is to *Accept Feedback*. It won't prevent you from making mistakes, but it will help deal with them. *Accepting Feedback* is both an inward and an outward solution. You shift your mindset because of the new information and/or suggestions (inward) and respond to the person or people that offered the feedback (outward).

If colleagues or community members tell you you're violating a social norm or being offensive, listen. Even if you think the social norm seems weird or unnecessary or antiquated to you. This is another instance to realize just because you grew up a certain way doesn't mean it's the right way.

It can be humbling to be told you're doing something wrong when you were just doing what you considered to be polite and normal. Being humbled is not a bad thing. It makes you teachable and open to new possibilities. This is the inward part of *Accepting Feedback*. Reflect on the feedback and see how you can implement it. See how it might have applied in previous situations. Resolve to heed it in the future.

The outward part of *Accepting Feedback* is how you immediately respond to the feedback or correction. Your knee-jerk reaction might be to get defensive. Avoid that. One way to respond is, "Thanks, I'm still learning." This phrase oozes humility. It acknowledges that the feedback giver has wisdom to offer and that the Transplant Teacher has lots to learn. "Thanks, I'm still learning" also sounds much better than defensively retorting, "How was I supposed to know," or "Nobody told me!"

Remember to be gentle with yourself. Nobody expects an oak seedling to be to withstand the weight of a tree swing. Nobody expects fruit from an apple tree seedling. The seedlings need to grow and develop to reach their potential. Feedback will help.

What matters? Positivity matters!

As you navigate different manners and social norms, it's important to *Stay Positive*. It can be easy to slip into negativity when confronted with different social norms. Sometimes it's a knee jerk reaction. Even if you don't say anything out loud, the negativity can creep into your thoughts. Find the beauty and goodness wherever you are and hold onto each meaningful moment like a treasure.

One of my precious Shishmaref memories is walking along the beach before the water froze. I think it was even before school had officially started. I started the walk alone, but a group of three or four junior high aged girls ended up following me. It was late at night, but the sun was low on the horizon in an extended sunset, and the light was gorgeous as it reflected off the water. We talked about random stuff, and they told me stories. We picked up shells along the beach and found giant starfish. I keep one of the big shells from that walk on top of our stove. It's an odd place to keep a shell, but it looks nice, and it reminds me of the beauty and connection available just outside our door.

Staying Positive in Your Thoughts begins with noticing. You can attempt to see good things, even if you have to start with small ones. I haven't been to every place on this earth, but I also haven't been anyplace that there wasn't beauty and goodness. If you're looking out for the goodness, you'll be more likely to see it. That will go a long way to help you *Stay Positive*.

You might make the conscious effort of physically listing positive things every morning, lunchtime, and after school. You might stop on the way to work and look around for something beautiful. You might ask your students what makes them grateful or happy and see if it resonates with you. Even these tiny efforts can move you into the realm of positive thinking.

It's especially important to *Stay Positive Publicly*. The miracle of the Internet makes it possible to share our Transplant Adventures with the world, and Transplant Teachers need to be aware that people in their new homes are watching them online and in person. Unless you've completely locked down your privacy settings, complaining online can be the equivalent of standing in the center of town and shouting negative things with a bullhorn. When you put negative comments and criticisms online, they can be seen by people you want to see them and by people you don't.

Don't be the teacher that publicly blasts your Transplant Home and loses the trust and support of your community. Don't set up a situation where you are not asked back for a second year or get yourself in a public relations mess that will make you miserable and not want to return for a second year.

You have every right to your own opinion, but be wise about how you share it. It's important to be authentic about your experience, but it's also possible to put a positive spin on things you share publicly.

I've written blog posts about the lack of indoor plumbing in

Shishmaref. I've described the processes associated with incinolets and honey buckets (you know, the human waste disposal mechanisms I talked about in the beginning of the book). I began those blog posts with factual information. "One of the biggest cons about living in Shishmaref is the lack of indoor plumbing. Yes, that's right, Shishmaref has no central sewer system. The school has flush toilets and running water, but the houses don't."

Using the word "con" is a little negative, but it reflects the sentiments of the people of Shishmaref, not just me. Most people in Shishmaref wish they had indoor plumbing too. They don't complain about it, but they do think villages with running water are lucky.

I also tried to balance the use of the word "con" by including some positive resolution to the situation: "Most people are absolutely disgusted and shocked when they hear about our plumbing situation. It's actually not that bad for the following reasons:

- Our bathroom is not heated. That makes for some very fast late-night visits, but it also prevents any smell normally associated with waste disposal
- Steve always takes the honey bucket out. I've only done it once, and it was to prove to him I could do it if I wanted to. (I simply don't. Steve doesn't want to do the taxes. I think it's a fair trade.)

Our plumbing situation definitely took some getting used to, but I rarely think about it anymore. At worst, it is mildly annoying."

In those posts, I took an aspect of life in Shishmaref that could have been portrayed in a disgusting and negative light and kept it informative and a little fun (even if I do say so myself).

It's not necessary to sugarcoat or perpetuate a romanticized version of reality, but you can share things in a "look at how they do things around here" sort of way. I strive for a tone of wonder and awe instead of judgment.

I have my share of frustrations and do my share of complaining, but not in a public forum. That's subject matter for a personal e-mail or message, a phone call to my mom, or a private conversation in my living room.

There's a time and a place to vent. I'm going to suggest that that time and place is never in front of students or even in the staff room where people can overhear you.

A wise teacher once told me, "Say whatever you want, but don't put anything in writing." It's easy to misinterpret the tone of the typed or written word. It's also easy for angry emails to be forwarded to others who may not have the context necessary to understand their true intent. If I'm angry about something, I prefer to talk about it.

Staying Positive Publicly has two benefits. First, it can help you avoid souring relationships in your Transplant Home. As you nurture your seedling, the last thing you need is a hurricane of people who were offended by your latest status update. Second, what you share outwardly can affect what you think. If you're taking the time to reframe things in a less negative way, it might help shift your thoughts in that direction. Coming up with a more neutral way to share things might soften your outlook.

There are an infinite number of social situations you may find yourself in as a Transplant Teacher. That means an infinite number of potentially awesome experiences, but also an infinite number of potential missteps. Focus on the potential awesomeness. You might still be nervous, and you might still make mistakes, but you can enjoy yourself (and others) in the process.

CHAPTER 8

Social Norms: Mind Your Manners and Mind Their Manners

Even if we were never explicitly taught manners, most of us grow up absorbing them from the people around us. They contribute to our idea of normal. Transplant Teachers can find themselves in a place where the manners they grew up with don't apply. Things that used to be considered polite suddenly aren't.

I've seen teachers from the Southern United States come to the village and expect to be addressed as "Sir" or "Ma'am." When the kids didn't automatically do that or comply when asked to, the teachers considered it very rude.

The strategy that applies here is *Withhold Judgment*. Those teachers from the South were taught to address adults as "Sir" or "Ma'am." That was expected of them. They were likely corrected or scolded if they didn't. They imposed that same expectation in their Transplant Home. The teachers could try to force that expectation. They could insist on being called "Sir" or "Ma'am" and spend time teaching, modeling, and correcting that behavior. Or, they could choose not to.

My students call me Angie. They call other adults by their first names, including the principal. That's what's normal here. That's considered polite. Even though this behavior might be rude in other places, my students grew up where it's perfectly acceptable. One way isn't better. One way isn't worse. They're just different. Some teachers want to be called Mr. or Mrs., and so they train their students to do that. It's okay if the teachers want to put their energy into that as long as they realize it's not a deficiency in their students that makes it necessary. It's the teacher's personal preference and expectation.

A new normal

As you observe social dynamics and situations, keep in mind that you're looking for a new normal. Things that seem crazy to you will seem normal to the people around you. As you observe, you will uncover assumptions you didn't even know you had. Then you can begin replacing these assumptions.

It can be tricky to determine the new normal. This is where it's essential to use the strategy *Withhold Judgment*. If your students or community members are doing something over and over (standing close to you, asking very personal questions, not making eye contact, etc.), don't instantly label it as bad or rude. Just take note. Then observe a while longer in different settings around town or school, in large gatherings and small, during formal and informal interactions to see if you see the same thing occur. Consider asking a trusted colleague or community member about what you're observing to get another perspective. What you consider rude and offensive may just be a different social norm.

A great example of contrasting social expectations is birthday parties. When a child in Shishmaref or Brevig Mission has a birthday, their family spends days baking goodies of all kinds. Pies, cinnamon rolls, donuts, blueberry delight (an amazing cheesecake-like concoction), cakes, and Jell-o. The family thaws tundra berries, and they sometimes make some into kammamak or agutaq (also known as Eskimo ice cream, a combination of berries, caribou fat, seal oil, and sugar. I find it delicious). Most of the time the family orders a "Nome cake" (a bakery sheet cake from Nome) and has it flown in for the party.

On the evening of the party, the parents start calling people. Close family members are called first and given the brief message "So-and-so's birthday party at our house." Then the family members come over and take turns sitting at the table to eat treats. When they're finished eating, they rotate to a seat on the couch or a chair so that someone else can take a place at the table. Family members sit and visit for a while before leaving. As space opens up in the house, the parents of the birthday child make more phone calls for another wave of guests. This process continues all night until the treats or the list of family and friends are exhausted.

In Shishmaref, the birthday child has a cup. Guests who come to the party put money in the cup as a birthday gift. If the child is young, a dollar or two is fine. If the child is older, the amount of money usually increases. If the child is really nice or special to us, we increase the amount of money. By the end of the night, the birthday child has a nice wad of birthday cash.

As guests leave birthday parties in Shishmaref or Brevig Mission, they often fill a paper plate with goodies to take home, especially if someone at home didn't make it to the party. If I go to a birthday party without Steve, the hosts often won't let me leave without filling up a plate and covering it with foil to take to Steve. Before we moved to Alaska, it never would have occurred to me to ask for or take a plate of goodies home.

Shishmaref and Brevig Mission birthday parties are very different from the ones where I grew up. Invitations for a party came on little cards in an envelope at least a week beforehand, not via a phone call as the party was happening. A last-minute phone invitation would suggest that I had been overlooked, or that I was a replacement for a no-show guest.

The invitations were for me as an individual, not for my parents or siblings. Bringing an uninvited sister or dad would have been rude and forced the hosts to awkwardly turn them away or scramble for an extra place setting and goody bag. Instead of putting money in a cup, I brought a wrapped present. Bringing money would have been socially acceptable only if it was in a cute or witty card.

If I were to judge a village birthday party by the norms of my childhood, I might miss out on enjoying all the wonderful differences. Steve and I received invites to birthday parties for almost every student we taught while we were in Shishmaref. Sometimes the calls came after we were already in our jammies and ready for bed, but we tried to go to as many as possible. We were touched that people thought to include us. It was a great opportunity to visit with people in an informal setting. Parties came with lots of laughter and stories, and the feelings of love and togetherness warmed my heart.

Birthday parties in Shishmaref and Brevig Mission are fun and amazing and beautiful, even if they're different from the birthday parties of my childhood. *Withholding Judgment* allows me to enjoy them for what they are. The same is true for other events.

Within the first few months of our first year, we attended Shishmaref's local Lutheran church. The setting was relatively familiar. There were pews. There was a cross at the front of the sanctuary (albeit one made of walrus ivory). There were hymn books. But during the sermon, I heard the pssssshhhh of pop cans being opened around us. I looked at the congregation and noticed adults passing pop and candy out of store bags to the children sitting around them.

I grew up going to church in congregations where parents passed out Cheerios and fruit snacks, but cans of pop and candy bars seemed over the top. I judged the people as rude and irreverent because I compared their behavior to the norms I was raised with. Similarly, I remember attending a local funeral at the church. The chapel was packed as nearly everyone in town attended. The funeral lasted for hours. Part of the program included an open mic session where anyone could get up and share a memory or request a song in honor of the departed or their family. Some songs were sung by the church choir, others were sung by groups of people or family members.

During the funeral people were constantly coming and going. Kids would play outside for a while and then come back in. Adults would walk out for a smoke break and come back in. I considered it extremely disrespectful.

These were prime opportunities to apply the strategy *Withhold Judgment*. As I observed more of the funeral, I noticed that even family members would take a break outside before returning, so clearly, the walking in and out wasn't because of a lack of love or respect for the deceased. I initially judged the behavior based on how I grew up. *Withholding Judgment* here was about recognizing what I saw differed from the funeral norms of my upbringing, but normal and appropriate in Shishmaref.

Another assumption I brought with me was that visiting kids are sent home before dinner. That's what happened in my childhood. Unless there was a pre-arranged visit like a sleepover, I always went home when it was time for my friends to eat. Likewise, my mom would send the neighbor kids home when it was time for us to eat dinner. In Shishmaref and Brevig Mission, you feed whoever is at your house when it's time to eat. I learned that when Kaitlyn and Levi come home from someone's house after five, they will have been well fed. I try to return the favor and feed the kids who happen to be at my house during dinner.

Withholding Judgment helped me not get irritated by kids who didn't automatically go home or parents who didn't call for their kids to come home at dinnertime. When I recognized it as a local pattern, I understood that the kids and parents were just doing what is usually done. I was able to slide into that pattern (outward) and adapt my expectations (inward).

Transplant Teachers don't have to completely change to fit all local norms, but they can adapt to work with the norms. One thing that shocked me when I got to Shishmaref was spitting. The kids spat all day long. It's not like it was on the floor or anything. It was in the trash can, but I could still see it (and hear it as it was expelled from their mouths). I forgot to *Withhold Judgment* here because I grew up with people spitting on the baseball field or outside on a walk in the country, but not inside. The more I got out and about in the community, the more spitting I saw. Even adults I considered respectful and kind would spit in the middle of a conversation. I realized my students weren't intentionally being rude or gross. They were just doing what their parents and everyone else in town did.

I decided I didn't want to fight to eradicate spitting behavior, and I found a way to work with it. I moved all trash cans away from my desk so there was no chance of the desk getting hit by poor aim or from some sort of spit bouncing. One veteran teacher established the routine of students spitting in a tissue and then throwing it in the trash can. We worked within the local norm without spending needless energy fighting it.

When being a teacher and being a person overlap

In Brevig Mission and Shishmaref, professional boundaries can differ from other places because of proximity. Teachers are community members and neighbors too. There's no going home to a separate world. In the villages you see your students everywhere. They're at the store. They're at the post office. They're walking around town whenever you go anywhere. They're at community feasts. They're at basketball games. They're at evening recreation time in the gym.

Some of them live next door to you. Some of them live across the street from you. When you need to borrow a cup of sugar, you go to their houses to get one. When you need a babysitter, you likely call one of them.

You Will encounter your students and their families even more if you're attempting to take part in community activities and develop relationships outside of the school (which I highly recommend).

Even when your students leave your individual classroom, they stay at the same school. Sometimes you may be their teacher year after year. I've had the current high school seniors since they were in seventh grade. That's six years, sometimes multiple hours a day.

With that kind of proximity and interaction, it follows that your relationship with your students will differ from what's normal in other places. Many teachers probably haven't been to their students' birthday parties. I do that all the time. Many teachers probably haven't been to their students' houses to mourn with the family after a loved one dies. I have. Most teachers probably haven't frantically altered prom dresses at the last minute when they didn't fit. I have. This is simply business as usual in my Transplant Home.

When I was growing up, it never would have occurred to me to visit my teachers. If I saw them at the grocery store, I would freak out. The idea of seeing them outside of the context of school blew my mind.

In Shishmaref and Brevig Mission, it is completely normal to visit teachers outside of school. From the moment we entered our house, we heard little hands knocking on our door and cries of "Can we visit?" once we'd opened the door. Piles of little shoes outside our door attested to the number of visitors we had regularly.

Even kids who seemed to hate our guts during the day had no problem walking into our entryway and asking to visit. I'm not sure what prompted the change of heart. Maybe it was their ability to slip into different behaviors in different contexts. Maybe they were just eager to interact outside of school.

My initial reaction here was not to *Withhold Judgment*. It was to think things like "they've got a lot of nerve…" "I can't believe they have the gall…" I considered the kids rude for overstepping what I considered proper boundaries.

Turns out it's different from what I grew up with, but it's normal here. Some people may argue that any kind of interaction with parents and students outside of school is inappropriate and unprofessional. I disagree. It's a natural extension of having an open heart, and it's no different from the way I would behave with my neighbors and friends if I lived in a different place. My neighbors and friends in Brevig Mission just overlap with my students and their families. If you were to draw a venn diagram of the people I know in Brevig Mission with my friends and neighbors on one side and my students and their families on the other side, there would be a great big middle section of people who fit in both categories. There are still certain boundaries I would never cross, but things look different than they might if I taught elsewhere.

You may teach in a more populated place. You may live miles from the school or in some other situation that makes out-of-school encounters with your students rare. The point is to be open to the possibility of shifting your perspective about interacting with students and their families outside of school and adapt to the norms of your Transplant Home.

Manners are relative. You may be shocked by what the people around you consider normal. What you do may seem shocking to them. A little awkwardness might be inevitable, but it doesn't have to stay that way. You can adjust your expectations and widen your definition of normal so your discomfort doesn't get in the way of making connections.

CHAPTER 9

Social Norms: Community Gatherings

One of the best ways I first got to know people in Brevig Mission was through church choir practice. I love to sing. My siblings used to pound on the walls and yell at me to be quiet when I inconsiderately belted out show tunes or Disney songs from the bathroom while getting ready at 6:00 am (my singing self-restraint is marginally better now).

I started by following one of my colleagues to choir practice. I would sit right next to her, and she introduced me to the other singers. After I showed up a few times, I was confident enough to go alone. I was familiar to the other ladies, and we could talk more.

One great thing about choir practice was that there was an activity to focus on, so I didn't have to try to maintain long conversations. I could make small talk in between songs and at the end of practice and just sing along the rest of the time. I was also doing something I find inherently enjoyable, so even if singing was the only thing I got out of choir practice, it was still a worthwhile activity. There were still uncomfortable moments when we sang songs I'd never heard before or that were out of my vocal range, but the setting allowed me to have fun and get to know people. The recurring nature of choir practice also helped. We practiced once a week, so I got to see and talk to the same people over and over.

I was doing something I enjoyed, getting to know people, and regularly showing up. It was the perfect setup to integrate into a community activity and make friends. I even learned to sing some songs in Inupiaq!

Every community will be different as far as what events are available and their openness to outsiders, but it's worth the effort to find out about them and show up.

First you have to find out about them

Finding out about community events can be tricky if you're not in the social loop. Pay attention to flyers and posters around town. Our post office always has several flyers posted in the entryway. Everybody has to go get mail, so people and organizations know it's a good place to reach people. In Brevig Mission, there are only two stores, so they're good points for publicity too. If you live in a bigger community with more stores, they are less likely to be central points of communication, but you may find other locations that serve as hubs.

Asking your students for ideas is a possibility too. Ask them what they do in the evenings and on weekends. If they're involved in any sports leagues or performance groups, find out when they play/perform and show up. This is a great way to show support for your students and get you out mixing with their parents and friends.

Your students might also clue you in on events that aren't publicized. Maybe they go to barbecues or family meals every weekend. Maybe they hang out at the beach or go hunting. It might not be appropriate for you to ask your students for an invitation to one of these events, but it gives you an idea for opportunities to watch out for. As you develop friendships, you can begin to ask about how to attend these informal events.

Think of yourself as a community member in addition to being a teacher. If you think of yourself only as a teacher, you might confine your world to your classroom and the school, and you'll miss out on opportunities to connect with the people around you and enrich your life.

Push through the awkwardness

Going to an event or activity for the first time can bring a certain amount of awkwardness. Push through the awkwardness as you use the strategy *Get Involved! Try Things! Participate!* It's normal to feel nervous or not know exactly what to do, but the benefits of forging connections outweigh the risk of embarrassment and awkwardness.

For example, feasts are important community events in Shishmaref and Brevig Mission. Each community has one on Thanksgiving and Christmas Day. The feasts are very communal experiences. Tons of people show up and eat together at long tables in the school gym. They're great opportunities to interact and share with the people in the community.

Going to our first feast was kind of scary. I didn't know exactly what to expect or do. It was a Thanksgiving Feast, and people were referring to it as a potluck. I imagined the church social potlucks of my childhood where food was lined up on folding tables and we all waited in line to fill our plates with the different casseroles and Jell-O salads. So, I made a tray of rolls to contribute to the table.

We weren't sure where to sit or if there would even be room for us. But we showed up anyway. We stepped into the unknown and risked standing around with nowhere to go. The first thing I noticed is that there was no central location for all the food, so there was no place for me to set my tray of rolls. Instead, people were gathered with their families around pots of caribou stew, sharing with the people around them. The young men in the community brought additional pots of stew around the gym, serving people at the tables.

Steve and I stood awkwardly in the entryway for a few seconds, with me holding my plate of rolls with nowhere to put them. We were pleasantly surprised that people invited us to sit with them, and we just kind of did what everyone else did. I shared the rolls with the people around us. They shared the caribou stew with us. We wished people a Happy Thanksgiving as they came by the table to shake hands and give hugs. It was fun, and the risk we took by showing up unsure was rewarded with kindness and confidence for the next feast.

Now we're at the point where we make arrangements with friends and family to sit together and save each other seats. It took a while to get there, but the more you practice, the easier it gets.

Transplant Teachers can't let the unknown stop them from participating in the community. If they did, they would never try anything! Push through the unknown. Push through the awkwardness. That's where the reward is.

There's no shortcut to connections, they happen a little at a time

The holidays bring a slew of community events in Shishmaref and Brevig Mission. Each one is an opportunity to *Make Connections a Little at a Time*.

One of my favorite Shishmaref traditions was the Church Ladies Party where we sang Christmas songs, shared food, and visited with each other. I was invited to go my first year in Shishmaref, but I hesitated because I didn't attend the Lutheran church regularly. The Ladies Group President encouraged me by saying, "Don't worry, lots of people come who don't go to church." Once I was convinced that it would be appropriate for me to attend, I gladly attended several times.

Part of the party was a gift exchange. Some years we drew names ahead of time and bought presents specifically for that person. Other years we each brought a gift and drew names once we got there, so it was all a surprise. I loved ordering fun stuff online and wrapping it up to give to one of the ladies in Shishmaref. It was especially fun when my gift went to somebody I didn't know well. It was like a little connection made.

Brevig Mission doesn't have a Church Ladies Party, but they have a community Name Pick. It's the Brevig Mission version of a Secret Santa Gift Exchange. City employees go around town and ask adults if they want to put their name in for the gift exchange. Then they come back around with a coffee can with the names on little slips of paper. I draw a name and buy a present for the person whose name I picked. I bring it to the church on Christmas Eve and label it: To So-and-So, From Namepick. The first few years I messed up and put my name on the From area. I guess that ruins the fun of not knowing who gave you a present… Now I know, and I label my present correctly.

I've picked people I know well and people I barely know. The challenge of trying to find out what kind of present they'd like is fun for me and forges another connection. Even if the recipient doesn't know the gift was from me, I still feel connected to them in a small way.

Going to the Ladies Party and taking part in Name Pick helped me *Build Connections a Little at a Time*. I didn't form a meaningful connection with every woman at the party. I didn't buy a gift for everyone in town. I didn't have to. I made a small connection with a different person each time.

It's important to remember that it might take more than one interaction for people to feel comfortable with you. Just showing up once doesn't move you out of visitor status. It's normal if you don't leave your first community event with fourteen dinner invitations and seven new best friends. Showing up multiple times and being open to interaction and sharing gives people the idea that you're sticking around and worth getting to know. Every time you take part is one more chance for people to warm up. Just like the strategy says, you *Build Connections a Little at a Time*, and those small connections add up.

Easy entry points

Every night in between Christmas and New Year's Day there are Inupiaq games in Shishmaref and Brevig Mission. They provide hours of opportunities to *Participate and Get Involved*.

In Brevig Mission, each night of Christmas events includes silly games and relay races. I have no problem making a fool of myself in front of other people, so I try to participate (when I'm not standing in line at the bathroom with one of my kids). One particularly memorable event was when they called for volunteers and told us to lie down on the ground, feet to head. I asked what we were doing, and they wouldn't tell me. Other people asked what we were doing. They weren't told either. I was lying on my back on the gym floor (along with the other brave volunteers) in front of the entire village, wondering what I'd gotten myself into. When they pulled out water bottles, I started to worry. Was I going to get wet? Was this going to be really messy?

I worried for nothing. The water bottles were closed, and all we had to do was pass them to the person behind us using our feet. The only thing I had to worry about then was if I was strong and flexible enough to lift the water bottle over my head (my chiropractor once told my husband I was definitely not a ballerina). Lucky for me, the person behind me was a very athletic young lady, so she had no trouble reaching forward with her legs to get the water bottle from me. Crisis averted, and I even had fun.

I've also held a toothpick in my lips and passed a thimble to the person next to me. I've passed an orange from under my chin to the next person. I've used only my face to retrieve a quarter from a bowl full of syrup. I've cheered as the people on my teams have done the same.

These informal opportunities to bond and interact allow the community to see a different side of me. I'm not just Teacher Angie in these moments. I'm not just a white outsider. I'm a good sport. I'm silly. I'm part of their team. I display a different facet of myself (although my students are probably not surprised at all by the silly part. They see that all the time). Holiday games are a great place to use the strategy *Get involved! Try things! Participate!* Some games are a little awkward and embarrassing, but more volunteers are always welcome, and it can be an easy entry point to stand up and walk out with the other volunteers.

Transplant Teachers can look for those easy entry points for participation. Do they need volunteers to set up chairs? Does it look like the people in charge are carrying heavy loads of supplies and could use a hand? Are they asking for people to come up and sing or dance or cheer in a group? Try it. Participate. It might be fun, and at the very least you look like a willing helper or good sport.

When it all pays off

Sometimes your efforts at participating and getting involved result in beautiful outward moments. One of my favorite traditions in Brevig Mission happens on New Year's Eve. When the clock strikes midnight, kids start throwing homemade confetti in the air, and the entire community circulates the gym wishing each other Happy New

Year while hugging and shaking hands. It's like starting out the year with a fresh slate of love and goodwill toward everyone. People I don't know very well will hug me and wish me good tidings, and I do the same in return.

I always make sure I make it up to the front row of chairs where the Elders sit during games. That way I can hug each Elder and wish them a Happy New Year. This past year, one of the most respected Elders in the community told me she loved me as I hugged her. The bustle and noise of the celebration melted away as I let that sink into my heart. Her words warmed and lifted my soul beyond imagining. To know that she thought of me that way meant an acceptance and appreciation for all of my efforts in being a part of the community of Brevig Mission. It wouldn't have been possible if I hadn't been willing to put in time and effort attending community events like Christmas Week.

When I hugged her husband, he said, "You're a good teacher." He's never been in my classroom, so I'm pretty sure he was complimenting my willingness to take part and be part of the community. Both comments were some of the most meaningful compliments I've ever received in my life. I'm honored that the Elders of my Transplant Home appreciate my efforts.

You don't have to do everything

Christmas Week is six days full of Inupiaq games and foot races for all ages. It can be grueling because races start at noon and Inupiaq games start at seven and last until late at night. In between is all the normal business of cooking and keeping a house. Sleep patterns get disrupted, and it feels busy all the time.

Full disclosure: I don't attend all the events. I absolutely never miss New Year's Eve because it's my favorite day of the year. I make sure to go on the days when my age group and my children race.

Then I pick a few other days to go, but sometimes I stay home, put my kids to bed, and relax. I push myself beyond my comfort zone, but if I'm not in the mood to go some nights, I stay home. I don't have to do all of the things with all of the people all of the time. I can do enough to get to know people, let them get to know me, even if I don't attend everything.

It's okay to have personal boundaries and meet your needs while participating in community events. I generally love big crowds and interacting with lots of people, but I have a high need for sleep and rest as well. I try to *Get Involved and Participate* as much as I can while taking care of myself too.

Building connections during sad times

Celebratory events are a fun way to get involved, but you can participate and connect during less festive times too. Funerals are an important part of life in Brevig Mission and Shishmaref. Because everyone is connected through family or social relations, deaths affect nearly all of my students and coworkers. Taking part in the mourning traditions is a way to support them, even if I didn't know the deceased very well.

Communal mourning for a person begins immediately after their death. Friends and family gather in the family's home to offer love and support. Sometimes the pastor comes with his guitar, and everyone sings church songs and prays. Bringing food to these gatherings is a way of supporting the family and helping them host all the mourners. When a young man recently passed away unexpectedly, Steve made plates of cookies, and I brought them to the house. I put them on the table before hugging his mom and telling her I was sorry.

Typically, when a person arrives at a mourning home in Brevig Mission, they first hug the person closest to the deceased, usually a spouse or a parent. Then they hug other close relations. I usually hug all the other people in the room too, offering my condolences and love. Then I sit on the floor and just be with the family and friends. Sometimes I talk. Sometimes I hug the children that come in and out. Sometimes I just sit there and be. If singing is happening, I sing.

The formal funeral happens after all the out-of-town family and friends arrive. At the end of the funeral, everyone gets in line to hug the family seated in the first few rows before viewing the body one last time. It's a time of lots of tears and sobbing. It can be hard on the heart, but some of my choicest experiences have been waiting in line to hug the grieving family.

I've held a sobbing child and told them everything would be all right. I've gotten on my knees to look someone in the eyes and tell them I'm sorry. I always tell the family members I love them and am praying for them. That might not be appropriate in all communities, but it is in Lutheran-majority Brevig Mission. I remember those moments when I am dealing with a misbehaving student that I've previously comforted at a funeral. I remind myself that I told them I loved them and that was a type of promise to continue to love them.

Mourning with the community is a very intense show of support and solidarity. It acknowledges the pain of the community and my willingness to be there in the midst of it. It shows that I'm not cut off and separate from the rest of the people of Brevig Mission, but that what affects them affects me as well. Each hug I give and each tear I cry is a root going a little deeper and interweaving with the roots of the people around me. They *Make Connections a Little at a Time*.

All community events have their own set of protocols, and it can be intimidating to step into a situation without knowing exactly what to do. Don't let your fear of awkwardness prevent you from *Getting Involved* or *Participating*. My best advice is to watch and copy. Observe what other people are doing and then do the same. This isn't a fool-proof method. In the example of a funeral, some people you observe might be close family members of the deceased, and copying them would be inappropriate for someone less connected.

For example, in Shishmaref family members of the deceased sit in the center pews in the church. In Brevig Mission, family members sit in the first three or four rows. In both places, the closer the family, the closer to the front they sit. If I were to copy a close family member, I might sit in the rows reserved for family. That's why it helps to have someone in town to help you learn the etiquette of events like funerals beforehand. (We'll talk about these allies in a little while.)

Going to community events is a great way to build connections. You get a chance to interact with others outside of the school setting, meet new people, and widen your view of your Transplant Home. Don't be discouraged if the growth seems insignificant. It takes time for strong connections to develop, but if you keep reaching out, it will get easier and lay the groundwork for meaningful relationships.

CHAPTER 10

Social Norms: You're Gonna Need Some Allies

When my mother-in-law planted her vegetable garden, she took great care in designing the layout. She arranged certain plants next to each other because they grow better together.

Just like broccoli grows better when thyme is nearby to repel pests, Transplant Teachers grow better with someone there to provide guidance, encouragement, and offer hope and an example that teachers can be successful in this environment. I call these people allies.

If your new community is more reserved, it might not be as easy to just show up at events. People in Brevig Mission and Shishmaref were and are thrilled every time Steve and I showed up to anything, but that will not be true in all places. One option for handling this situation is to develop local allies that can bring you to things. It can be acceptable to attend an event with a local person.

Your allies (both local and Transplant Teachers who've been around for a while) are also a good source of information when determining if an event or activity is public or requires an invitation. In Brevig Mission, it would be completely acceptable for a new teacher to just show up at church choir practice, but if someone just showed up as a family was preparing to go berry picking, it would be weird. Your allies can help you learn to tell the difference.

Sometimes, even if an event is public, it can be scary to go by yourself. This is another instance when your allies come in handy.

Early in our years in Shishmaref, I felt inspired to take part and support people who are grieving the death of loved ones. I asked one of my allies if she would call me next time she went to sing at someone's house. She did. I showed up with her, someone passed me a song book, and I started singing along. Once I had shown up the first time, it was normal to see me at similar events, so I felt comfortable going by myself.

Allies can also clue you in on how to behave at community events. If you feel comfortable with someone, you can *Ask for Help* without being embarrassed (or, at least, a little less embarrassed). Allies can explain the reasons behind the different protocols and traditions so you know what's going on. You can also copy what they do and know they'll be mindful of showing you the appropriate way to take part.

Allies can introduce you to new things. As you become friends, they might feed you new foods, and you might even get to be around for the preparation. Your allies might speak a heritage language around you, and you'll have a chance to ask about the words and phrases. You might get to hear family stories and look at pictures. Maybe you'll be around as they make things or do housework in a way that's unusual to you.

Allies also make it easier to *Accept Feedback*. The burning face and stinging eyes might lessen if the correction comes from someone you know and like.

Keep an eye out for coworkers or neighbors that will make good allies. Developing a friendship with them will enrich your life and give you insights into how the community works. The bonus is that they might be able to take you to events that are more private. Don't use people just to get invites because that's not cool, but focus on developing meaningful relationships, and invites will happen naturally.

Don't hang out with only teachers

The people you choose to spend time with are important. The right people can provide guidance and enhance your experience. Your fellow teachers are an important source of interaction and support. They can take the place of extended family when you're far from your original home, but it's important to expand your circle beyond just teachers.

I've seen teachers come to the village, stay for years, and only interact with other teachers. This provides them with adequate social opportunities, but they miss out on the richness available by including other community members. If all of your social needs are met with your teacher-only network, you may not feel the need to extend into the community. If that's happening to you, try to expand your reach, even if it means moving out of your comfort zone.

A first step can be as simple as not always sitting by other transplants at staff meetings. This is part of *Get Involved! Try things! Participate!* Seek someone else to sit by and chit chat with while you wait for the meeting to start. It's handy to have a few ideas of conversation starters. I enjoy asking questions to get people to talk about themselves or something they know about. This also prevents me from talking too much if I get nervous. I few questions I might use are:

- Is it always this warm in October?
- Who should I talk to about finding some sealskin gloves?
- I've seen fish hanging on racks down by the beach. What kind are they?

There's always the old standbys of "How about this weather?" and "How's your week going?" Those might work, but you might as well use the casual conversation to increase your knowledge of your new home.

If the person seems willing to talk, ask some follow-up questions to keep the conversation going. If the other person seems resistant to the questions, back off. They might not be comfortable enough to have a conversation or might be nervous too. Don't write them off forever, just sit by a few different people before you come back around. Sometimes it takes more than one attempt to get a warm response. The idea is to *Make Connections a Little at a Time*. It's okay if it's just a little bit at first.

The same approach can work at community or school events. Seek out people who aren't teachers to sit by. Maybe one of the staff members that grew up in the area is at the event with their family. A comfortable start might include sitting by them and meeting their kids. You could ask questions about the kids and to the kids directly.

Looking for a friendly face and sitting by that person is also a good strategy. Start by asking, "Can I sit here?" The worst that will happen is that they will say no, and you'll move on to the next friendly face. If the friendly face says yes, you can sit down and introduce yourself. A fun question to ask in Brevig Mission is, "Who are you related to here?" They'll likely laugh and say, "Everybody!" Then I ask them for specifics by saying, "Like who?" Asking about relations is completely normal in rural Alaska and is a great way to help people feel at ease.

The "how are you related" question is more relevant to a small community and might not work as well in a larger place. In that case I might ask, "What's your connection to people here?" If they don't understand what I mean by "connection" I would offer examples like "Are you related to anybody here? Good friends? Neighbors?"

If you discover someone super friendly and fun to talk to, you can seek them out again at another event. They could turn into an ally that helps you grow into your Transplant Home.

Depending on the age of your students, they might be able to suggest people to get to know. Some questions I might ask my students are:

- Who sews and might let me watch them?
- Who would I ask if I want to go hunting?
- Who do you think would take me berry picking?

Of course, these questions are tailored to the Alaska Bush. You will have to adapt them to your Transplant Home. Pick an activity or place you're curious about, and ask your students who would be a good person to ask about it or take you.

You may also consider starting your own events and doing the inviting. The events don't have to be huge or elaborate. They can be as simple as a game night or a dinner. Steve has a weekly guys' game night on Wednesdays. He invites guys from around town to come and play board games that last hours. There's always a lot of laughing and joking, and it's a good way to get to know people. Not all of the invites are accepted, but he keeps inviting.

You can do the same thing with whatever you enjoy. Invite someone over to watch a movie, make art, or sew. Not every invitation will be accepted, but that doesn't mean it's not worth the effort. The more invitations you extend, the more likely it is people will accept, and they'll get the idea that your home is open to visitors. Even unaccepted invitations can be part of *Making Connections a Little at a Time*.

Veteran transplants

It's also helpful to have an outsider who's been around for a while as an ally. These allies are great for when you feel embarrassed asking a question you feel you should already know the answer to. They'll remember what it was like to be new and unseasoned, and they'll likely be happy to fill you in on what they've learned about participating in the rituals and traditions of community events.

A Veteran Transplant can tell you to slow down and shut up if you want to learn anything. They can relate to feeling uncomfortable when the local people are working in almost telepathic synchrony because they're doing things the way they've been done for generations. A Veteran Transplant's experience of adapting to your Transplant Home can support you on your own journey.

My first year in Shishmaref, I was struggling with the junior high girls. I couldn't hook them into participating in class, and they were constantly criticizing my lessons and appearance (which I took personally). I was indignant about their behavior. After sharing my woes with the assistant principal, he said, "Yeah, they can be really mean." (Those were not his exact words, but definitely the sentiment.)

That statement did more for me than any advice. I was relieved that he knew! He understood! It felt so good to know that it wasn't just me. The girls really were being mean. Once I didn't feel the need to prove their behavior was unacceptable, I could put energy into figuring out how to deal with the problem. I certainly could have made that shift on my own eventually, but the assistant principal's comments helped me get there.

(By the way, those girls have grown into lovely adults. We're friends. Sometimes we joke about how we didn't get along when we first met. It's funny now.)

That assistant principal was a good ally. He offered a balanced perspective about what was hard without complaining. Other colleagues have been similarly supportive. One veteran teacher let me watch her reading class to show me how she adapted the scripted curriculum to make it relevant and enjoyable for her students. It inspired me to make my own adaptations rather than dismiss the entire curriculum as useless. The same teacher told me that sometimes teaching is more about teaching students about life than it is about academic achievement. That advice helped me ease up on my determination to shove content standards down the students' throats.

Colleagues noticed and complimented my efforts in a way that made me want to amplify them. Others shared resources and examples from their own classrooms. These people were allies because they encouraged me and prompted mind shifts or renewed efforts. Like companion plants, they enhanced my growth. The connections I built with them couldn't replace the connections I was making with the community, but reaching outward to my fellow Transplant Teachers made me a stronger and healthier teacher.

Avoid toxic plants

Just as allies strengthen a transplant, certain plants will cause harm. For example, gardening folklore says planting onions next to beans and peas is a bad idea because they have different soil chemical requirements. Tomatoes and corn shouldn't be planted next to each other because they spread infections to each other easily.

This can happen to Transplant Teachers too. I've seen new teachers come to the village and get sucked into the clutches of toxic staff members. Negative comments and judgmental attitudes of toxic staff members can influence new teachers, who start criticizing the people and circumstances of their new home. They blame the school, the administration, the curriculum, and the community for all of their struggles. The blame poisons their perspective and blocks potential growth. These new teachers soon find themselves surrounded only by other negative people, and the cycle continues.

It's important to tell the difference between companion plants and toxic plants because each can make a big difference in your Transplant Experience. One way to differentiate is to check the content of your conversations and how you feel afterward. If your associates offer mostly negative comments and criticisms, they are likely toxic plants. If conversations consist of complaining and pointing out what's wrong with other people, the school, the community, etc., they're toxic plants. If you feel yourself getting indignant or self-righteous after talking to them, they're probably toxic plants.

Conversely, if the advice they offer leaves you feeling hopeful, they're an ally. If they help you find solutions rather than dwell on problems, they're an ally. Allies help you *Stay Positive* in your thoughts and publicly. Not in a Pollyanna way, but in a "let's get up and keep moving" kind of way. In a "there's a way to figure it out" kind of way.

Some people might be toxic in one context but valuable allies in another. It's up to you to navigate interactions with those people and see when and where they might offer support and when and where they might drag you down.

Keep in mind as you turn to your allies that everyone has their own biases based on their individual experiences. Some background information I accepted as true from some of my allies turned out to be less than the gospel truth. I don't think they lied to me, they just gave me information from a distinct perspective. The longer I was around, and the more people I connected with, the more I discovered other perspectives.

Gathering information from multiple perspectives is a good thing. It can help you get a more balanced view of the people and situations around you. Widen your circle enough to include different people from different situations. You'll be better positioned to get good information and make good decisions.

Benefits of allies

I've been lucky in both Shishmaref and Brevig Mission to be surrounded by women who became trusted sources of information. I knew they would be honest with me, and they were often my foot in the door to join activities that required an invitation.

My local allies also started thinking of me when they planned to do something cool. One of my favorite days in Shishmaref was the day my friends called me to watch them butcher seals. I grabbed my camera and ran right over! I got tons of fascinating photos, and they told me all about the process. I even got to go to their house later that night and watch them kapsraq (kapsraq is the Inupiaq word for removing the blubber from the seal skins). The tools they used had been passed down from their grandmothers and great-grandmothers. They were doing the work that Inupiaq women have done for thousands of years. It was a moment that could have been in a *National Geographic* magazine, and I got to be there in person. I got an authentic glimpse of the Inupiaq subsistence lifestyle. It was only possible because I had shown an interest in cultural activities and developed relationships with my allies who thought to invite me.

The more you participate in local gatherings and experiences, the more likely you'll get an invitation to another one. This starts a cycle of connections that perpetuates and grows. The more you *Get Involved! Try Things! and Participate!*, the more *Connections You Make a Little at a Time*.

Venture out of your house and go visiting

So how do you develop and nurture relationships with people that will turn into your allies and friends? Getting out of the school and your house to attend community events is helpful. Visiting on an individual level is also helpful.

As I mentioned before, in Brevig Mission, it's socially acceptable to just show up at someone's house to visit. Local people visit each other all the time. It was initially scary to do this because I wasn't sure who lived where. There are no house numbers, addresses, or street signs to tell me I'm at the right house. What I end up doing is asking someone to point me in the general direction of a specific house. As I get closer, I ask another person (a kid if I can find one) which house is so-and-so's. If nobody's around, I summon up my courage, knock on the closest door and ask, "Is this so-and-so's house?" If it's not, they usually tell me where it is. I thank them and continue the process until I arrive at the correct location.

Most people in Brevig Mission don't knock on doors when they're visiting. They just open the door and walk in. If I had done that when I was growing up my mother would have been horrified. I still can't walk into most houses without knocking. But expecting people to come to the door and open it for me would be weird, so I compromise. I knock as I'm opening the door, and then I shout out, "It's Angie!" as I'm walking in. This allows me to at least give (very) brief notice that I'm coming in without inconveniencing my hosts by interrupting them.

If it feels weird to just drop by, do some planning to give your visit a purpose beyond chatting. As I mentioned when describing birthday parties, I really like the dessert blueberry delight. It's sweetened blueberries on a light crust with a cream cheese topping. I had some at a birthday party for one of my students, so I called up his grandma and asked her if she would show me how to make it. She agreed and told me what supplies to bring.

I brought my bag of supplies over to her house on a Sunday afternoon, and we made it together and talked about her memories of school. We got to visit for a longer amount of time than usual, and I left feeling like I knew her better. It was a connection building experience. It was an opportunity to *Make a Connection a Little at a Time*.

Your entry point doesn't have to be making food (although that's a good one). It can be dropping off food. Maybe you make some treats to share. Maybe you show up on someone's doorstep with a loaf of bread. You could drop off a flyer or school calendar. You could bring an awesome piece of art or writing that their son or daughter created. If they invite you in when you stop by, accept the invitation! Even if it's a short visit, it's another small connection.

A natural extension of being a visitor in other people's homes is allowing visitors in your home. Your home is your personal sanctuary, and you get to set the boundaries about who and what is allowed in your home. I suggest you at least consider the social norms of your Transplant Home when making these decisions.

I've seen teachers with strict no-visitors policies, and I've seen teachers with kids at their house at what I considered inappropriate times. Steve and I shoot for something in the middle. Adults are welcome in our home at any time. Adults bringing their children are welcome as long as our kids are not trying to go to sleep. We are a little more selective about kids only visitors. Steve doesn't allow kids to visit when I'm not home because he wants to maintain a sense of propriety and prevent any rumors. Exceptions to this rule are our kids' close relatives whose families we know really well. When I'm home, we allow kids to visit that are close to our kids' ages that our kids actually want to play with. Older relatives that our kids have relationships with are invited in as well.

Sometimes the visitors join us for dinner. Sometimes they don't. If the little kids don't listen or respect our rules, we ask them to leave. If the kids don't leave when we ask them to (like when it's bedtime), they don't get to come back another time.

It's been a good system for us. Our home is open for moderate amounts of interaction. Our kids get a chance to play with their friends, cousins, and siblings, but Steve and I don't feel like we're babysitting or overwhelmed with a never-ending flow of visitors.

I wasn't always so wise when it came to visitors. Early in our first year in Shishmaref, I let anyone who wanted to visit come inside, no matter how many kids were already there. I insisted to Steve that this was necessary for us to get to know people and be seen as friendly. As a result, our tiny house became a for elementary school children.

There were as many as fifteen of them over at one time, and we didn't really have anything for them to do after they finished fighting over who got to sit on our recliner, so they got creative. I can't remember how they got in our bedroom in the first place, but they did. They started digging through our closet and trying on our clothes.

I knew that was too much. I knew Steve was right. We needed to set some boundaries. I wanted to be open and friendly, but not at the expense of our privacy. We started to limit visitors to one small group of kids at a time. If more knocked on the door, we simply said, "We already have visitors" and gently turned the new ones at the door away. The bedroom became off-limits. The visits became more enjoyable, and we were still perceived as open and friendly, even without kids wearing my shoes and Steve's dress shirts.

There are many moderate options between the extremes of nobody and everybody and many options for informal interactions that will allow Transplant Teachers to *Make Connections a Little at a Time*. Everybody has different tolerance levels and personalities, so find what works for you.

Transplant Teachers need allies. Not only can your sprouting friendships guide you through the social mores of your Transplant

Home, but they make the journey more fun and interesting. Not everyone has to be your best friend, but a wide network of allies can support you in a variety of situations. Start with the people that offer you kindness and interest, but don't stop there. Extend the same kindness and interest in your interactions with others.

CHAPTER 11

Social Norms: Communication or What you think you said and heard may not exactly be what you said and heard

Everybody in Shishmaref spoke English when we got there, but certain Inupiaq words and phrases were very much a part of everyday life. On our first day, we went on a walk on the beach with a couple of elementary school girls. They kept asking if we knew certain Inupiaq words. Of course, I answered, "No." They tried to get me to say the words, but I didn't because they kept laughing. I had a hunch they were trying to get me to say something naughty or silly. Turns out they were only trying to get me to say *anaq*, which is the Inupiaq word for poop. It definitely could have been worse. My experience with local communication continued (and still continues!) through the years in Shishmaref and Brevig Mission.

Learning how to communicate differently is part of the Transplant Experience. Everything else that you're trying to do will hinge on your ability to understand and be understood. It can be confusing to work with a new language or slang, but it can also be fun and interesting. You can use the same strategies with communication as you do with the rest of the areas of your Transplant Life.

Local dialects and slang

Even if you speak the local language or have researched some words and phrases, be sensitive to the local dialect. I've found resources for learning Inupiaq, including a Rosetta Stone course. However, most of them are in the North Slope dialect, which makes sense because that's where the highest concentration of Inupiaq speakers live in Alaska. Shishmaref and Brevig Mission each have their own distinct dialects of Inupiaq, and the people are very proud of them. If I had waltzed in speaking North Slope Inupiaq, I would have gotten lots of corrections and comments like, "We don't say that here." Approach language with cultural humility. Use what you know, but *Accept Feedback* and be open to correction and learning.

You'll also have to deal with local slang and colloquialisms. Shishmaref and Brevig Mission are both full of those. Some I've had to learn include these:

cheap = of poor quality or unfair or lame

honda = any kind of four-wheeler or ATV

snow-go or snow machine = snowmobile

put-put = barely working

gaa = an expression of annoyance

cooked = broken or all gone

always (as in, "Do you always buy carvings?") = habitually or often tomorrow next day = the day after tomorrow

follow = to go with (as in, "I'm going to the store. Wanna follow?")

puddle boots = rubber boots

raw = really (as in, "You kids are raw loud!")

try see = shortened form of "try and see" (as in, "try see if the batteries work")

I never = I didn't (usually an exclamation after getting scolded, as in, "I never hit him!" Or an answer to a question about something naughty, "Did you take the erasers?" "I never!" Can also be used calmly, as in, "I never go to the store yet.")

mopey = angry or grumpy

sticky fingers = tendency to steal (as in, "He got sticky fingers for pens.")

post = post office (never used with the article "the." "I'm going post." "Wanna go post?")

babytell = tattle

bugging = annoying

    I could figure out the meaning of most of the slang words from the context without having to ask outright for the definitions. Some of the words were familiar but used in a different way than I was used to. This was a good opportunity for me to *Withhold Judgment* and *Stay Positive*. Instead of labeling the slang as "wrong" or "improper," I just viewed it as unique to the villages where it is used. My efforts to use local phrases are a way to *Try Things! and Participate!* People still crack up when I use the word "cooked" to describe something that's not working.

Some of the words used in Shishmaref and Brevig Mission are harder to figure out because they are Inupiaq. For those words I had to *Ask for Help*. Finessing my pronunciation and understanding of Inupiaq words is a way for me to deepen my connection to local culture.

I made a list of some of the Inupiaq words used all the time in Brevig Mission and Shishmaref. I will spell these words three ways. The first way will use the Standard Inupiaq Alphabet. The second way will be spelled phonetically in a way that most speakers of Standard (or Standardish) American English will be able to sound them out. The third way will use the actual International Phonetic Alphabet for anyone serious about pronunciation and/or will be impressed that I know how to (mostly) use the phonetic alphabet. The definition will be given after the spellings.

> *kanitaq* = kuhneetuck = /kʌnitʌk/ = the entryway outside of a house that one most pass through in order to get to the door leading to the interior of the house. Also known as an Arctic entry.
>
> *kugluk* = kooglook = /kʊglʊk/ = startle or surprise
>
> *anaq* = uhnuck = /ʌnʌk/ = poop

amaq = uhmuck = /ʌmʌk/ = to carry a baby or small child on your back

kataq = kuhtuck = /kʌtʌk/ = fall down

qii = kee = /ki/ = go, hurry

nanaqsuq = nuhnucksook = /nʊnʌksʊk/ = scold

Fun side note: Some Inupiaq words are used so often that the English equivalent is never used and sometimes unknown. When we were in the Lower 48 one summer when Kaitlyn was about five years old she told some kids she was going to amaq something (carry it on her back). I told her she needed to explain what that meant because not everybody knows what it means. She said, "Amaq is Inupiaq for amaq." She didn't have another word to describe the concept.

Another fun side note: Some slang words have roots in Inupiaq. "Gaa" is a shortened version of *akkaa*, which means too much. Other slang words have cultural roots. "Cooked" originated from drying skins for making parkas. Women began hanging the skins near the wood stove to dry, but if they got too hot the skins became brittle and unusable. They referred to these skins as "cooked." The word has since transferred to anything that's been ruined. Familiarity with that kind of local knowledge is another way to connect with my Transplant Home.

I've learned not to be shy about asking what words mean. My natural curiosity about language worked well for me in this regard. It felt natural to ask because I sincerely wanted to know. If I ask my students, they usually laugh and look at me with disbelief, but then they describe what it means. Adults are generally more polite and will just tell me.

I know many Inupiaq words now but stumble on pronunciations and hearing the different sounds. A couple of years into our time in Shishmaref a Young Elder in Shishmaref gave me my Inupiaq name, Quwiasuk, which is the root word for "happy." If I pronounce it wrong, it means I have to pee. That still causes me some anxiety when I introduce myself in Inupiaq. I don't want to tell people that my name is "I have to pee." I keep trying and accepting corrections to my pronunciation as graciously as possible, even when I want to crawl under a rock and hide from embarrassment.

Part of using the strategy *Try Things!* involves experimenting with local language and slang. It may feel uncomfortable, but just as you need to do with any new activity or event, attempt to push through the discomfort. It can be humbling to be corrected or inadvertently pronounce a crude word, but mistakes are an opportunity to *Accept Feedback* and keep trying. The most important thing is that you care enough and respect the culture enough to want to learn.

Non-verbal communication

Non-verbal language is also an important part of communication. In both Brevig Mission and Shishmaref, raised eyebrows mean "yes." A scrunched nose means "no." Children and adults use these facial gestures all the time

One time Steve kept one of his third graders in at recess and was scolding him. It was near the beginning of our first year, so we were still navigating unfamiliar social and behavioral terrain, and Steve was still trying to get to know his students.

Steve explained why the student's behavior was not okay, and then he asked, "Do you understand?" The student raised his eyebrows. Steve asked again, "Do you understand?" The student raised his eyebrows again. Steve started getting frustrated and assumed defiance. Steve demanded that the student answer him before realizing that the kid had been answering him all along. Oops.

I've adopted raised eyebrows and a scrunched nose into my own communication style. It's a very efficient way to answer questions during quiet time in class. Students indicate a question or a need, and I'm able to respond non-verbally without disturbing the peace in the classroom.

I've adopted these mechanisms so completely that I sometimes use them outside of Brevig Mission and Shishmaref. I'll be at the Anchorage airport Starbucks, and the barista will ask if I want whipped cream on my vanilla bean Frappuccino. I'll raise my eyebrows. Then we'll awkwardly stare at each other for a while before I realize that she's expecting an audible answer. I'll stammer "yes" and slink away embarrassed to wait for my drink.

Eye contact is another thing that's different. I was raised to look adults directly in the eye when asking for something or when being scolded. The scolding would be worse if I didn't look the adults in the eye. ("Look at me when I'm talking to you!") The kids in Shishmaref and Brevig Mission do the exact opposite. I'm not sure if it's taught or just something they pick up, but they look away deferentially when asking for something or being scolded. It's not out of disrespect. That can be problematic if a teacher is demanding a student look at them when the student has spent their entire life looking away out of deference.

Each place will have its own set of unspoken rules about non-verbal communication. Notice what people do and don't do and the contexts in which they do or don't do it. When you observe and *Withhold Judgment* you might learn enough to communicate more effectively.

Exploring and practicing local ways of communicating is a good way to *Make Connections*. Most people will like that you're trying to use local words, phrases, and nonverbal communication. *Accepting Feedback* and *Asking for Help* with pronunciation can be good conversation starters. Understanding what people are saying or asking will help your efforts to *Participate! and Try Things!* An investment of time and energy in communication can pay rich dividends.

CHAPTER 12

Transplant Challenge: Logistical Systems are Different

I talked earlier about how not having house numbers and street signs is complicated when finding people's houses. It's also complicated when convincing online merchants that our made up address is our functioning address, even if the USPS system can't confirm it. I try to tell people that even if the package had only my first name and the zip code, it would still get to me. One time I ordered something for my dad and accidentally had it sent to Brevig Mission. The postmaster recognized Dad's last name as my middle name, and the mail ended up in my hands. But, sometimes sellers are reluctant to mail items to unverified addresses, and we have to work to allay their fears or find another way around the problem.

It's not just addresses and mail, though. There's voting, working visas, driver's licenses, and an assortment of other issues. Part of adjusting to your Transplant Home includes navigating logistical systems like shopping, transportation, law enforcement, government, and health care. Things that seemed so simple in your previous life may be utterly confusing and complicated in your Transplant Home. Learning to work within these new systems is a key to thriving.

One strategy for dealing with new logistics is to *Be Flexible and Adaptive*. I've mentioned before how desperately clutching your expectations can cause frustration and keep you from focusing on possible solutions in the context of social norms. This is totally true about logistics, too. Insisting that you ought to be able to order certain things at certain times will do nothing to change the reality of your situation, so you might as well figure out how to deal with it. A positive way to handle this challenge is to work inwardly to accept your reality and work outwardly to respond to it.

Asking for Help is another valuable outward strategy. The inward work is your responsibility, but you don't have to figure everything out on your own. Asking your allies how to do something, or for help doing it, can save you time and energy. Get over the fear of looking stupid by admitting that you really don't know the answer. Then accept guidance.

Dealing with new systems will often require the strategy *Plan Ahead*. This strategy is an inward-outward hybrid. Inwardly you'll map out what you'll need ahead of time. Outwardly you'll gather information about the processes and systems involved and take action. There's nothing like red tape and delays to make you wish you started working on something three months before. Sometimes things take time. Sometimes you make mistakes that make them take even longer. Give yourself some wiggle room to figure things out by thinking in advance.

Plumbing: the time we got a flush toilet in our living room

Occasionally something as basic as plumbing requires *Adaptation*. I've mentioned before that Shishmaref has no central sewer system. Using honey buckets and incinolets was an adjustment all its own, but that wasn't all we needed to *Be Flexible* about.

During our third year, we got a flush toilet. It sounds pretty exciting, and it was, but the district plumber and his colleagues installed it in our living room. They built a platform less than ten feet away from our front door, put a toilet on it, and then built walls around the platform. They mentioned something about it being easier to hook into the existing plumbing that way…

We had expected the new toilet to go in the unheated room where we kept the honey bucket, but that was apparently not an option. This development ended Steve's weekly treks across town to empty the honey bucket, but we didn't have a door to the toilet closet for the first few months. It was kind of awkward when people were over. One time Steve was playing games with a group of boys, and he had to go to the bathroom. All the boys had to wait in our bedroom and shut the door while Steve used the door-less flush toilet closet in our living room. Classy.

The location of our toilet was firmly out of our control. We weren't given a say in where it would be installed, and we didn't have the skills to move it ourselves. Complaining about where it *should* have been and how it *should* have been installed did nothing to change the situation (perhaps you remember how useless *should* statements are from our discussion earlier). The best way to handle it was to make the best of our living room toilet and be grateful we (meaning Steve) didn't have to haul the honey bucket across town anymore (although, I must admit the living room toilet remains one of our favorite stories to tell because most people find it absolutely unbelievable).

Your Transplant Experience may include logistics you can't even imagine (like figuring out how to deal with a toilet in your living room). Adapting is part of the journey. Some logistics of the Alaska Bush may be unique to our corner of the world, but your Transplant Home will have its own peculiarities. Embrace the peculiarities so you don't make things harder than they need to be.

CHAPTER 13

Logistics: Food and Supplies

One realm of logistics that might require some *Adaptation* is food and supplies. In my quest to supplement groceries available in Shishmaref, I turned to Amazon.com. I'd never really used Amazon to order anything but books (remember, this was 2005), and I was thrilled to have access to a wide range of cooking supplies. My cart was overflowing with ingredients, and I checked out, satisfied that I had mastered online food shopping. It wasn't until the boxes started arriving and I started checking packing slips that I realized one seller had charged sixty dollars in shipping for a jar of minced garlic and a bottle of lime juice! I hadn't checked the shipping costs of each individual item in my cart. It was a rookie mistake that proved I had a lot to learn.

Food sources might be different in your new location. I recommend you use the strategy *Try Things!*, even if they seem overwhelmingly different. Shishmaref and Brevig Mission have introduced my palate to marine mammals. I had no idea that something could have the texture of beef but the flavor of fish before I tried seal. I have tried everything that's been offered to me, including fermented walrus flipper (usruk) and whale skin and blubber (maktak).

Maktak is my favorite. The first time I tried it was during the Inupiaq Days celebration in Shishmaref. Someone brought maktak to share and offered me a taste. The bite-size pieces had a layer of dark whale skin topped with a thicker layer of pinkish white blubber. I was really curious about it, so I accepted the offer immediately. I asked how to eat it. The ladies around me told me to put it on a cracker with a little salt. I followed their suggestions, and it was really good. Almost like eating a nutty cheese with a really chewy center. I like it so much that now I eat it plain. I even have some in my freezer right now.

As a newcomer, you might be gifted local foods. Accept gifts graciously. I was walking down the street in Brevig one day when the mother of some of my students stuck her head out the door and asked if I wanted some meat. She was butchering a moose, and she cut off a chunk and put it in a Ziplock bag for me to take home. My oldest daughter's uncle has shown up on our doorstep with a leg of caribou, and her grandparents send seal oil to the house to be used as a condiment. My son's mom saves tundra berries for his birthday parties.

Students in our school district are allowed ten subsistence days for hunting or fishing, counted as excused absences. One of my students took a subsistence day to go moose hunting. I asked him the next day during third hour if he got anything. He lit up and told me, "Yes." I asked where my share was, as a joke, and he laughed. After going home for lunch, he returned with a frozen chunk! He was so excited to give it to me. It was adorable! The next day he asked me how the meat was. I told him it was still thawing out, but we would eat it as soon as possible. He even talked to Steve about the meat. He was so happy to share.

Sometimes the gifts require some help. When coworkers first gave us geese, I didn't know what to do with a whole bird that had all of its guts intact and feathers attached. I had to *Ask for Help*. After some Google searches and consultations with local women, I dipped the whole bird in boiling water before removing the feathers (well, most of them, I got a little lazy toward the end). I slit open the abdomen and removed the stomach, intestines, liver, and a host of other organs. Then I roasted the goose with potatoes and carrots. It was yummy and made for a great Sunday dinner.

Some friends dropped a box of caribou meat off at our house. It had a random assortment of parts, including the tongue and the heart. I'd never cooked tongue and heart before, so I called Kaitlyn's grandma and asked her what to do with it. "Make soup!" was her instant reply.

I asked her some questions, and she walked me through the process mostly by saying, "You could," when I asked if I could add certain things. (Brevig Mission cooking is less an exact science and more a set of principles that can be applied across a variety of dishes.) I cut the heart and tongue up into little strips, fried them for a while, and then added water and vegetables. After simmering until the meat was done and the vegetables were soft, I served the soup to all the children at my house.

Levi's brother happened to be visiting, and he said, "It tastes like soup." That's how I knew I had nailed the recipe, and his comment remains one of the best compliments I've ever received about my cooking. (It turns out I really like heart and tongue soup. The texture of tongue is different from anything else I've ever eaten, but the flavor is amazing.)

In each of these food adventures I had to *Be Flexible and Adapt* to new foods (whale, moose, geese, caribou heart and tongue) and new ways of acquiring the food (while walking down the street, while coming back from lunch, handed to me as I left after visiting, and dropped off in a cardboard box). I also had to *Ask for Help* to make use of the gifts. Besides literally feeding our family, these experiences nurtured our connection to the land and the people around us.

Ordering food, or Amazon delivers out here!

You will likely need food that you can't get by walking out the front door. Shishmaref and Brevig Mission do not have their own flour mills, nor are they producers of sugar or other baking staples. We can get lots of red meat locally, but if we want chicken or pork, we have to find a way to get that in. Greens and berries are plentiful in the summer and can be frozen, but other types of fruits and vegetables have to be imported as well. We have not figured out how to milk a musk ox, so dairy products are another thing we get from outside the village.

I recommend that you find out how people in your community order and buy food and then do that. It's good to get information from a mix of local people and veteran transplants. One of my friends that grew up in Shishmaref was a gold mine of information and insight, but she would have no idea how to get fresh milk because she grew up on boxed milk and even drove around looking for it when she went to college in Anchorage.

Keep in mind that what works in one place, be it a website or regional store, might not work in another. Some villages have great luck having items shipped out from a grocery store in Fairbanks. Every time we tried that in Shishmaref, we had to wait ages for our groceries to arrive. One airline out of Nome is great about getting our food and produce orders shipped out immediately. Other airlines, less so. A reliable airline out of Bethel might be notoriously understaffed and behind schedule out of Kotzebue. Local information that pertains specifically to your community will be the most helpful.

Also expect things to change. Amazon orders used to arrive in Brevig Mission in a matter of days, but we've been through periods of time when it takes weeks. Alaska is a special case because travel and deliveries are inherently erratic due to the weather. But, sometimes retailers and airlines change their policies and that impacts how food and supplies arrive. *Be Flexible*, and when something stops working, do something else.

There is also great variance in the condition of goods. Some pilots and airline agents are mindful of packages marked fragile, but others just toss things around like nothing matters. We've had boxes of produce left on the steps of the school by a substitute airline agent, and the boxes were invaded by students before we even knew they were there. Luckily, the company that sent the produce accepted full responsibility and gave us a refund because the goods didn't make it into our hands.

Working with companies that guarantee their goods and the shipping is crucial for us. Otherwise we spend hundreds of dollars on produce that gets frozen and is unusable. That's not a risk I'm willing to take, so I give my business to companies that will work to replace or refund damaged goods. That may not be a possibility in all places, but it's something to consider.

You paid how much for that?

Because it's so much effort to get food and supplies into the village, prices are higher than in a grocery store in Anchorage. Here's a smattering of food prices I've recorded over the years:

> Fruit snacks (twenty-eight little pouches)- $8.49
> 32 oz. Gatorade- $4.89
> 48 oz. Apple juice- $9.89
> 18 eggs- $5.39
> 5 lbs. of potatoes- $10.79
> Yellow onions- $1 each
> Low quality white bread- $3.29
> 4 apples- $5.65
> 16 oz. of cream cheese- $8.55
> Can of pop- $1.35

One of my first memories of Shishmaref is going to the general store and internally freaking out about the cost of cooking spray. Even in Nome prices are relatively high. You'll pay seven dollars for a gallon of milk and five dollars for a pound of butter there.

When my mom visited Brevig Mission, I paid $20 for a whole chicken to make for Mother's Day dinner. She freaked out and didn't want me to buy it (she's extremely frugal). I had to explain to her that this is just the way it is up here, and if we didn't buy it, we wouldn't have anything for dinner. I've had to *Adapt* to the prices. If I insisted on only buying things at prices comparable to my pre-Transplant Life, I would have to go without.

When people travel to Anchorage from Brevig Mission, they generally return with loads of groceries and household goods. Many people travel with coolers to bring back produce or frozen goods. Our family uses plastic tubs. We go to Costco as close to our flight as possible and fill the tubs with frozen meat, cheese, and produce.

We've *Adapted* by traveling with zip ties, packing tape, and permanent markers to keep the tubs closed and label them with our last name and phone number. The tubs can be checked as baggage on Alaska Airlines. The baggage claim in Nome (which is nothing more than a metal ramp that airline employees hand toss the luggage onto) is full of coolers, tubs, cardboard boxes, and bulk size packages of toilet paper. Nobody bats an eye. It's a normal part of living in the bush.

This method of securing supplies means that every food and household item is precious. I have a hard time throwing anything away (besides food waste products) because I can't shake the thought that I might need it someday. There are no big box stores in Brevig Mission where I can pick something up on my way home from work. I can get pretty much anything on Amazon, but then I have to wait for it to arrive. Life in the Alaska Bush has taught me to save anything that might be remotely useful. If I don't need it, somebody else might.

You're gonna wanna plan ahead

Planning Ahead is a necessity in the Alaska Bush. Without those big box stores that stock seasonal goods, you have to order Halloween costumes in August or September. Ordering Valentine's Day cards in January is a good idea. If I want to do a special art project in my classroom, I need to plan for it weeks in advance. If I want to make something special for a birthday dinner, I need to know the menu in time to order the necessary ingredients. If you don't plan ahead, you might be out of luck (unless you can call enough friends to find what you need).

I'm going to share my list of how we (but mostly I) *Plan Ahead* to give you an idea of the kinds of things you may want to add to your list. It reflects the holidays and events important to my family and the ones important in Brevig Mission. Yours may look different depending on what kinds of holidays you celebrate and what holidays and celebrations are important in your new community. I've learned over the years what I want to have on hand for Brevig Mission events. You may not be able to fill out your checklist completely when you first arrive in a new place. Just keep the thought of preparation in the back of your mind, and reflect on what you might want to do differently in the future.

The list is also based on a school year that starts in August and being outside of Alaska for the summer months. You may have to adjust to fit your school schedule.

July:
- start shopping for non-perishables to take up to Alaska

August:
- order Halloween costumes

September:
- order Halloween candy
- decide on a theme for Levi's November 18th birthday, order supplies
- order gifts for Levi's birthday
- start thinking about pumpkins for jack-o-lanterns

October:
- stock your freezer up with butter for holiday baking and cooking
- plan your Thanksgiving cooking so you can figure out when and how to get all of the supplies
- start ordering Christmas presents
- order wrapping paper, tape, and bows to wrap presents as they arrive
- check supply of paper plates for Thanksgiving and Christmas feasts. Order if necessary

November:
- order Christmas cards and stamps

December:
- cross your fingers that everything makes it in time…

January:
- now that Christmas is over, order Valentine's Day cards
- decide on a theme for Kaitlyn's March 22nd birthday
- order gifts for Kaitlyn's birthday

February:
- When is Easter this year? If it's in March, start ordering Easter supplies. Make sure you get your hands on lots of eggs to dye.

March:
- order gifts for Steve's May 3rd birthday
- order gifts for Steve and my April 29th anniversary

April:
- make a menu for Steve's birthday, start ordering supplies

Why bother doing this? So you have what you need/want. Around the holidays in Brevig Mission, mail delivery tends to take longer. What typically takes two to three weeks can take over a month. Everyone in town is ordering gifts, and sometimes the piles of packages get backed up in Nome.

As a parent, I don't want to deal with the trauma of a Halloween costume that didn't arrive. It's not the hugest deal in the grand scheme of things, but it makes my life easier if my daughter isn't sobbing about her missing princess shoes. Planning ahead to allow for unexpected events or weather situations ensures that we have costumes, gifts, and party supplies on hand when we need them. (You'll notice there's more advance planning/ordering for celebrations that focus on our kids. That's because Steve and I take the disappointment of delayed mail a lot better than our children.)

One of the most significant factors that can keep supplies from arriving on schedule is the weather. If the weather is bad, the planes don't fly. That means mail doesn't come. And freight for the store doesn't come. And packages from Amazon don't come. We've gone days without planes. The shelves in the store get bare, the postmaster gets bored because there's no incoming mail to process, and I get anxious waiting for my Amazon boxes to arrive that I know are just eighty miles away sitting in an airplane hangar. One year in Brevig Mission we didn't get mail for almost two weeks before Christmas. Mail and freight finally arrived on December 23rd with everyone's Christmas presents. The weather almost stole Christmas that year.

Sometimes our *Planning Ahead* gets a little out of control. Steve gets nervous if we have less than one hundred pounds of flour in storage. We currently have fifteen cases of canned mandarin oranges sitting by the front door because I eat them every day for lunch and hate the idea of not having fruit.

We also end up with Christmas presents sitting around for months. We used to be able to stack the closed Amazon.com boxes in our bedroom, but now our kids get out scissors and cut open the boxes. There is only so much room on the top shelf of our closet. Some years we ask neighbors if we can store some of the gifts in their spare bedroom. Our kids seem less inclined to open presents that are already wrapped, so some years that's the only thing preventing early Christmas.

When in doubt, ask for help

When we arrived in Shishmaref, people repeatedly asked us if we needed food. The owner of one store even offered us credit to buy what we needed. Apparently many teachers arrive broke because of the high cost of plane tickets. Don't be afraid to *Ask for Help*. Chances are people in your community have seen new teachers arrive before, and they may even feel some compassion for you.

We had a friend that arrived in Shishmaref with her own canned food but didn't have a can opener. She didn't eat for days before someone else figured out what she needed. She had no idea that she could have opened a credit account at the store. She didn't know who to ask for a can opener. *Asking for Help* might be a little embarrassing, but it can be a great opening line to introduce yourself. "Hi, I'm Angie. I'm going to teach high school here. This is going to sound really weird, but do you know where I can find a can opener?"

If you need help, use it as an opportunity to make a connection.

These experiences are clearly specific to the Alaska Bush. Not every place depends on air freight for food and supplies or has to deal with weeks between placing an order and receiving it, but every Transplant Home will have its own systems and quirks for getting food and supplies.

We've learned to function amid bad weather and long delays. To get what we need and want we have to work within the system, as frustrating and finicky as it is. Our literal survival may not depend on figuring out how to order oranges and milk chocolate chips (although one could probably argue that in the case of the chocolate chips), but having those things contributes to our well-being.

If you don't get what you need, you won't thrive. If you feel deprived, you won't thrive. You can change your expectations and desires (remember that from earlier?). You can also figure out how to work within the systems of your Transplant Home to get those things.

CHAPTER 14

Logistics: Transportation

Transportation is another aspect of life that we've had to adjust to, and it's been nothing short of adventurous! Our travel in and out of the village is by plane. Not the kind of planes where you have seats that recline and beverage service, but the kind of planes that run with propellers and hold nine people besides the pilot. The kind of planes where you have to give your weight before getting on, and the pilot might tell you where to sit based on that number.

Planes like these are a lot more sensitive to the weather than the reclining-seats-beverage-service type. Snow or wind or fog can ground planes for days, meaning we can't get out of or into Brevig Mission or Shishmaref for that time. We've been on both sides of those delays. One Christmas Break we were supposed to fly into Brevig Mission on December 29th in time for New Year's Eve (since, as you remember, it's one of my favorite days of the year in Brevig Mission). Bad weather shut down the airport in Nome, and we didn't make it home until January 2nd. We're lucky enough to have friends in Nome that we stay with, but others might have to get a hotel room when they're stuck in Nome.

Being Flexible and Adaptive helps in situations like this. There's nothing you can do to change the weather. There's nothing you can do to make planes fly. Agonizing over the delays will make you miserable. It's better to make a new plan and find something to do while you wait.

Being stuck in Nome also means being on constant watch for the weather and the airlines' reaction to it. The day usually begins with a call to the local airline to find out if they're flying. If they tell you they're on weather hold, you call back every hour for an update. If there's a chance they might fly, you go to the airport and check in. This involves hauling all of your suitcases/boxes/tubs/coolers to the lobby of the airline to have them weighed and placed in a pile in the hangar. Then you sit in the lobby. Every hour the airline does a weather check and announces if they'll be flying or not. If they cancel the flights for the day, you get to ask for your bags back and try to find lodging for the night.

If they don't cancel flights right away, you might spend the several hours sitting in the lobby waiting on the hourly weather reports. Keep in mind that the airline lobby consists of three rows of chairs, a coffee machine, and no wifi. There are no restaurants or bookstores, and bad weather days are usually crowded because days' worth of passengers fill the lobby hoping to get home. Imagine all of that and add a couple of squirmy kids to get an idea of why we dread delays.

Even if you get on a plane, you're not guaranteed to get all the way home. I've flown all the way to Brevig Mission, only to have the pilot say it's too windy to land. In situations like that, it's back to Nome to unload all your baggage and try to find a place to stay for the night before starting the process again the next day. The absolute worst was when it was too windy to land in Brevig, so they flew to a neighboring village to drop off freight before returning to Brevig Mission, still unable to land. We headed back to Nome. It was all the hassle of a long plane ride with none of the joy of getting home.

It's also worth mentioning that bush planes are less comfortable than commercial airliners in other aspects. The rows consist of one seat on either side of the aisle. This means that you cannot sit directly next to your small child. When Kaitlyn was just over two years old, she had to sit in her own seat. I held baby Levi on my lap, and Kaitlyn was terrified to be in the seat in front where she couldn't see me. While in the air, Kaitlyn wiggled out of her seatbelt and crawled back to my seat. I held her on one knee and Levi on other while praying we wouldn't encounter bad turbulence. I didn't want to try to hold on to two babies if the plane started bouncing around. Luckily, that hasn't happened since. I like to think it was a once-in-a-lifetime experience.

The airplane seats can easily be removed to accommodate freight. If the plane is carrying lots of boxes, the seats on one side, or rows in the back, will be replaced with cargo. Oh, and there is no bathroom. Or snacks. And in the winter, you wear full cold-weather gear in case the plane goes down and you have to wait on the tundra to be rescued. It's a good idea anyway because sometimes there's no heat. One of the worst flights of my life was when Steve and I decided not to wear winter boots. I think we were headed out of Alaska for Winter Break, and we didn't want to carry our boots around for the rest of our flights. Our feet were so cold on the flight that Steve took his gloves off and put them on his feet. I cried out of pain the entire way to Nome. We never tried to skip boots again.

If school is in session while you're stuck in Nome, you have to use personal days for those you miss (unless you're flying on district business, then the district picks up the tab). The school has to find last-minute subs to cover your classes, and if you didn't leave enough sub plans, you have to frantically find an Internet connection to send plans to one of your colleagues for them to print out and make copies for the students. Any time I leave the village while school is in session, I make my sub plans more robust than I know the students can finish while I'm gone in case I don't get back on time. This *Planning Ahead* has served me well when I've come back a week late because of poor weather.

Recently, I've taken my *Planning Ahead* to the next level by creating a large box of sub plans at the beginning of the year. I try to come in early or super late when I can take over the copy machine. Each unit has a labeled file folder with an assortment of assignments. A checklist at the front of the file folders allows the subs to check off each assignment as students turn it in. The next time I'm gone, students can pick up where they left off. There's enough work in the box that even if I'm gone for fifty days, the students will still have something to do!

Being stuck in Brevig Mission when you have somewhere else to be is equally frustrating. You make the same hourly phone calls to the airline in Nome, checking the weather. You can wait all day and then be called by the local airline agent that the plane will arrive in fifteen minutes.

It's also possible to wait all day and have the flights cancelled. If you have a connecting flight in Nome you have to call Alaska Airlines and beg them to switch your ticket without charging you extra money. If it's a busy travel time, there might not be any available seats for days. If you have medical appointments in Nome or Anchorage, you have to reschedule them. If it was a specialist appointment in Nome, you might miss the window when they are in Nome and have to wait until the next quarterly visit. It's a hassle, but everyone up here is so used to being at the mercy of the weather that you just have to mention you've been weathered out (or in), and they understand.

The strategy *Be Flexible and Adaptive* is key for waiting at home too. Sitting by the phone crossing your fingers and hyperventilating as the weather changes isn't helpful. You might have to keep the phone nearby, but you can find something to do in the meantime. Sort that pile of mail. Dust the tops of your light fixtures. Jot a quick letter to your grandma. Organize a section of your pantry. Keep teaching your students and relish the extra time they get to spend under your tutelage (if the waiting is happening at school).

It's not just getting into and out of the village that's different. Transportation around town can be different. In Brevig Mission it happens by snowmobile or honda (you'll remember that's what we call an ATV or four-wheeler in Brevig Mission). The school has a truck, as do one of the airline agents and the owners of one store. When the snow is packed down, the trucks and hondas can make it around just fine. When the snow is soft and unplowed, snow machines are the only way to go. During summer months the dirt roads are bare, and the trucks and hondas are the only way to get around. Parking lots are not a thing. When there's an event going on at the school or community center, the hondas and snow machines pile up outside of the entrances. Traffic jams are not a thing unless everybody is trying to fill up their gas tank before the store closes.

Our daily commute is about five minutes when walking with our kids (that includes stopping to stomp on the occasional puddle or look at the stars during the winter). If we had a honda or snow machine, our commute would probably be reduced to thirty seconds (not counting the time the vehicle takes to warm up outside the house, which would make it five minutes and thirty seconds).

Your Transplant Home might not need four-wheelers or snow machines. You might have to navigate public transportation or travel by car or lots of walking. Whatever your transportation situation is, the same strategies apply. *Ask for Help* to figure out the system (why mess up if you don't have to?). *Be Flexible and Adaptive* to what the system is (complaining will not fix it, just learn to deal with it), and *Plan Ahead* for potential challenges.

CHAPTER 15

Logistics: Law Enforcement, Government, and Health Care

Late one night in Shishmaref the phone rang, and Steve answered it. It was our friend asking if Steve wanted to be the jail guard for the night. Apparently, he was having a hard time finding someone to fill the position and desperately called our house on the off-chance Steve would agree. It worked, and Steve ended up spending the night in the tiny city jail checking on the prisoner every fifteen minutes. Steve got called a few times to be the jail guard because he always answered the phone and didn't fall back asleep after agreeing to come in. He even got to escort a prisoner to Nome.

Besides just enlisting my teddy-bear of-a-husband as a jail guard, law enforcement was different in ways I never really thought about. Something as ubiquitous (in my life before the Alaska Bush) as calling 911 doesn't work in Shishmaref and Brevig Mission. Law enforcement is typically provided by Village Public Safety Officers or VPSOs. They carry tasers and work in cooperation with Alaska State Troopers stationed in Nome. If a serious situation develops, the VPSO will apprehend the suspect (if it's safe to do so) and keep them in a holding cell until the troopers arrive. Sometimes troopers come in to do the apprehending.

VPSOs in the Norton Sound region are hired by a regional nonprofit called Kawerak, Inc. VPSOs are assisted by Village Police Officers (VPOs) that are hired by each city. In Brevig Mission, the

VPOs work the night shifts, are on call for emergencies, and enforce the local curfew.

Most court proceedings happen in Nome where the judges are. Depending on the specifics of the case, some people fly in to take part in hearings and trials. Others participate in the VPSO office via teleconference. Each village also has a tribal court that gets involved in certain situations.

Transplant Teachers probably don't plan to be involved in a legal case, but it happens. It's one of those things you might not think about until something unfortunate arises. It's important to *Ask for Help* in these situations as soon as possible. Better still, seek out information in advance so you know who to call and where to go for help if something occurs.

Government

Most of the things I learned about local government in my high school government class are very different from the reality of Brevig Mission (and I actually paid attention in my high school government class. For real).

In Brevig Mission we have, not one, but three local governing entities. The first body is the City Council. This is composed of the mayor, some other officers, and council members. The City Council is in charge of city statutes (like curfew, whether alcohol is allowed, and how to handle the never-ending problem of loose dogs). The city also manages local cable television and water and sewer. City elections are open to all registered voters.

The next local governing body is the Traditional Council or the Native Village of Brevig Mission. They derive their authority from the Indian Reorganization Act and are recognized by the federal government as the governing body for the native people in Brevig

Mission. The traditional council is in charge of tribal registration, tribal court, tribal adoptions, and the administration of federal grants they've received to promote and preserve local culture and traditions. Traditional Council elections are only open to registered members of the tribe who are at least eighteen years old.

The third governing body is the Brevig Mission Native Corporation. They derive their authority from the Alaska Native Claims Settlement Act. They manage the surface rights of the land in and around Brevig Mission. They also run the Native store in Brevig Mission through a partnership with other Native stores across Alaska. Brevig Mission Native Corporation pays annual dividends to shareholders based on the profits of the store. Their elections are open to shareholders of the local corporation.

Every so often the three governing bodies meet together to coordinate their efforts. In Brevig Mission, the City Council, Traditional Council of the Native Village of Brevig Mission, and Brevig Mission Corporation all have different (sometimes overlapping) roles within varied realms of authority. The City might control the use of the Multipurpose building, but the Traditional Council secures the grants that pay for community events at the Multipurpose building. The Corporation controls surface land rights, but the City might hire the people to build the community basketball court on that land. The way these entities operate can change based on available funding and who is elected to serve on each council.

It's easy for Transplant Teachers to get confused about who's supposed to do what when systems and institutions look different than they're used to. You might expect one entity to be responsible for services in a particular area when it's really not within that entity's jurisdiction. When you have a concern or need permission for something, you need to know which governing body to go to. That requires *Asking for Help*. Rely on your allies to guide you through the maze of permits/visas/statutes/licenses you need to deal with. Your allies will especially help you *Plan Ahead*. They can give you a good idea of how long the paperwork and procedures might take, so you can allow yourself plenty of time and minimize potential freak-outs.

Each system of government has its own quirks. And no matter how irritating the quirks are, it's usually easier to adjust to the existing systems instead of fixating on how you think things should be done.

Health care

Health care in my Transplant Home is taken care of by a handful of health aides at the local clinic. They ask questions predetermined by a manual and then call the results into Nome where a doctor at the regional hospital makes recommendations and writes prescriptions. Patients with emergencies are medevaced into Nome or Anchorage on planes dispatched by the regional airlines.

When Levi was small, he pushed his feet against the table and knocked his high chair backwards. He hit his head on the linoleum, splitting it open and causing blood to gush everywhere. We contacted the health aide on call, and Steve rushed him to the clinic. The health aides were able to put staples in Levi's head so he didn't have to fly to Nome. They also delivered a baby safely a few months ago. The clinic does what needs to be done!

Most babies are not born in Brevig Mission. About three weeks before their due dates, expectant mothers go to Nome. They wait in a hostel across the street from the hospital until they deliver the babies. The fathers try to fly into Nome when contractions start but may or may not be there during the birth depending on the weather in the village and the number of other children that need to be cared for at home. At the first sign of any possible complications, pregnant women are put on a plane to Anchorage to deliver at a hospital better equipped to handle complicated deliveries.

The health care system is not always efficient. One December the Shishmaref clinic was concerned I had appendicitis as I was getting ready to leave for Winter Break. The health aides were worried my appendix might rupture on an airplane, so they wanted me to get it checked before I flew down to the Lower 48.

I flew into Nome and went straight to the hospital. I spent twenty minutes arguing with the woman at admission about whether I was supposed to be there before she realized I was referred by the village clinic and in the system already. I waited forever to be seen by a practitioner and sat in an ultrasound room for two hours before a technician showed up (I think they had to call one in, but I've always been puzzled by the long wait because there's no place in Nome that's anywhere close to two hours away from the hospital).

The technician spent two minutes with me before declaring it wasn't appendicitis, and I took a cab to the airport with just barely enough time to catch my flight. (For the record, I also did not want my appendix to burst in the air between Alaska and Seattle. It just would have been cool to have the examinations happen differently.)

Prescriptions come out of the pharmacy in Nome. They get put on an airplane and delivered to the clinic in Brevig Mission. Then one of the health aides calls and lets you know you have meds waiting at the clinic.

Getting prescriptions this way requires constant double-checking with the pharmacy in Nome. Sometimes the prescriptions don't get filled because of an insurance issue. Sometimes they don't get filled because they need permission to charge $2.38 on your credit card on file. The pharmacy doesn't always call to tell you about the holdup. You get to wait and wonder why the prescriptions haven't arrived.

I've learned to *Adapt* by calling the pharmacy to verify everything. I feel kind of obnoxious, but it's what I have to do to make sure I have medicine when I need it. I've also learned to call and verify all of my appointments the morning they happen in case there's a last minute cancellation because they're missing a health aide. Bundling up and braving heavy winds to be told you don't have an appointment after all is a drag, so I do what I can to prevent it.

Transplant Teachers may find themselves in health care systems with their own peculiarities. Things don't always work the way you're used to. Things don't always make sense or seem efficient to you. If you *Learn to Be Flexible* and *Adapt* to the system as it exists, not as you think it should be, you can focus on getting the care you need.

CHAPTER 16

Bonus Challenge: Nurturing Kids

Kids need to go through their own process of Nurturing the Seedling. Your kids' experience may not go according to your plan. What you think will be a huge adjustment may not even be a thing. What you consider no big deal may make your kids totally freak out. When we moved houses within Brevig Mission my son really missed the old house. We couldn't figure out why he missed it because the new house was closer to the school and had a room for him so he didn't have to share with his sister. I finally got him to tell me what specifically he missed, and he said it was watching Curious George with the computer and the mouse. We still watch Curious George at the new house. We just use the TV and a remote instead of a keyboard and a mouse. The difference seemed inconsequential to me, but to Levi it mattered.

Kids will need support as they step out and stretch beyond their comfort zones toward thriving. Just like with Transplant Teachers, the process requires nourishment and gentleness. The inward and outward strategies Transplant Teachers use as they Nurture the Seedling are kid-friendly too!

Stay Positive and non-judgmental

The most important thing you can do when you transplant your children is to teach by example. If you want your kids to enjoy living in your Transplant Home, you need to enjoy living in your

Transplant Home. That means, for example, watching your kitchen-table conversations and the way you describe your new home to people when you're talking on the phone. Your kids will pick up your attitudes and judgments. If they hear you talking about all the things you don't like, they will likely adopt the same attitude.

I watched a teacher tell her high school daughter that she wasn't like "these kids" and she was better than "these kids" while referring to kids who grew up in their Transplant Home. The daughter internalized her mom's messages, and it affected how she treated the other kids. It is no wonder that the daughter struggled socially.

Choose instead to be a positive support to your kids and help them process environmental and lifestyle differences. Conversations with your kids are important to help them rearrange their mental furniture. One conversation we've had with our kids is about soda pop. Pop is a common beverage around town, but we only drink it every once in a while. When our kids ask why, we explain that we want to keep their teeth healthy and pop has a lot of sugar in it. They accept that. We don't tell them that pop is bad. We don't tell them that people who drink pop are bad.

An important lesson for kids (and all people!) is to not judge people according to their own personal standards. This is the internal *Withhold Judgment* strategy from earlier. Things may be different than your kids are used to. Behaviors might be foreign. That's not necessarily a bad thing. Sometimes it's just a different thing. It's common for kids to grow up thinking all families or communities do things a certain way (I remember being shocked when I found out some families don't go to church on Sundays). Being in a new place can be an opportunity for kids (and their parents) to be exposed to different ideas and ways of doing things.

Your kids can observe what is considered normal without making fun of other kids when they operate within those norms. They can avoid labeling their Transplant Home normal as dumb or lame and talking about how much better everything was where they used to live. As your kids tell you about their observations and experiences help them note the differences without instantly labeling them good or bad.

Another important thing parents can do to help their children transplant successfully is emphasize the positive aspects of their new home. Kids who move to Shishmaref or Brevig Mission from bigger places might lament the lack of movie theaters, malls, and restaurants. Parents could help kids *Stay Positive* by pointing out the things that are available and maybe not as common in other places. In Brevig Mission, the entire village and surrounding area are basically available for kids to explore. Outside has water, rocks, sticks, and dirt to play in. Unstructured play time abounds. Beautiful surroundings offer plenty of opportunities for adventures.

As parents outwardly express and emphasize the positive aspects of their Transplant Home, kids will internally begin to notice the positive too. That doesn't mean your kids won't ever complain or dislike anything, it just means that maybe their default mode will be to notice the good.

Building connections

Help your kids *Get involved! Try things! and Participate!* in and out of school. Within the school setting this might look like encouraging your kids to join a school team or club. It might mean encouraging them to raise their hands to answer questions or prepping them on how to approach someone to play with at recess or sit by at lunch.

Outside of school this might mean enrolling them in sports or lessons. It might mean taking them to a nearby park or letting them run around the neighborhood with the neighbor kids. It might mean taking them to the mall or the pool or wherever kids hang out or helping them join in on communal activities or celebrations. Get your kids out there interacting with other kids.

There's not a ton of structured leagues or lessons in Brevig Mission, but there are a number of opportunities for kids to interact with each other outside of the classroom. The gym is open every night for free play. Different age groups are assigned different times, and kids can come and chase each other around, toss balls, or play basketball. The boys and girls club is a small building that hosts kids activities. When it's not blizzardy there are a ton of kids running around outside or biking when the snow's gone. Any of these are great places for kids to start to make friends.

As you help your kids participate, you can help them develop cultural and social sensitivity. Making friends is easier if your kids can pick up on social *Feedback* and *Adapt*. Your child doesn't have to abandon how they were raised or hide who they are, but they can be aware that not everybody is talking about how much money their parents make or sharing long stories about the novel they're writing (those are kind of extreme examples, but I think they make the point). Kids that are aware of how people are responding to them can avoid alienating potential friends.

To support your kids in this area, ask questions that help them reflect on their interactions. "How did the kids react when you did that?" "How many other people were sharing stories?" "Did the other kids seem interested in hearing about that?" "Was everyone else talking about vacations they've taken?"

Parents can also help nurture friendships and *Build Connections a Little at a Time*. When people reach out to your kids it's imperative to help them reach back! The reaching out might be subtle. It may be less formal than a scheduled playdate or dinner appointment. It may be as simple as an offer to walk your child to school or take them to an activity. Jump on those opportunities and reciprocate by inviting those kids and families to play, eat dinner, or do something together. With a little nurturing those opportunities can grow into friendships.

As Transplant Kids deal with the social ups and downs, you can guide them through the process of examining their own actions (inward) and what kind of impact they might be having. Then you can help them decide if they want to change anything before trying to connect again (outward). It may require some give and take, but the process is valuable to help your kids move toward thriving in your Transplant Home.

Focus on what you can control

As Transplant Kids navigate new cultural and social landscapes, it helps to direct their attention inward to what they can control.

Let's say that your son is the only kid in his school with light blonde hair and green eyes. His hair and eyes could be a novelty that other kids are fascinated by and curious about. They could also be points for teasing. Your son can't control the teasing, just like he can't control the color of his eyes or hair. He can control what he says in response, so you can help him craft a few statements he could use in those situations. Maybe something like, "That's just the way I am," or "Hair can be all different colors," or "In my family most people have green eyes." You could even help your son practice using the statements. Do a little role playing, so your son feels inwardly prepared for the outward interactions.

Similarly, your daughter can't control if other kids don't automatically sit by her at lunch. She might feel sad if she sits alone, and that's when you can suggest some solutions that are under her control. She can go up to someone and ask, "Can I sit here?" She can invite someone earlier in the day to sit by her at lunch. The first step is for her to accept that there are some things she can do. It might take a little brainstorming and practice to prepare for these scenarios, but then she'll be better equipped to reach out.

Helping your kids focus on what they can control will help them in all sorts of situations. For example, the food tastes funny or people don't seem to like them. Maybe their classmates are hard to understand or they're scared during the walk to school. They will always encounter things beyond their control, but they can learn to look for something they can control and take action on that.

Tough stuff

Conversations will help kids deal with possible ridicule or ostracizing. This too is an opportunity. Parents can help their kids explore how it feels to be treated poorly or ignored for looking or acting different. Avoid generalizing statements like "kids around here are like that" or "these kids are just mean." If you avoid blaming the community, it will be easier for your kids to avoid it too.

Our daughter had a makeup set stolen by one girl in town. It would have been easy to complain about the family or the village, but we didn't want negativity to poison her. We told her that some people make bad choices and steal. We also told our daughter she didn't have to play with that girl anymore. We validated our daughter's pain and offered some protection but tried to keep the negative feelings from overflowing to all people and Brevig Mission in general.

I was on the giving and receiving end of meanness as a kid. Either situation can be an opportunity for life lessons. How to respond to rude people. How to make unpopular decisions. How to empathize with others. How to stand up for what you believe in. How to minimize how much you care about what other people think.

Remember that kids get teased and mistreated in lots of places. I'm not trying to excuse the behavior or minimize the pain of the kids on the receiving end. I'm just hoping Transplant Teachers won't vilify their Transplant Homes if their kids have difficulty adjusting (or if the other kids have trouble adjusting to them!).

I've seen some Transplant Kids thrive and others who were targets of ridicule. There's not always a rhyme or reason. Sometimes kids slide right into the new social rhythms of their Transplant Homes, and sometimes they don't. The personality of the Transplant Kid and the social dynamic of the kids in their age group both play a role, but some things are unexplainable. (See the chapter How to Know if it's Time to Go for considerations on making the decision about whether or not your Transplant Home is the right fit for your family.)

Giving your kids a Transplant Experience is a gift that will enrich and benefit their whole lives, but it requires extra guidance and support. Ongoing conversations will help guide them in positive directions and bolster them when things are tough. Efforts to help your kids look inward and reach outward, just as you're doing, can help their Transplant Experience be a positive one.

Plant Health Checklist

Once a plant has been moved to a new location in your garden, you'll continue to evaluate how it's doing. Is it droopy? Is it pale? Is it being eaten by bugs? Is it weak? Based on what you observe, you can make adjustments. The plant might need more compost or fertilizer. The plant might need less. It's a constant process of evaluation and adaptation to ensure the plant gets what it needs to thrive.

The same is true for Transplant Teachers. Instead of droopy, you might be exhausted. Instead of pale you might be constantly stressed. Instead of being eaten by bugs you might be devoured by negativity. Instead of fertilizing yourself you might need more personal connections or more time out in the community. Making inward and outward adjustments is something you'll do throughout your Transplant Experience. To be successful in your Transplant Life, you will keep the things that are going well and change what you can about the things that are not.

Sometimes I get so caught up in day to day happenings that I don't take the time to check in with myself and see how I'm doing. That's dangerous. In the garden, that could lead to the plant withering, growing in the wrong direction, or failing to bloom. For Transplant Teachers the danger lies in the possibility of chronic discouragement, bad habits, and unhappiness. Try not to let yourself get or stay unhealthy!

The following checklists are a good starting point to help Transplant Teachers evaluate their Transplant Health.

Signs of health:

- ☐ I'm observing, exploring, and finding out more about everything around me.

- ☐ I consider different perspectives and don't freak out when things are different than I'm used to.

- ☐ I am working to learn and operate within the norms of my Transplant Home.

- ☐ I accept feedback and act on it.

- ☐ I build connections a little at a time.

- ☐ I sit by different people at staff meetings and school events and seek out people to start conversations with.

- ☐ I'm open to trying local foods.

- ☐ I try to understand and use local language and slang.

- ☐ I get out of the school and my house and do other things.

- ☐ I show up repeatedly to community events so I become familiar (not in an annoying way, just in a way that shows I'm sticking around and making an effort).

- ☐ I find allies to help guide me through local events and protocols.

- ☐ I try new hobbies and skills and offer to help in order to learn.

- ☐ I extend invitations even when they're not always accepted.

- ☐ I'm not trying to do all the things with all the people all the time.

- ☐ I ask questions and am learning to work within existing systems for supplies, travel, law enforcement, government, and healthcare.

- ☐ I plan ahead to meet my needs.

- ☐ I avoid toxic people that fuel negativity.

- ☐ I stay positive in the public arena, both in person and online.

- ☐ I find beauty and goodness and hang on to meaningful moments.

- ☐ I'm generally happy (not 24/7 every minute of the day happy, but mostly happy. I laugh and enjoy my family, students, and colleagues).

Notice what's contributing to your Transplant Health. What from this list are you doing especially well? Leverage that. You will not be A plus perfect on every item on the checklist (and if you are, write your own book!), so take advantage of what's going well. Do more of it. Build on it. Let it bring you even more satisfaction, and maybe it will propel you in other areas too.

I was really good at *Get Involved! Try Things! and Participate!* If something was going on in town, I wanted to be there. I dragged Steve along most of the time, and we showed up even if we had no idea what to expect. People got to see us. They asked who we were (a lot of people assumed I was Steve's daughter!). They offered a place to sit. We learned names and talked to people.

I wasn't very good at *Considering Different Perspectives* and operating within the norms of my Transplant Home, but I kept showing up to events and gatherings. Gradually I made connections to people at the events which led to more events and conversations. I had fun. I made friends and spending time with them opened my eyes to why things were different and that different might be okay.

Building on my strength helped me grow in other ways. Don't get discouraged if you can't check off all the items on the above checklist. Look at what you can check off and do it more.

This next list is some signs that your plant might be unhealthy. (Don't get confused and think of this as a to-do list. That would definitely not lead to thriving.) Think of these as warning signs that you might need to make adjustments.

Warning Signs:

- ☐ I expect the norms/manners of my own upbringing and judge my surroundings by that standard.

- ☐ I use the word *should* a lot. (For example, "They should provide more curriculum." "They should be quiet on their own." "I shouldn't have to ask for this." "They should take care of this.")

- ☐ I get defensive when I receive feedback.

- ☐ I mostly talk to other teachers or transplants.

- ☐ I'm uninterested in local food, language, and events.

- ☐ I haven't tried anything new.

- ☐ I stay home a lot.

- ☐ I'm super crabby and start getting mad at little things and overreacting to them.

- ☐ I get frustrated when the systems of my Transplant Home don't work according to my expectations and schedule.

- ☐ I complain a lot.

- ☐ I don't enjoy my family, colleagues, and students for long stretches of time.

When you pick up on a warning sign, take action! For example, if I notice that I'm staying home a lot that means I need to go somewhere! I need to do something! I need to talk to other people and strengthen relationships. I need to add variety to my life instead of sitting in my jammies at home. I realize that I am an extrovert, so interaction with other people generally energizes me. Other Transplant Teachers may have other needs, but strengthening community relationships is generally a good idea.

If I've been cooped up in my house without interacting with anybody beside my family, I try to make myself get out and go do something. I promise myself it only has to be one little thing, and it really can be little. I can go to the post office. I can go to the store. I can walk around town. I can do anything that will get me out and around people. A place where I'll be forced to at least say hi and wave. Overcoming that initial inertia is hard! I don't want to go. I don't think I'll enjoy getting out, and it seems like such a hassle to get bundled up in my beaver hat and fur mittens just to do something I don't want to do.

Usually it's not as bad as I think it will be. Getting up and out the door is the hard part. After a little positive experience, I might have the energy to tackle something bigger. Maybe I'll decide to stop by a neighbor's house on the way home from the store, or I'll make another loop around town on my walk. Maybe I'll call a friend and invite them to dinner or make plans to do something later. The extended experiences tend to uplift me even more.

Addressing the warning signs doesn't necessarily require herculean actions. It can mean making small changes. Even minor adjustments can yield dividends, and once you get started, you may find you able to do even more.

Here's a checklist specific to having Transplant Kids. Because this book is written for Transplant Teachers, not Transplant Kids, the items are phrased about what you can do with or for your kids. This isn't the kind of list that you would interview your kids with. It's another self-reflection list that can help you gauge what you're doing well to help your kids transition to Transplant Life and where you might focus more effort.

Transplant Kids Checklist

- ☐ I have regular conversations with my kids about all the things that are new and different.

- ☐ I help my kids avoid judging everything according to our family's norms and expectations.

- ☐ I emphasize positive aspects of our Transplant Home.

- ☐ I arrange for my kids to try new things and take part in formal and informal activities.

- ☐ I ask questions that help my kids reflect on their own behavior and interactions and pick up on social feedback.

- ☐ I nurture friendships by reciprocating when someone shows an interest in or makes an effort to include my kids.

- ☐ I help my kids practice conversation starters or replies to use in uncomfortable situations.

- ☐ I avoid vilifying all kids or our entire community when something mean happens.

Part III

Nurturing the Seedling in the Classroom

Just like life outside of school, the main challenge Transplant Teachers will face in the classroom is dealing with different, and you may be surprised at what is different. I didn't expect to have to keep kids after school until a polar bear warning expired, but I did that first year. Steve didn't expect to be responsible for arranging class shower time so kids without running water at home could shower at the school, but he was.

Some of what's different will be out of your control. Whether you're a classroom teacher or an administrator, there will be policies and procedures that are decided by someone else. There will be environmental factors that you can do nothing about. Traditions, habits, and norms may have a long history.

Many of the strategies for thriving in your Transplant Classroom are similar to the strategies for life outside of school. Some strategies help you look inward to change yourself. Others help you look outward to connect and deal with those around you.

Inwardly, you can *Withhold Judgment*. Even if you've been teaching for forty years, the procedures and expectations you're used to in the classroom are not the only way to do things. The policies and management of the school system as a whole may look different from any you've experienced in your career, and that's not necessarily a bad thing. There are different ways to do things, so train yourself to *Withhold Judgment* without labeling things as wrong or bad.

You can also inwardly *Focus on What You Can Control*. While you may be deluged from all sides with uncontrollable factors, there are always things you can control (most notably, yourself). Teachers are the most powerful force in their classrooms, even when they're dealing with regulations, mandates, or policies from above. If you save energy by not fighting against things that may never change, you'll have more energy for the things in your control.

Along with that, *Be Flexible and Adaptive*. Dealing with different may mean doing things you've never done. If you're open to switching up your teaching and classroom management, you'll be in a better place to deal with uncontrollable factors.

Outwardly, be willing to *Seek After, Ask For, and Accept Help and Information*. You may face new curriculum, new rules, new procedures, new coworkers, new paperwork. You don't have to figure all of that out on your own! If you don't know something, ask. Find out more. Letting people help you can save you time and trouble.

Likewise, *Accept Feedback*. We talked about this in the last chapter, but it's important here too. Feedback may come in a formal observation or evaluation, but it can also come informally from your colleagues or students. You don't have to try to make everybody happy and embrace every suggestion that comes your way, but if you can resist getting defensive, feedback can help you adjust to life in your Transplant Classroom.

Your classroom is a great place to *Make Connections a Little at a Time*. You will want to reach out and connect with your students. Maybe your students will automatically respect and adore you. Maybe they won't. Trust is often established bit by bit. Repeatedly showing an interest in your students and finding out about their lives will help you make those connections.

CHAPTER 17

Getting to Know Each Other

Making Connections a Little at a Time in the classroom begins with getting to know your students. This can start when you first arrive. Find out what they like. What do they watch? What music do they listen to? What do they do in their spare time? Who do they live with? What are they interested in? Any way you can find the answers to these questions formally and informally, you're gathering information that will help you *Make Connections a Little at a Time.*

If you can figure out what lights your students up, start connecting everything you teach to those topics. In Shishmaref and Brevig Mission it was hunting and basketball. Everyone loved going outdoors and participating in subsistence activities, and everyone loved basketball, especially the NBA. Any time I could connect my lessons to either of those topics, engagement was higher, and everyone (including me) had more fun. During a lesson on the types of propaganda, students had to create advertisements using propaganda techniques against a rival NBA team. We laughed at the clever insults and enjoyed applying the concepts of the lesson.

Knowing your students also helps you identify connection points with each of them. Maybe you root for the same team. Maybe you love the same albums. Maybe you can swap fishing stories with some of them. The formal and informal points of connection will strengthen your relationships with them and create a sense of community in the classroom. Even if the connection is small, it counts!

If there are no apparent connection points, you might have to do some research. I am really not interested in professional basketball, but my students drink it up, so I try to stay on top of who the hot teams are and what people are saying about famous players. Sometimes I'll look at an NBA headline and start a conversation with one of my students the next day. "Could you believe that buzzer beater in last night's game?" They'll usually reply enthusiastically. Then I'll do something dumb like refer to LeBron James as James LeBron, and my cover is blown while the students roll on the floor laughing at me. But, it's all still a bonding and connecting experience.

Let your students get to know you back

As you get to know your students, let them get to know you. My back classroom wall is covered in photos of my immediate and extended family. Every once in a while a student will point to a picture and ask me the story behind it. I get to talk about my grandparents, my brother-in-law, or a family reunion. It's fun for me, and the students seem to enjoy it.

One particular photo that's gotten a lot of attention is a framed photo I have from the summer after I graduated from high school. I'm barely eighteen, and I'm with my parents and siblings. At least once a week one of my students asks, "Is this really you?" Then they go through all of my brothers and sisters and ask who they are and how old they are now. My students marvel that we all have the same smile, and they can't believe I was so young and skinny. It's kind of humbling, but I value their interest in me and my family.

The other walls of my classroom are covered in photos of trips I've taken around the world. My students love looking at the traditional dress of tribes in Thailand, the animals I saw on safari in Botswana, and the food I tried in Morocco. Every question they ask starts a story. I get to share a little of my passion and introduce them to something from another place. Double bonus (and perfect for my social studies classroom)!

I'm also a storyteller. I love telling silly stories about things my kids have done or sharing funny conversations I've had with Steve. I showed them pictures of my failed birthday cake attempt for Levi's first birthday, and they still talk about how ugly it (the cake) was.

The students laugh (usually) and sometimes share stories of their own. It takes a few minutes of class time, but the investment in my relationships with them is worth it. The *Connections are Made* one story and one question at a time.

Learn from your students, they might teach you about walrus hunting (or is that just me?)

One thing I wish I had done right away in Shishmaref was to actively learn from my students. I was so busy thinking of myself as the teacher and all the information I wanted to impart to them, that I didn't stop to think about what they could teach me until the last day of school before Christmas Break (you know, when I broke a broom playing Inupiaq games).

If your students have lived in their community their entire lives, or even most of their lives, they will be infinitely more familiar with the customs and culture than you. Tap into that! I knew zero Inupiaq words when I arrived in Shishmaref. None of my students were proficient in Inupiaq, but they all knew words and phrases regularly used in the village. I could have had them teach me a word a day or a word a week. I could have kept a running list of all the words, maybe posted on the wall. I could have practiced saying them and allowed the students to correct my pronunciation. I would have built up an impressive store of local knowledge, and I think the students would have enjoyed sharing that with me.

I have a distinct memory of sitting spellbound at the front of the classroom in the spring of our first year while my fourth hour students described walrus hunting. I don't remember how the subject came up, but we spent the better part of the class period talking about it. I asked questions, and the students answered enthusiastically. Even the boys who usually sat in the back and didn't say much were contributing.

They described getting close to the walrus in boats and then shooting as much as possible to try and penetrate the thick walrus skin enough to take the walrus out before it attacked the boat. They shared how they butcher the walrus right on the ice so that they can take it back to the village in chunks because a whole walrus wouldn't fit in a boat. They told me how good the walrus blubber, called kauq (pronounced like "coke"), is. I was fascinated by every detail, and the kids fed off my fascination by sharing more and more. I was the student that day, and it was electrifying for everyone in the room.

Some things that are foreign to you are normal for your students, so let them be your teachers whenever possible. If you're allowed to go off-campus, let your students take you on a tour of the community. They can point out where people live, where the important places in town are, areas to avoid, and anything else they consider important. This can be an important part of *Seeking After Information*. Your students can be the sources of information. Let them!

Now that you know, you can adjust

As you get settled in your classroom you may encounter student behaviors that surprise or repel you. Don't let your attitude toward the behaviors get in the way of getting to know and like your students.

Just like other aspects of your Transplant Home, student behaviors may not be as universal as you expected. Behaviors you've never seen before might happen regularly in your new location. What would never happen in your Transplant Home might have happened regularly where you grew up or taught before.

Remember that expectations list you made before you left on your Transplant Journey? If you're frustrated with student behaviors, it might be a good time to pull it out again. See if there's anything on the list about student behaviors or student reactions to you. There might be nothing on the list about those things. Those expectations might have seemed so obvious or universal to you that you didn't write them down.

Take some time to add to your expectations list. Think back before you arrived. How were you expecting the students to behave? Then think about any frustrations that have come up recently. How are you expecting your students to behave now? Once you have the expectations written on paper, you can compare them to your reality. Maybe make a separate column where you list your reality in comparison to your expectations. If they don't match, you have likely found a primary source of your frustration.

You might be tempted to insist that your expectations are reasonable, and it's the students' failure to live up to them that's the problem. Remember that just because you grew up a certain way or had a certain expectation doesn't mean it's the right or only way. Different expectations exist in different places in the world. Your familiarity with some doesn't make them better or more valid.

In Brevig Mission, the expectation is that people will know how to drive a four-wheeler and/or snowmobile by the time they're in junior high. I'm still not very good at driving either of those things. Does that make me stupid? Does that make my family irresponsible for not teaching how to drive a four-wheeler or snowmobile? No. It just means that my family didn't consider it a priority and instead taught me things that were more relevant to my life at the time (although the time I spent learning to tap dance is debatable).

The beauty of recognizing that your expectations are the source of your frustration is that expectations can change! It's not some universal cosmic law that you have to fight against. It's something inside of you that's very much under your control.

To people who continue to insist that they're expectations are "correct" and that everyone *should* live up to them, consider this. Some universal values exist, but defining them is not always as clear cut as you might think. You might suggest that valuing life is a universal ideal and that people *should* not kill. Okay, sounds reasonable. What about accidents? If you kill someone on accident is that the same thing as killing someone on purpose? What about terminating life support? Is that killing? If a patient signs a Do Not Resuscitate order, are they killing themselves? Does the death have to be quick to be bad? What about people who don't exercise? Are they slowly killing themselves? Should they be punished?

Valuing life is a little more complicated than it might seem at first. The same is true of student behaviors. Teachers sometimes consider their expectations to be universal truths in the classroom. Consider the statement "students *should* bring a pencil and pen to class." Okay, what if they don't have pencils at home? What if there's no place in town to buy pencils or pens? What if the only pens for sale are $8.00 for a pack of crappy ballpoints?

Try "students *should* bring their books home and back to class." What if they don't have a backpack large enough to fit a five pound history book? What if it's so snowy sometimes that carrying a book in your arms to school would cause a ruined book? What if there really are no shelves or desks at home to keep the book so it ends up on the floor?

Did you notice the word *should*? We talked about should statements a few chapters ago. Just as when dealing with school systems and coworkers, using the word *should* sets up a right and wrong situation. It can be helpful to replace the word *should* with "prefer," like this:

> I would prefer that students bring a pencil and pen to class.

This revised statement acknowledges that it is a preference. It might be a very strong preference. It might be based on some very good reasons, but it's still a preference. This subtle shift can help you deal with students who show up without pencils. Instead of your students violating some epic law, they are just acting differently than you prefer. This bit of perspective can temper irrational anger or frustration and allow the curiosity to find out more about the situation and its causes.

Nothing is as universal as it seems. It's not as easy as slapping a good or bad label on behaviors and trying to convert people to your point of view. It's about *Withholding Judgment*, *Seeking More Information* about what's going on, and *Adapting* to the reality.

Your classroom will be filled with all sorts of personalities and temperaments. Your job is to get to know the students and figure out how to work with them. It doesn't have to be a chore. Your students have a lot to offer individually and as residents of your Transplant Home. It's worth the effort to adjust your expectations and perceptions so you can get a kick out of who they are and what they know.

CHAPTER 18

There Are Things You Can Control and Things You Can't

During those early years in Shishmaref (and even now, actually) it was impossible for me to predict what would go careening through my day like a wrecking ball. Like the time I got a phone call during class telling me there was a baby seal in the gym. As soon as I got off of the phone, the kids demanded to know who it was and what they wanted. When they heard there was a baby seal involved and that it was at the school, my lesson was done for. I joined all the other teachers and brought my class into the gym to see the baby seal that someone had brought in a plastic tub so the kids could see it. It was adorable. I took pictures of it and tried not to think about what might happen to it once it left the school. The kids were jazzed. They stood around the tub and crinkled their noses at the smell (I think the seal had pooped in the tub).

It was just one of the many times I learned that I had to *Be Flexible*. You can't predict when someone will bring a baby seal in a tub into the school, and you can't miss out on those opportunities either. Sometimes you have to stop what you've planned and attend to the opportunity at hand.

If it wasn't a baby seal in a plastic tub, it was the dentist in town, and all day long kids would leave my classes to go to their appointments. The National Guard would visit and want to hold an assembly. Physicals for the high school athletes would be set up while a physician's assistant was at the clinic. A journalist from Europe was here to interview people and wanted to visit our classrooms. On three separate occasions our U.S. Senators and a Representative from the U.S. House made appearances in Shishmaref, and we all got to go to the gym for impromptu speeches and question and answer sessions. The U.S. Secretary of Education even visited my classroom once to observe a Civil War battle game (I'm not even joking). I stepped back to let my students do most of the talking, mentally willing them to avoid saying anything that might embarrass me in front of a member of the president's cabinet. The kids animatedly described the game to Secretary Spellings and delighted in her positive response.

Something was always happening to throw off my plans and schedule. It used to drive me crazy. I felt like my instruction time *should* be preserved. I felt like I *should* get more notice of events. I felt like my day *shouldn't* get interrupted. I complained passionately to the principal and demanded that he preserve my class time. I resented any and all interruptions.

It was a waste of time and energy for me to get mad. And although there is an appropriate time for feedback, it was better and easier to just roll with things and try to turn the unexpected into teachable moments. My self-righteous complaining produced no results aside from irritating my administrator, and the interruptions kept coming. Continuing to fight for undisturbed class time was a futile effort.

It took time, and didn't happen all at once, but I accepted the idea that interruptions were going to happen. I had to train myself to look for ways to turn the unexpected into good experiences with and for my students. If something was happening that was particularly interesting to my students, or if they wouldn't focus on anything else, I shifted gears and integrated it into my lesson. If most of the class was gone, we would take a tangent to an enrichment activity. If it threw off my lesson plans, I tried to remind myself that it just means

I had lessons ready for the next day.

Learning to *Be Flexible* extended into other areas. A very common concept in both Shishmaref and Brevig Mission is inside shoes and outside shoes. Students generally keep a pair of inside shoes at school and wear a different pair of shoes or boots to and from school. Basketball shoes are most definitely considered inside shoes and kept pristine by only being worn on the gym floor.

I had a pair of inside shoes too our first years in Shishmaref. I generally kept my inside shoes in my classroom. I would take off my snow boots and slide into my teaching shoes first thing every morning. One Monday my teaching shoes weren't there. I looked all over my classroom. Nothing. I didn't want to waste my prep time running home and looking for them. I also didn't want to spend all day in my snow boots because those things were super warm, and I knew my feet would get sweaty.

So, I just taught in my socks. My students laughed at first, but they got over it, and the day continued as usual. When I got home, I looked for my shoes to throw in my bag for the next day. They were nowhere to be found. Our house wasn't very big, so I didn't understand why I couldn't find them. I figured I must not have checked my classroom thoroughly.

I repeated this process for an entire week. I couldn't just run to the store and buy a new pair of shoes. Anything I ordered would take weeks to arrive. I didn't know what to do besides just keep teaching in my socks and hope that the shoes showed up.

I never would have done that in a Lower 48 school. I never would have had to. But, learning and teaching still happened. I eventually found the shoes under my bed. I had checked under the bed multiple times, but the shoes were just barely under the bed at the edge. I didn't see them when I checked under the middle of the bed, and they were covered by our oversized down comforter on the outside.

(I'm still not sure how they got home in the first place, but I'll just have to file that away with some of life's greatest unsolved mysteries.)

I *Adapted* to the shoe situation. I didn't fixate on it (inward), and I kept on teaching, albeit with slightly colder toes (outward). Transplant Teachers can also choose to *Be Flexible* to circumstances. You won't be able to predict what will throw a wrench in your schedule or lessons (I never would have anticipated a baby seal in a tub!), but you can roll with it.

What you can control

One key to *Being Flexible and Adaptive* is to *Focus on What You Can Control*. First, you must decide what is in your control and what isn't. Ask yourself if there's anything you can do to directly impact the situation. The answer to this question will help you determine how much control you have.

There's a kind of continuum of things you can control. On one end are things you have almost no control over, things where your actions won't directly impact the situation. This includes mandated curriculum and what your students do in their lives outside of school. On the other end are things that are almost completely under your control, things where your actions directly impact the situation. This is like how prepared you are, the rhythm of the class, and classroom management techniques.

Don't fall into the trap of assuming you have no control over your situation. There are a lot of things you can control in your classroom, no matter what students bring to the door with them or what administrators mandate. Even when something is out of your control, you can still take steps to deal with it.

Remember when we talked about weather? That's the ultimate example of something you can't control. Nothing you can do will change the weather, but you don't go outside in a blizzard wearing shorts, throwing your hands up saying "There's nothing I can do. I can't control it."

You take steps to deal with the uncontrollable weather. You wear a heavy coat, gloves, and a hat before going outside. You limit the time you spend outdoors, and you make sure your house is warm enough to keep out the cold. In the classroom there are other things you can do. You may not be able to control the external world, but you can control your response to it. Let's look at a few examples.

You can almost always control something!

Take mandated curriculums. They're pretty far on the no control end of the continuum. The textbook or program for your classes will likely be chosen before you arrive at your Transplant School. You may one day serve on a committee that selects the next curriculum. You may one day get the opportunity to fill out a survey about the curriculum and how it's working. You may be able to send an email to the Curriculum Director about your concerns. But, anything beyond that is likely a waste of time. You could spend your energy documenting all of the curriculum's failings and complaining about it, or you could spend your energy figuring out how to make the best of it.

When I moved to Alaska, the district used a reading curriculum I really didn't like. I hated the canned, scripted nature, and the number of student questions each day was unreasonable for the reading level of my students. Instead of using every question provided in the manual, I started picking only the ones I thought were most important. I focused on those during class time and didn't worry about the others. I couldn't control everything in that situation (the reading curriculum), but I could control some things (the adaptations in my classroom). Curriculums and programs can be adapted to meet the needs of your students. You don't have to throw away the entire thing and go all rogue in your teaching. You can make adjustments and substitutions that make sense for your classroom and your students while still using the mandated curriculum.

What your students do outside of school is pretty far toward the no control end of the continuum. You can encourage certain activities. You can introduce possibilities, but ultimately the students and their families control what happens once the kids walk out of the school doors.

Many of my students are perpetually exhausted. Some of them fall asleep in class. I gently try to rouse them. I offer to let them walk around the classroom or splash water on their face. If that doesn't work and they still sleep, I contact their parents by writing a note home or making a phone call. I like to keep parents informed. They may not know that their son or daughter is so tired during the day. If they know they might be able to support getting more sleep. If the sleeping is affecting their grade because of incomplete work, I note that on grade reports.

It would be easy to say, "If they weren't so tired, I could teach them." There's a grain of truth in that statement. If the students weren't so tired, it would probably be easier to teach. But, they are tired, and complaining about how it should be won't change that. Instead, I can work with the tiredness. I can build more movement into my lessons. I can sprinkle interactive experiences into each class. I can avoid talking in front of the class for long periods of time. Those are things I can control.

(Almost) always in your control

Some things in your classroom are solidly in the controllable zone.

If weather is an example of something you can't control, the food you eat is an example of something you can control. You decide what you put in your mouth. You decide what to prepare for breakfast and dinner. You decide what to snack on. But, there are some limits. You can't just wave a magic wand and say, "Strawberries!" The type of food you want has to be available. You have to be able to afford or harvest it.

Situations in your classroom are like that. You have a lot of control over some things, but certain conditions must be met. Think about how to leverage what you control based on what's available or possible and you'll make your life much easier.

Routines: teach and reteach, repeat as necessary

You control classroom routines. The school day is full of opportunities for routines. What will your students do when they first walk into your classroom? What will they do when they're ready to leave? How do they get out and put away materials? Classroom routines can be kind of like the stakes that gardeners tie to tomato plants to help support the plant if the tomatoes get too heavy. It doesn't guarantee that all will be well with the plants, but it supports their growth.

The first step in creating a good routine is identifying exactly what you want students to do step by step. If you're unclear about what students should do, then they're definitely going to be unclear about how to do it.

Next, set up the room and supplies in a way that makes it easy for students to follow the routine. Do the students need a designated place to put supplies away? Do containers need to be labeled? Does something need to be moved higher or lower to be more accessible? Whatever you want the students to do should be as easy as possible.

Once the room is all set up, explicitly teach students each step and have them practice while giving them feedback. Don't skip this step. Just putting up a sign or verbally giving directions once isn't enough.

Students need to physically go through the routine so you can confirm they're doing it right or offer minor corrections to help them. I've known early elementary teachers who have all students physically practice sitting in the thinking chair so they know the routine for when they are naughty (or, excuse me, need some time to think). Other teachers practice getting out and putting away microscopes or art supplies multiple times. You may have the students practice all at once or one at a time. You may offer verbal praise or high fives or smiley faces on the board as students successfully complete the routine. The goal is for all of your students to know the routine and have some experience completing it.

The last step is to reteach the routine as necessary. Even after the routine is established, students will sometimes lapse. That's normal. It doesn't mean you're a failure at routines or that your students will never learn them. Your students might just need some reminders. It also gives you a chance to reflect and see if there's anything you can do to improve the routine.

For example, I implemented a routine for the beginning of each of my classes. I wanted my students to walk into my classroom, grab an entry task, and sit down and work on it while I welcomed the rest of the class and took attendance. Those were the exact steps I wanted them to follow.

To make it easy for the students to follow the routine, I moved a plastic paper sorter right by the door. I labeled the slots by class period so students could easily identify which paper to grab (as long as they remembered which class period it was…).

The first day I implemented the new system, I taught the routine to each student as they came into class. I stood by the door and pointed to the paper sorter. I said something like "grab one of the entry tasks out of the first period slot."

I offered feedback when a student (or students) started walking in without grabbing one by cheerfully reminding them, "Don't forget! We grab an entry task on our way into the classroom."

We practiced every day with a new entry task, and I continued to give verbal feedback as I corrected and reminded and thanked them for doing a good job. The students started to follow the routine automatically until I didn't have to point to the entry task and verbally remind them. Reteaching happened anytime there was a lapse in the routine, and it usually consisted of pleasant verbal reminders to individuals or to the entire class if a lot of students were forgetting.

It's not an earth-shaking routine, and it doesn't solve all the problems in my classroom. But it buys me some breathing room at the beginning of each class. While my students are engaged, I can take care of all the beginning of class business.

Routines can also help solve pain points in your classroom. I've struggled with getting my students to clean up at the end of class. Somehow by the time I realize class is almost over and we rush to finish up, my room ends up looking like the aftermath of a hurricane. I'm left trying to deal with pencils, papers, and random Gatorade bottles.

Instead of throwing my hands in the air and complaining about my messy students, I *Focused on What I Could Control*. I identified my ideal routine: students log out of their computers, return their pencils to the pencil bin, and put their notebooks in their cubbies before standing in the "kid zone" (my name for the area inside an invisible boundary that keeps them from crowding around the door).

Then I thought about what would make it easy to follow the routine. I realized I needed to give them more time to clean up. This is super obvious, but it took me a while to figure it out. I used to expect them to clean up even if I gave them thirty seconds. They would freak out about leaving on time and stash their notebooks somewhere, leave books piled around, and abandon pencils.

Now I try to start the clean up process earlier. When students have enough time, they are more likely to follow the routine. If we end up with ninety extra seconds at the end of class when everything is cleaned up and put away, I ask them trivia or vocabulary questions.

Allowing plenty of time for clean up also gives me a chance to make sure everything is where it's supposed to be. If it's not, I can offer feedback and give reminders. If I notice that the class is getting collectively lax and leaving a lot of stuff out, I remind the class before I instruct them to clean up. Then I position myself in front of the door and watch for everything to get put away. When kids start to whine, I remind them that it goes faster when everybody helps.

I have to reteach the clean up routine about once a week, but my students are doing a much better job than when I first started teaching.

Another change I made to support the routine was moving my cubbies to the wall closer to the door. I initially had them across the room, but students hated walking to the far side to put their notebooks away before walking back across the room to the door (a difference of about twenty steps, but, you know). Instead, they shoved their notebooks on top of shelves or in drawers or left them on the tables. The kids who made the long trek to the cubbies just threw their notebooks on top.

Moving the cubbies close to the door side eliminated most of those behaviors. Now, students can put their notebooks away on their way out. A simple change, but it made the routine easier.

Routines are not a cure all for every problem in your classroom, but they can be a support. Stakes aren't the only thing tomatoes need to grow either. They still need sunshine, nutrients, and water, but the stakes provide support in addition to all of that. Give yourself that support. Bring in the stakes (metaphorical, of course)!

Micro consequences: little itty bitty consequences

Sometimes routines aren't enough to deal with unwanted student behaviors. But even in these situations, there are things you can control. Micro consequences are one strategy for dealing with irritating misbehaviors. A micro consequence is just what it sounds like, a very small consequence that can be enforced fearlessly. This isn't something you'd want to use for major behaviors, but it's perfect for small infractions that happen over and over.

One of my favorite micro consequences is a fifteen-second delay after class ends. Students who misbehave in a very specific way get to spend fifteen seconds after class with me. If I hear a student making duck noises during class (this is sometimes a real problem because my classroom is full of avid duck hunters), I warn him or her that each quack will earn him/her fifteen seconds after class. The next time I hear a duck noise, I make a tally mark on a slip of paper and say, "That's one."

Fifteen seconds really isn't a big deal, so I don't hesitate to apply the consequence. If the duck noise happens again, I make another mark and say, "That's two." Sometimes the students will stop the annoying behavior after a couple of marks. Sometimes they'll test me to see if I mean it. That's okay because, even if they quack twelve times, it's only three minutes.

As I dismiss the rest of the class, I instruct the quacker to take a seat. Then I watch the clock and let them go at the right time. The micro consequence isn't so big a deal that it provokes anger, but it's enough to provoke annoyance. Most students serve only a couple of micro consequences before they decide quacking is not really worth it. If they slip back into the behavior, another fifteen or thirty seconds is a good (and relatively painless) reminder.

Absolute consistency is key with this strategy. The tiny nature of the consequence helps because it allows me to enforce the consequence every time without worrying if I really want to raise the stakes with detention or a call home about something like a duck noise.

Don't try to do it all at once

Whether you're using micro consequences or some other intervention, it's important not to try to solve every challenge at once. It can become overwhelming, and you'll likely run out of energy and patience without being able to follow through with every consequence. I want to give you permission to start with just one thing. Pick one behavior that you'd like to change and focus on it. You can even start with the behavior that's contributing the most crazy to your classroom. Maybe your students shout out answers without waiting their turns. Maybe they pop their gum. Maybe they forget to put names on their papers. Maybe they chew on their pencils and spit out the erasers (I don't know, kids do weird stuff sometimes).

Let me show you how I would tackle this. Say I'm ridiculously annoyed by my students' swearing. A good first step would be to gather some data. One day I'll keep track of every time my students swear. I'd probably make a little tally mark on some scratch paper and divide the paper up by class period. The next day I would ask the kids to guess the total number of swears. We could even turn it into a little game to see who could get closest. When I revealed the real number, I'd use it to start a conversation.

We would talk about why getting swearing under control is a good idea. It might go something like, "When you're working at a job, you can't just swear any time you want to. If you swear at a boss or a customer, you could get fired. Part of growing up is learning when certain language is appropriate and when it's not."

I'd ask the students what they think should be the consequence for swearing. If the students were used to sharing ideas and respectfully discussing them, we would verbally make a list together. If I was worried the students would attack or insult each other's ideas, I would have the students write their ideas on pieces of paper, turn them in, and I'd make the big list.

We'd discuss the pros and cons of each idea, and I'd cross off any ideas that were not feasible to enforce (for example, fine them a million dollars or do an hour detention after school). Then the students vote for a consequence on slips of paper or with hands raised and their heads down.

We'd implement the winning consequence the next day. For the next week or so, I would really focus on that single behavior. I wouldn't allow my classroom to become a free-for-all as long as they aren't saying bad words, but I would try not to scold and punish every instance of misbehavior. I would focus on working the system and consistently enforcing the consequence for swearing.

If the consequence doesn't seem to be working or it's too much work to enforce, I would bring the issue back to the class. I'd explain the difficulties, and we'd brainstorm new ideas and start again.

Once the consequence implementation is going smoothly, I would target another behavior and follow a similar pattern.

This is part of *Focusing on What You Can Control*. You can't control everything all at once, but you can make changes and interventions that begin to shape your classroom.

Preparation and presentation

One thing that's more on the I-can-control-it side of the continuum is how you deliver content in the classroom.

You get to decide how prepared you are and how much time and energy you put into your lessons. Of course, your supply of free time and energy is finite, but within that limit, you can control how much of it goes into lesson prep.

When I have activities and backup activities planned in case the first ones bomb or wrap up quickly, I feel more confident. When the students aren't waiting for me to find the copies or load a video, they get less antsy. When I allow myself time to give the lesson more than a glance, I have a greater opportunity to enhance or personalize it. I can think of examples that are locally relevant and how the content connects to my students' lives. I can control how much I prepare, so it deserves my focus.

You control the rhythm of the class. If my students get restless with long chunks of independent work time, I can break up those chunks. If small tasks start taking a long time, I can create a little bit of urgency.

I once had a Composition class that journaled at the beginning of the class period. Each week I raised the minimum number of sentences required for journal entries. This worked really well until the students started dragging out journal time. They constantly had to be refocused, and journal time got longer and longer. Now I set the timer for journals. They have a certain number of minutes to write in their journals, and when the timer goes off, it's over. They are welcome to go back to their journals if they finish their other assignments, but I don't let journal time take over the class anymore.

You can control the different activities you use during class time. If the students don't respond well to listening to you talk for forty minutes at a time or doing thirty-five straight questions out of a book, you can introduce more variety in your activities. Try group work, sketch notes, games, art projects, scavenger hunts, playing review games with the content, simulations, brief clips from YouTube, foldables, movement, and a host of other things. There's nothing wrong with direct instruction, but it doesn't have to be the only technique.

(I totally understand classroom activities might fall toward the no control side of the spectrum depending on your school or administration. Some curriculum programs have mandatory activities, and some schools have restrictions about what can happen in the classroom. YouTube may be blocked in some places, or there may be a lack of supplies... Any number of other factors could limit your teaching freedom. If that's the case, refer back to the sections about finding small things you can control, even amid uncontrollable situations.)

A few years into our time in Shishmaref, I started to hit my stride with classroom activities. My thinking shifted from "what am I going to do in the classroom" to "what experiences am I going to give my students in the classroom." I started one year with map projections on the first day of school (we were studying World History that year). We examined different projections in little booklets, and then the kids drew latitude and longitude lines on mandarin oranges I had hauled from Anchorage. Their challenge was to peel the mandarin oranges in the shape of one projection. It was awesome. They were totally engaged and got to eat the oranges at the end. Perfect first day of school.

We also had a lot of fun studying ancient civilizations. When we studied the use of paper in ancient China, I borrowed a blender and we made paper pulp out of scraps. We strained the pulp with some makeshift sieves and dried it into clumpy sheets of our very own paper. I printed off various Mandarin kanji from the Internet, and the kids practiced writing them on their clumpy paper.

As we studied explorers, I filled little condiment cups with different spices. The students smelled the spices and tried to match the spice names with each numbered cup. A few of the boys decided to be clever and started licking the spices. Not only did I get great pictures, but we all laughed as they turned in the most accurate guesses.

The pinnacle of my Ancient History unit was when we mummified Cornish game hens (it was supposed to be chickens, but they were too expensive in Nome). I bought a lot of salt, and we followed the directions from the Internet about how to dry the chickens out using double gallon-sized Ziploc bags. We documented the whole thing with pictures and patiently waited the thirty days for the salt to do its work.

The kids named each of their mummified "chickens" (the only requirement was that the name had to be bird related) and painted inner and outer sarcophagi for each mummy. When the birds were dry, we wrapped them in gauze, hiding amulets in the wrappings, just like the ancient Egyptians did.

The ground was frozen solid by the time we finished the project, so we had to wait until the beginning of the next school year to bury them. Looking back, I can't believe I stored a bunch of dry Cornish game hens in my classroom for almost a year. The kids were so excited when we finally got to bury them. It's definitely the most long-term lesson plan I've ever done.

That one time my students and I created a *Law and Order* episode

One of my best examples of being *Adaptive* in my teaching our first year in Shishmaref was when my classes made a *Law and Order* episode. One Level 4 Social Studies standard required knowledge of the steps of a trial. The End of Level Assessment listed them as: arrest, preliminary hearing, indictment, arraignment, jury selection, trial, verdict, and sentencing. That's a lot of steps and a lot of long words.

I tried everything to help my students master the vocabulary of the steps. We took notes. We filled out graphic organizers. We made flashcards. A wise mentor suggested we use the mnemonic device APHIAJTVS (it sounds crazy, but it actually stuck with them—and me. I used it to write the steps in the paragraph above!).

Even with APHIAJTVS, my students weren't reaching the level of mastery I felt was necessary to mark them as proficient on that standard (that was back when our district decided not to give out grades. We measured mastery of standards instead). I needed to give my students an experience to help them internalize the steps. I tried a mock trial with the principal presiding as judge, but that was a flop. The students weren't prepared enough to fulfill their roles as prosecutor, defense attorney, bailiff, etc. I had the Village Public Safety Officer come in and perform a mock arrest and talk to the class about his role in the justice system. That was fascinating, and the kids loved it, but it didn't encompass all of the steps.

But then one of the other teachers taped (as in VHS!) an episode of *Law and Order* for me, and we watched it in my classes. That helped because the story was riveting, and I could pause the video at important points and remind the students which step was happening.

An idea started to form. I love video editing. Ever since taking a class on the subject in high school, I'd dabbled in creating videos of all kinds. I had my own video camera. I had an Apple laptop with iMovie on it. I had a bunch of junior high kids with lots of energy and personality. What if we made our own episode of *Law and Order*?

Could it work? It would be an involved project that would take up lots of time. Would it even be worth it? Would the kids cooperate? Would they hate this idea as much as almost anything else I'd tried with them?

I finally asked the kids what they thought about the idea, and they were hooked! We brainstormed story ideas (I vetoed the overly graphic death scenes), and the kids claimed roles they would play.

We started shooting immediately. I would take the day's footage home, edit it, and bring it back the next day for the kids to watch. They loved seeing the progress and laughing at each other on film. Then we planned the next phase of shooting and repeated the process.

We showed the final product to a school-wide assembly and got to hear the entire student body laughing at our silliness and enjoying our bloopers reel.

The project was a lot of work. There were nights I was too exhausted to finish editing the day's footage, and I had to disappoint the kids by making them wait another day or two to see it. But, we persevered and had an experience that people in Shishmaref still talk about today.

This experience taught me to have the courage to try new things when old things don't work. I was *Adaptive*. I really thought that graphic organizers and flashcards would be enough for learning to happen. They weren't. I tried other methods in an almost desperate attempt to encourage learning. When I still didn't get the results I needed, I tried something entirely different. It was the right move for my students and presented the content in a way that reinvigorated them.

The *Law and Order* experience also showed me how fun it could be to teach using my strengths. I was already a good video editor. I already enjoyed capturing footage and turning it into an impressive end product. Bringing those things into the classroom brought the fun and enjoyment with them. I looked forward to the classes when we were shooting footage. I woke up in the morning excited for the next step in the process.

This is not to suggest that big, involved projects are the only way to teach. It's always an effort to balance the time and effort an experience will take with the learning it will produce. One could argue that it was a waste of time to create a video that taught only a basic understanding of the judicial process. But, one could also argue that the accompanying community-building effects were worth the effort.

Not every lesson was amazing. I still had plenty of limitations within the school day and curriculum, but I took advantage of *What I Could Control*. If I moaned and groaned about what I wished I could do or what I didn't like about the standards, I wouldn't have opened my mind to the possibilities. Once I shifted into the mindset of looking for what I could do, I found ways to make the content engaging. It started with my own attitude toward what I was teaching in my classroom (inward) before I could connect it with my students (outward).

There are a million and one forces that may affect your classroom, and your job is to deal with them. You don't have to be the victim of what's out of your control. Use adaptive lesson planning and classroom management to adjust to whatever's thrown your way. You'll save yourself the trouble of raging against the unchangeable and have more energy for creating solutions and experiences for your students.

CHAPTER 19

Feedback from Students

If I ever need a dose of honesty, I know I can look to my students. They have absolutely no trouble telling me that it's been a while since I waxed my eyebrows or that my red knee-high boots make me look like I should be on farmersonly.com. Those examples are only low key hurtful and about my personal appearance, but students can be a good source of feedback about important things too, like your teaching. The feedback won't come formally, but it will come in their response to you and your classroom activities. This is a perfect opportunity to apply the strategy *Accept Feedback*. Even if the feedback is negative, it's a cue that you need to do something different. If you're teaching the same way you've always taught and it's not working, you need to try something else! Insisting "that's the way I teach" is unhelpful. Refusing to change in the classroom is as ridiculous as trying to order food in English in a country where the people speak a different language because "that's the way I speak." Transplant Teachers must change their attitudes (inward) so they can *Be Flexible and Adapt* their teaching to the environments of their Transplant Homes (outward).

Are they interested or not?

One form of useful feedback is interest level. If the entire class is uninterested in an assignment, it's worth reflecting on why. Was it too hard? Too easy? Too disconnected from their reality? Too much at one time? Too many unfamiliar words? Were they all tired? Were they preoccupied with something that happened the night before?

There are countless possible reasons for their disinterest. Rather than blaming the students and labeling them lazy or apathetic, dig deeper and see what you can learn for next time. You can adjust your attitude (inward) to approach the situation differently and look for what you can do (outward) rather than insisting it's not your fault. Maybe a small modification is needed (like breaking the ginormous packet of primary sources into smaller chunks) or maybe an entirely new approach is more appropriate.

Interested students are a sign that things are going well in my classroom. Like when the entire class begs for more Inupiaq spelling practice. Or when they are furiously finding facts about U.S. Presidents so they can improve their times in a matching game. Or they are cheering and hollering as the Communist Party distributes candy "resources" during the economic systems simulation. Those intense moments don't happen every day, but when they do, they are a good sign. The rest of the days I'm looking for a generally happy buzz in my classroom as students talk about the content and willingly do the work.

I'm not suggesting you do only the things your students want to do. Part of being an adult and a teacher is providing guidance about what is healthy and beneficial, even if it's unpleasant (think of any kid who doesn't want to eat vegetables or get vaccinations). However, interest levels and engagement are worth considering when you make instructional decisions for your classroom. *Accepting the Feedback* from your students and *Adapting* to what you learn can make you more successful in the classroom.

Did they all fail it? That's a cue!

Another form of feedback that comes from students is their success level with the work you're assigning. That doesn't mean they're all earning A pluses or one hundred percents. It means a high majority of them are able to participate in the activities and show some kind of measurable growth. It means most students are finishing the work by the due date.

If almost everybody failed something in my class, I know I need to go back and reteach the concept or clarify the directions. Maybe the students need some more examples. Maybe I need to break the assignment down into more manageable chunks. Maybe I need to change the requirements.

One year, my classes did a types of government mini-simulation. I encouraged the students to take notes in their notebooks to help them with the written assignment afterwards, but none of them did. When it came time to complete the written assignment, they couldn't remember the relevant facts.

I let them struggle with it for a little while (because I thought it was an appropriate natural consequence). Then I did the activity again and suggested that this time they take notes. They ran to their cubbies and frantically grabbed their notebooks before I got started. The adaptation of doing the assignment again led to more student learning than if I'd said, too bad, so sad and moved on.

I use similar techniques if most of my students miss a deadline or are off task. Maybe they didn't know what to do. Maybe the volume of the work overwhelmed them and completion seemed impossible. Maybe the work seems irrelevant. Maybe they just need more time.

Sometimes I'm not a great judge of how long an assignment will take. I'll plan an assignment for the last third of the class period, and they end up needing five days to complete it. Sometimes I'll budget forty-five minutes for an activity, and seven minutes later the students are looking at me as if to say "What now?" Admitting that some of these errors are my responsibility helps me shift blame away from my students so I can better identify the real issue and address it.

The key here is to *Accept* student success–or lack of success–as *Feedback* (inward) and *Adapt* your teaching (outward). You are not necessarily to blame for a lack of student success, but it's not about blame. It's about finding what your students need to move forward. It's about *Being Adaptive* by *Focusing on What You Can Control*.

Student complaining can be good for something!

I've heard students complain about lots of things including not getting seconds on corn dogs, the font I used on an assignment, and the fact that they have to walk across the room to get a pencil. Most of the time this complaining makes me roll my eyes so hard that I get a headache, but some complaints contain useful grains of feedback. That's right, complaining can actually be helpful. One or two students complaining generally doesn't concern me. In those cases the complaining usually has more to do with that student than it does with me or my classroom. However, when almost everybody is complaining, I know something needs to change.

It's hard not to let student complaining bother me personally. I remind myself not every single student is going to like my class every single day. That's okay. But, when there's a pattern of complaining by multiple students, I take extra time to consider what's happening in my classroom. Answering these questions helps me evaluate:

- Is it boring?
- Do the students know why this is important for their lives?
- Is it the same thing over and over?

- Is there a way I could make this more interactive?
- Can I switch gears during the class period so they're not doing the same thing all hour?
- Are my policies reasonable?
- Do the students know the reasons behind the policies?
- Are there any structural changes* I could make so following the policies easier?
- Am I enforcing consequences consistently?
- Am I correcting my students more than I'm noticing the good things they do?
- Is anything making the students uncomfortable (stifled/unheard/unfairly treated)?

If I'm honest in my answers, they can be a useful guide to target areas for improvement.

(*A quick note about structural changes. That could mean giving my art class more time to clean up at the end of the day so that they're not scrambling and cutting corners when cleaning and caring for supplies. It could mean moving the cubbies to the counter by the door so that students can put their notebooks away as they leave rather than stashing them in random places because they don't want to walk across the classroom. See the previous section on routines).

Student feedback is a valuable source of information, even if it's not 100 percent positive. Not every student likes my class. I'm not everybody's favorite teacher. That's okay. I don't consider myself unsuccessful in the classroom because a couple of kids think me and my class are meh. Similarly, some off-task students are fairly normal, as are some kids off task for a little bit here and there. My students aren't completely and enthusiastically engaged at every moment. Sometimes students have bad days or come to school exhausted. Sometimes things are chaotic at home or in the community or around the school.

I don't use flawlessness to judge my classroom. I don't tabulate complaints to make sure I have an average of less than 2.67 complaints per class period. If the vibe in my classroom is generally happy and friendly and students generally like my class, I consider things to be okay.

CHAPTER 20

Classroom, Community, and Connections

I've talked about the things I did during my student teaching and how they weren't appropriate in a new setting. Wearing dress suits and nylons, assigning descriptive assignments about individual bedrooms, and expecting parents to rave about how much their kids loved me during parent-teacher conferences were all part of my former teaching life. My teaching life now needs different things. It requires a softer voice, a calmer rate of speaking, and a willingness to give kids space instead of demanding instant compliance.

The way you've always taught before and the way you've shown up may not work in a new location because you're not teaching in your old reality. You're teaching in your Transplant Home, and if you want to thrive there, your teaching methods need to reflect that.

Teaching and learning the local way

Teaching the local way means presenting content in a way that reflects local norms (with a story, in small groups, individually, quietly, loudly, with lots of personal examples, etc.). It means using culturally appropriate means of correction and feedback. It means being sensitive to the ways your students express knowledge or indicate they need help.

Figuring out how to teach in the local way is a time to *Seek After*

Information by observing. Transplant Teachers who are out and about in the community can see what life is made up of in their Transplant Home. They can see how people spend their time and what skills and traits are admired and important. Transplant Teachers who observe how parents, parapros, and students interact can tap into those patterns.

It can be as simple as giving an example of an unjust situation and using hunting or a snow machine in the example. It can be using an old regional story to illustrate plot structure. It can be using local words to describe a new concept. I experience higher engagement levels when I incorporate cultural stories and examples into my lessons, and the kids pay more attention when it connects to their reality.

Observation is an important part of Inupiaq learning. When children learn to cut fish or butcher seals, they first spend years watching their parents and grandparents do it at camp. When the child is older, they get to try for the first time side by side with those same adults. The teaching isn't verbally explicit, and children are expected to observe carefully before they try on their own. One of my favorite Elders in Shishmaref was not allowed to cut some parts of the seal when her mother was alive, even as an adult. She was still in the observation phase.

This pattern can be translated into classroom practice. Instead of rattling off a list of instructions or showing my students how to do something once, I can allow them longer periods of observation. When the students do try to do something independently, I can be right by their sides, continuing to show them how. This pattern is familiar to my students and yields better results for them than the way I was taught in school.

When I taught an art class for the first time, I would generally do demonstrations at the center table in my room. The students gathered around me as I showed them how to use watercolors with salt or rubbing alcohol or masking tape to get different effects. After the demonstration, I expected them to scatter around the room and independently use the techniques. That didn't happen. The students preferred to crowd around the table, staying right next to me, and using the techniques while watching me at the same time. Eventually, I started planning my lessons that way, and the demonstrations always transitioned into periods of me working side-by-side with the students so they could look over and check out what I was doing.

Transplant Teachers also need to keep local learning patterns in mind when asking students to demonstrate their learning. Students in Brevig Mission and Shishmaref don't often give quick verbal responses. Taking time to think is standard practice. Some teachers assume this is because they don't know the answer to a question. Sometimes it's just that the students are processing what the teacher said. Sometimes it's because the students are feeling out the social situation and deciding what and how to share in a way that's culturally appropriate and not boastful.

A teacher met with silence from the students after rapidly firing off questions that require students to make inferences may assume that the students don't know how to make inferences. That might not be true. Our students make inferences all the time. They observe body language and infer how someone is feeling. They observe a teacher's words and attitudes and infer how the teacher feels about them. They hear pieces of information or stories and infer what's going on and how that affects them and their families. The problem isn't always the skill of inferencing. The problem might be in the way they're asked to share it.

Learning patterns are different around the world. A Transplant Teacher's students may not learn the same way my Inupiaq students do. It's up to the Transplant Teacher to *Seek After Information* and observe the learning patterns appropriate to their Transplant Home. This takes being out and about in the community and talking with parents and local coworkers. Keep in mind that parents and local coworkers may not think to mention the learning patterns. It may be such a part of who they are that they don't recognize it as different or noteworthy.

It's okay if you don't nail it every time. Shifting into learning and teaching patterns that are different than you're used to is a complex process. It's not something that's ignited once and stays lit for the rest of your career. Like everything else in the Transplant Life, it's a process that requires trial and error, reflection, and adaptation.

Reaching out to local experts

One way to connect your classroom to the community is to invite in local experts. The experts don't have to be formally trained or certified, but every community is full of people who know a lot of stuff.

Getting to know people informally and listening to their stories can give you a good idea of who might make a good classroom visitor. I had no idea the mother of one of my high school girls moved from Shishmaref to Brevig Mission by dog sled when she was a little girl until I was sitting at her kitchen table listening to her tell stories of her childhood.

You can also discover experts by asking around. This is a time to use the strategy *Ask for Help and Information*. Find someone you have a relationship with and ask "Who would know a lot about (insert topic here)?" or "Who remembers (insert specific historical event here)?" Their answers will point you in the direction of new people to get to know. Asking these questions of each new contact has led me on a veritable treasure hunt of resources. I didn't know that some of the young Elders in Brevig Mission attended Native American boarding schools in the Lower 48 until I asked someone else about who has a good story about school.

Your students are likely familiar with community members and can give suggestions about whom to invite into the classroom as a guest speaker or interviewee. This is a great time to *Ask for Help and Information*. If the kids think the person has worthwhile information to share, they will probably be more interested in engaging with that person. The students can also make suggestions about how to contact these resources. Maybe some students would even be willing to make the contact for you!

Once you've arranged for a local expert to visit, prepare your students by generating background knowledge and questions as a group. I've even printed a list of student-generated questions for my students to refer to when the visitor arrives. It's also a good idea to review ways to be respectful to the guest speaker (actually listen, not getting up while they're talking to get water, only laugh at what they say if they're trying to be funny, etc.).

If you get the sense that the local expert is uncomfortable with the idea of standing in front of the class and giving a speech, change the format. I've gotten good results by having the students sit in a circle with the local expert and making it more of a conversation. If the expert is showing my students how to do something, we sit around a table in the center of the room. I've also invited a couple of local experts in at the same time and put them in separate corners of the classroom. My students rotated in small groups to each expert. Smaller groups can be less intimidating.

Another technique is to invite a few experts to come in together so they can bounce off each other and tell stories together. We had a group of women from the community share stories with a gathering of high school girls during our weekly girls' meeting. The women talked about the importance of getting along and resolving conflicts. They stressed the importance of preparing to be a community of women that will need and help each other. The group setting facilitated a conversational approach that involved the girls without feeling like a lecture.

My favorite Elder experience ever was when a pair of cousins came in. They laughed and laughed as they remembered stories from the past together. Each story triggered a new memory, and the process started again. The kids were fascinated, and we all laughed with them.

Like everything else, I've learned to *Be Flexible* when dealing with local experts. Weather conditions and family responsibilities trump appointments with my class. If the weather is nice, the local expert might choose to go hunting or fishing at the last minute. If a family member needs help or a babysitter, the local expert will often choose to help their family.

I always have a backup plan in case something comes up. I call the local expert in the morning or at lunch to see if they are still coming in. If they are, I say, "Great, can't wait to see you!" If they aren't, I say, "No worries, we'll try again tomorrow," and do the planned backup activity with my class. My initial instinct can be to guilt the local expert by saying, "I was really counting on you" or "My class is expecting you," but I resist that. I want to make sure the local expert feels appreciated for even their willingness to come in, and I want to preserve the relationship so they will be inclined to try again.

People may be hesitant to come in if they are unsure what they will say. It can help to give them a few written prompts or questions ahead of time so they can think about what they're going to say and feel confident that their comments are what you want.

It may also be possible and appropriate to bring your class to the guest speaker. Elders sometimes feel more comfortable in their own homes, and as long as we call in advance, I feel okay about bringing small groups of students to visit with them. Students can also visit people as they're cutting meat or carving, as long as the workspace is safe and large enough.

There are people all around your Transplant Home that can enhance your lessons and benefit your students. You have to know enough to know who to invite. You have to be brave enough to do the inviting. You have to be flexible enough to accomodate once you've invited them. Prepare yourself inwardly so you can reach out. Remind yourself that local connections and relevance are worth the effort. Then go out on a limb and try to make it happen.

Mini field trips

Mini field trips are another valuable resource. I'm lucky in Brevig Mission that I don't have to deal with buses and transportation. With a consent form on file, I can make sure the students are dressed warmly, and we can walk any place in town.

Initially I didn't think there was really any place to go in our tiny village that would relate to anything I was teaching. One of my skilled professors helped me see otherwise. We did an exercise in one of my graduate classes where we walked around and matched content standards to local places. Even math standards were able to be matched (finding right angles in buildings around the community! Measuring rate and flow of local water! Measuring volume of heating oil barrels and water tanks! Observing changes in temperature across different locations! Adding decimals at the store!). Mini field trips don't have to be elaborate. They can be simple and nearby.

As I widened my perspective I started to see places where I could take my students to see examples of classroom content in action. I could lecture my students about the 1918 flu pandemic, but it would be a lot more powerful if we talked about it at the mass grave of pandemic victims. We could write descriptive pieces of our favorite places, but the students might be more engaged if we take paper and clipboards down to the beach, write drafts of descriptive pieces of our surroundings, and compare all of the things we noticed. I can drone on and on with my passion for primary sources, but sending the kids on a scavenger hunt to find them around town is way more fun and memorable.

Flexibility is key with outings too. If the weather is bad, we can't go out. If a majority of my class came to school without boots or outside shoes, I'm not going to take them walking around in the snow. I've learned to have backup plans for any scheduled outings. I whip them out if conditions are less than favorable, and we do the outing another day.

It's easy to find excuses for why I can't take my kids out of the classroom (it's cold, it might be windy, it might snow, there's nowhere to go, I don't want to…), but none of those factors are insurmountable with a willingness to *Be Flexible* and *Adapt*.

Odds are, your Transplant Home is full of interesting people and places. Don't use inconvenience as an excuse to not make these connections. Take advantage of your surroundings and integrate them into your teaching so that what's going on in your classroom is relevant and connected to your students' lives.

Plant Health Checklist

It's important to reflect on your life in the classroom, just as you reflect on your life in other areas. You don't want to thrive outside of school and be droopy and shriveled in the classroom (you know, like in an unhealthy plant). Taking the time to step back and look at your classroom can help you decide what's going well and what you need to adjust. The adjustments might be your attitudes or perceptions (inward). They might be routines or consequences for your students (outward). A big part of your overall Transplant Health is your Classroom Health.

Here's another checklist to help you consider the Health of your Transplant Classroom.

Signs of Health

- ☐ I am getting to know my students and connecting with them a little at a time.

- ☐ I am letting my students get to know me.

- ☐ I ask questions and let my students teach me about local customs, culture, and surroundings.

- ☐ I examine my expectations for student behavior to see if they are appropriate for my Transplant Home.

- ☐ I observe local patterns in teaching and learning and integrate them into my classroom

- ☐ I look for ways to deal with seemingly uncontrollable factors.

- ☐ I establish routines in my classroom and reteach as necessary.

- ☐ I focus on one behavioral intervention at a time when solving problems so I don't get overwhelmed.

- ☐ I'm prepared for my lessons.

- ☐ I use a variety of methods and activities in my lessons.

- ☐ I accept disengagement and widespread complaining as a cue to adapt my teaching.

- ☐ I reteach and adapt if many students are unsuccessful.

- ☐ I invite local experts to be a part of my classroom.

- ☐ I look for ways to take my students on relevant outings.

- ☐ Students are generally interested and on task in my classroom

As you look at this list, you might start to feel overwhelmed. Try not to let the list feel like something that's burying you. Let it inspire you. Take time to celebrate what's going well and consider how to build on it. Let one of the items you don't check off be the vision for where you want to head next.

Warning Signs:

- ☐ I expect my students to behave the way I did when I was in school or the way my students behaved in a different place.

- ☐ I blame my classroom problems on things I can't control.

- ☐ I teach the same way I always have.

- ☐ I use the same methods over and over, regardless of student success or interest.

- ☐ I don't introduce new routines or behavior interventions because I don't think they will make a difference.

- ☐ I dread going to work or teaching certain classes.

- ☐ My students are regularly bored, confused, or off-task.

If you find yourself checking off warning signs, look for ways to make changes. All is not lost if a plant is struggling. There's still a chance to nourish it back to health.

Remember, bad days don't necessarily indicate that something is horribly wrong. There are countless reasons a student (or two) might miss a deadline, be off task, or complain. Sometimes you make a mistake in how you explain something and students are confused or frustrated. Isolated and occasional incidents are a normal part of classrooms, and while there's always room for improvement, you don't have to feel like you're doing it all wrong when it happens.

If your classroom is unhealthy, nourish it! Doing nothing will likely not make it better and may make it worse. Remember the strategies and *Accept the Feedback* you're getting from all sources, *Focus on What You Can Control, Seek After Help and Information* to figure out what you can do, and *Adapt* your teaching.

Part IV

Putting Down Deep Roots

After you've been in your Transplant Home for a while, you'll have the chance to put down deep roots. You're not fighting for survival anymore, so you can spend time developing and deepening your understandings and connections. Putting down deep roots isn't a one-time event. It's a continual process that requires regular growth and nourishment.

As a tree puts down deep roots, it expands and strengthens. The wider root network makes the tree less vulnerable and prepares it for even more growth. Transplant Teachers do the same thing as they widen their network of personal connections and strengthen relationships. They extend the work they did when Nurturing the Seedling. This makes them less vulnerable to difficulties and prepares them for more growth as people and teachers.

Deep roots are the difference between being a guest at a birthday party and being a regular visitor. As I mentioned earlier, Steve and I were invited to countless birthday parties during our years in Shishmaref. It was customary to invite teachers, and we were among the many people who stopped in, ate treats, and visited.

Being a birthday party guest was a good way to meet people and start to get to know them, but I started putting down deep roots when I returned as a visitor on my own. Showing up this way signaled I wanted to visit on a more personal level. Conversations were more focused, because there weren't a thousand other things going on and grew beyond pleasantries and small talk. I listened to stories about growing up in the village. I asked questions about how everyone was related and connected. I admired sewing projects and ate and was surrounded by normal life. All of this helped me forge deeper connections and understanding.

Putting down deep roots is a chance to learn even more from your community and includes rising to meet the challenges of Deepening Relationships and Meeting Your Needs.

The inward strategies that will help are familiar: *Humility* and *Focusing On What You Can Control*.

Just as it was before you arrived and when you were first making your way in your Transplant Home, admitting you don't know everything is the first step to learning more. You might overestimate what you know because you've been around for a while, but there's still lots to learn. Teachers don't stop learning once they get their first teaching certificate. They improve and grow their entire careers. Consider approaching your Transplant Life with a continued awareness of all that you still have left to learn. *Humility* will help you keep an open mind and serve you well as you learn more about your community and the people around you.

Focusing on What You Can Control can help you in a myriad of situations. If something about your living situation is uncomfortable, *Focus on What You Can Control*. If you're missing someone or something, *Focus on What You Can Control*. Difficult or annoying situations might come up as you get to know more, and you might be tempted to label things as right and wrong. Sometimes it's a matter of needing to adapt expectations. *Focusing on What's in Your Control* is a better use of energy than focusing on what's out of your control.

Outwardly you can *Build More and Stronger Connections* so you can understand. There's a lot to learn about your Transplant Home beyond what you can walk around and see. Relationships are the key to revealing what's under the surface.

Putting down deep roots is a good time to *Stay Positive*. Learning more about your Transplant Home may expose you to new ideas and perspectives. Working with your colleagues for a while may mean dealing with unsavory personality traits and habits from time to time. *Staying positive* will help keep the distasteful from getting in the way of everything else you're trying to accomplish.

Through it all you can *Be Flexible and Adaptive*. This will happen as you think about things in a new way and consider possibilities and solutions that your pre-transplant self may never have thought of (inward). It will also happen as you make those possibilities a reality and put those solutions in place (outward).

CHAPTER 21

Deeper Understanding

It's important to look for deeper connections in the right places. A few years ago one of the other Brevig Mission teachers and I applied for a teacher's grant to travel abroad to research and observe teaching methods in other places. I had read about some New Zealand educational reform efforts that targeted Indigenous student achievement, and we thought the country would be a great fit for the grant since we taught an Indigenous population in Brevig Mission.

We spent days crafting a compelling proposal that encompassed classroom observations, interviews with educators, and cultural experiences around New Zealand's north island. Our proposal included a component of modeling our own efforts after the efforts in New Zealand. Our application highlighted the unique situation of Brevig Mission as an Indigenous community filled with non-Indigenous teachers and situated the New Zealand educational system as a relevant model.

We were elated when our proposal was funded. We frantically made airline and hotel reservations and started arranging cultural experiences. As part of the preparation, I contacted one of the lead scholars in Indigenous education and reform in New Zealand, and she was gracious enough to meet with us for a few days and arrange school visits and experiences for us with other educators. We planned to learn about Kia Eke Panuku, a reform effort focused on observing teacher interactions with Maori students.

Our hostess invited us to a scheduled meeting with the executive committee for Kia Eke Panuku as the final event of our experience. We were all seated around a large conference table, and attendees included officials from the New Zealand government and universities. Some attendees were Maori, others were not. They were all much older than us. We had just finished a light lunch of sushi and finger sandwiches, and we were spending some post-lunch time with the group before they continued on with presumably important business. We were given the opportunity to ask the esteemed group questions and listen to their thoughtful answers. At the very end of the discussion, the lead scholar I had contacted made some comments. She told us that the most important thing was to listen to the Indigenous people around us and that they may not take too kindly to the fact that we went all the way to New Zealand to seek answers that might have been available to us in Alaska.

Her comments stung like a slap in the face. We were so excited about what we could learn from our New Zealand adventure and their efforts, but we hadn't taken full advantage of the wealth of information and perspective in our own Transplant Backyard. It was a very humbling moment, but it was also formative in turning my focus to the people of Brevig Mission and what they want and think.

I came back from New Zealand with much more than some kiwi bird stationary and a map showing New Zealand and Australia on the top and everything else on the bottom. I came back with a renewed desire to learn from members of the community where I live and teach. I started taking notes during staff meetings whenever local staff members shared their thoughts or stories. I tried to record their perspectives and ideas so I could ponder them.

You don't have to be low key humiliated by a foreign education expert to look to your Transplant Community for insight and answers. You can be humble and open to their insights without the reprimand. Don't just look for outside and "expert" perspectives.

Look within and among the people you work and live with. Deep roots come as you *Connect* with those people, hear their perspectives, and let it inform your work in the classroom.

Deep culture

In the efforts to put down Deep Roots, Transplant Teachers will need to go beyond the tip of the iceberg of culture. We mentioned the iceberg analogy in the Prepare the Soil chapter and the idea that there are aspects of culture that are easily observed on the surface. Other aspects are deep culture that are not easily observed.

One wise principal had our staff sit in circles during staff meetings in a mix of people who grew up in Brevig Mission and people who came in later as teachers. We discussed different topics and Inupiaq values and gave those raised in our village a chance to share and explain what those topics and values mean to them.

Sometimes the circles were safe places that resulted in insightful conversations, and sometimes the conversations veered away from their intentions and we missed an opportunity to learn more about deep culture. The veering was generally due to teachers who wouldn't stop talking about their own upbringing and history long enough to listen. If someone is bulldozing the conversation, other people may sit back and let them talk. It also happened when well-meaning teachers tried to avoid silence by rattling on. The blabbing cut off the conversation for everyone but the blabber.

Insightful conversations resulted from waiting for the conversation to flow naturally without trying to jump in and control it. They resulted from allowing lulls in the conversation without speaking up just to fill the silence. Some of the most meaningful moments came after people were quietly thinking.

One such circle was the day the local staff members talked about humor, and the rest of us got a glimpse into one aspect of deep culture in Brevig Mission.

What's funny in one place may be offensive in another. The people of Brevig Mission love to joke around, and there are specific Inupiaq words for teasing different family members. The people in our circle recommended not taking the joking around too seriously. If you look at the person's expression, look at his or her face, and hear them laugh at the end, you can know they are joking

Those closest to you will tease you more. You can expect more teasing from your best friend than from an acquaintance. The people of Brevig Mission will also use humor in tense situations. If they're offering a criticism or suggestion, they might make a joke about it instead of attacking the issue directly.

Certain topics are inappropriate to joke about, including death and suicide. A Transplant Teacher may not immediately know what topics are off limits. Pay attention to the reactions of the people around you. If you make a joke and people are uncomfortable or quickly change the subject, it might mean that the joke was inappropriate.

Cultural humor changes over time. The Young Elders in our circle commented that there used to be more joking in large groups, but kids are more sensitive today, so the joking has backed off a bit.

The principles unearthed in that conversation helped me better understand and interact with my students. I understood that it was a compliment when the high school boys called me Twitch (I'm excessively animated in my body language and gestures, and they thought it was hilarious how I would flail around when I was startled).

Likewise, when I told a class the story about ending up with seven stitches as a four-year-old because I slipped off the kitchen counter while playing Super Angie in my Sunday shoes, they called me Super Angie. It meant they were comfortable with me.

My improved understanding of humor helped me recognize when it's used to deliver low key criticism. When a staff member made a joke about Levi running in the hall after school, I knew she was suggesting that I should do something about it. She used humor to make the point instead of scolding me.

I don't know if it's possible to completely understand the deep culture of a Transplant Home, but I do know it's possible to go beyond the surface level. Develop your connections and deepen your relationships (outward) to reveal deeper levels of culture. Reflect on it for greater perspective and understanding (inward).

As you get more involved in your community, you may start to sense and observe facets of deep culture. They may include:

- Ideas of justice. What is fair? What is unfair? What restitution is appropriate when someone is wronged? Who decides consequences?
- What is honorable, and what is not. What kinds of things are considered disrespectful? What kinds of things dishonor a family or individual? How does one defend the honor of their family?
- Relationship expectations. What is considered faithful in a relationship? Who bears the responsibility of maintaining the relationship? What happens when expectations are violated? What are appropriate ways of ending a relationship?
- Familial obligations. Who has the responsibility of caring for children? Who has the responsibility of caring for aging parents or grandparents? What is the role of the family when someone's spouse/child/sibling dies? When does caring for family take priority over other responsibilities?
- Patterns of deference. Whose opinion carries the most weight when making family or community decisions? Is there room for

discourse around decisions? Is it appropriate to question decisions? Who has cultural authority in matters of tradition and language? Who takes correction from whom?
- Expressing gratitude. How do you honor what someone has done for you? Should you expect expressions of gratitude?
- Conflict resolution. When do you talk to someone you have a conflict with? Where are appropriate places to work out conflicts? Do conflicts require a mediator? Do you talk directly to the person with whom you have a conflict?

There's an entire world under the surface of the water. Don't be satisfied with only experiencing and learning about what's easily visible. The roots of a tree are deep below the surface too, and part of putting down deep roots as a Transplant Teacher is understanding deep culture and starting to operate within it.

Learning about deep culture comes as you outwardly *Build More and Stronger Connections.* Only through relationships will you get a window into the deep workings of your Transplant Home. The stronger your relationships, the more you'll observe and learn about deep culture.

Once you've observed, you can look inward to see how things compare to your own deep culture and decide how you will function within it. You don't have to adopt the culture. You don't even have to agree with it, but you need to be aware of how it impacts the people around you and your reality.

Dismissing cultural norms because you don't understand them or think they're unnecessary might get in the way of what you're trying to do in your Transplant Home. If you're challenging Elders because you think you're right, are people even going to listen to your points if they think you're being disrespectful? If you're thanking people in a way that's meaningless to them, do they feel your gratitude? If you're demanding a conflict be resolved in a way that people won't engage with you, is there a chance for resolution?

Deep culture is right under our noses, waiting to be discovered. Observing and reflecting on deep culture (inward) will help Transplant Teachers function within that culture and make meaningful contributions as teachers and community members (outward).

Local history

One thing that can help your understanding is learning about the historical and cultural context of your community. Current reality doesn't exist in a vacuum, and there are roots and reasons for current conditions. Without knowing the history and background of the school, the community, and the people, you're seeing an incomplete picture.

Focus on local stories and implications. Regional resources may provide a nice overview, but they may not mention how certain events and conditions affected your specific community directly. One example is the 1918 flu pandemic. Regional (and other) resources point to the epidemic as a turning point in the history of the Seward Peninsula because so many people died. That's good to know, but it's even better to know that Shishmaref experienced no deaths during the flu pandemic because they placed armed guards outside the village and refused to let anybody in. Contrast that with Brevig Mission that lost all but six people. Two villages near each other, two very different stories. If I had assumed what was true for one was true for the other, I would have missed out on understanding some pretty important historical context.

Shishmaref used to be one of the smallest villages on the Seward Peninsula. Now it's one of the largest, in part because it didn't sustain the losses that other villages did during the flu epidemic. Shishmaref has maintained stronger linguistic and cultural traditions because they didn't lose a generation of people the way Brevig Mission did. People in Shishmaref are very proud of that fact, and they told Steve and me the story of the armed guards multiple times during our five years there.

People in Brevig Mission don't talk about the flu pandemic as much. Maybe because it's painful. Maybe because it feels like there's not much to say beyond "our village almost didn't survive." I'm not sure. When I ask people about what important events shaped Brevig Mission, they almost always respond with more recent events like the deaths of Elders or when the village got running water in the homes.

As you get to know people and have more opportunities for visiting, start asking what important events shaped the community then listen to the stories. Start asking around for who has stories about these events. Even if they happened a long time ago, there might be a story that's been passed down. There's an Elder in town whose mother lived in the orphanage in Brevig Mission after the flu pandemic. She's not alive anymore, but her son knows her stories. What a wealth of information that is.

I'm ashamed to say that it was graduate research work that initially got me into more homes asking about historical stories. I wish I could say I started it on my own. Once I started hearing stories of Brevig Mission's past and how they connect to present conditions, I was hungry for more. I wanted more pieces of the puzzle. As a bonus, I started figuring out how everyone in town was related, and that has been really fun.

It's one thing to listen to stories socially for entertainment. It's another thing to allow those stories to inform your understanding. Stories are sources of deep culture. Some things may not be stated explicitly in the stories, but the underlying lessons or references can be valuable information.

I listened to an Elder tell stories of her time as a health aide decades before. She described radioing to doctors in Kotzebue for advice and trying to provide care with equipment so sparse she didn't even have a blood pressure cuff. During emergencies she had to light coffee cans full of oil along the runway so the pilot could tell where to land while praying the plane would come quickly.

Hearing these stories made me grateful for the resources we have now and allowed me to appreciate the relative ease of getting health care. But they also emphasized the lesson that I can find a wealth of information and experience within my community, and these connections foster deep roots that help me thrive.

Be a mindful listener. Connect with the storyteller as you listen carefully, ask questions as appropriate (outward), and think about the things shared even after the story is over (inward). Reflecting will help you integrate what you're learning into a wider understanding of your Transplant Home.

Educational history

Don't forget to explore educational history. What has school been like over the years in your community? What kind of teachers have come and gone, or come and stayed? What was the local perception of the school and the teachers? How people view the school and teachers now can depend on what the school or teachers did in the past.

An important component of the educational history in Brevig Mission is that the village did not have a high school until the 1980s. Before that, kids had to go to boarding schools, some of them out of state, if they wanted to go to high school. This took kids away from home during a portion of their formative teenage years, which they could have spent solidifying their knowledge and use of Inupiaq language and cultural skills. In the 1970s, the state of Alaska established regional high schools that allowed kids to stay closer to home but still required leaving their home village and staying with host families.

Thinking about the dilemma faced by fourteen- and fifteen-year-old kids to pursue high school or stay home helps me understand why some chose to forgo a high school education. They had lives and family responsibilities and familiarity with everything in Brevig Mission. Families living a subsistence lifestyle relied on young people to contribute. Teenagers often played crucial roles in watching children, caring for Elders, and doing chores. Fourteen years old is not very old to be leaving that all behind in pursuit of something outsiders insist is important. The fact that anybody at all had the courage to leave home for four years and finish high school is remarkable.

Young Elders from Brevig Mission that attended the Regional High School in Shishmaref generally have good things to say about their experience. Shishmaref School had a strong bilingual/bicultural program, and many former students say that was the first time they learned the Inupiaq language in school. The host families were viewed positively by former students, and they often maintain connections to this day.

Again, I want to emphasize taking advantage of local resources. Get out and talk to people! Sitting around the kitchen table with one lady in town and her cousin, daughter, and niece as she described her favorite teachers was a hoot. She remembered their daughter and how they gave her a live chicken when they left. I laughed at the idea of a young girl trying to raise a chicken in the Arctic, but the way she talked about her favorite teachers was instructive as well. It helped me see what kinds of things stay with students into their adult years. She didn't mention any particular worksheets or lectures that the teachers gave. She remembered that school was fun, and they were always busy. She remembered the relationships. The details of what I teach may be less important than the feeling in my classroom and the interactions with my students.

The stories you hear about the educational history of your Transplant Home may reveal recurring problems. This is a chance for taking time to understand before offering immediate solutions. Problems like tardiness, sleeping in class, chronic absences, and apathy may appear to have clear-cut solutions that simply require consequences, but that is rarely the case. New teachers who arrive preaching that things should be this way or that way are seldom effective in those efforts and often feel frustrated. Don't be one of those teachers. Be the one who asks questions and listens to stories of the past before opening your mouth to tell people what they should do. In fact, maybe don't open your mouth to tell people what to do at all. Use the strategy of *Humility* and open your mouth to be an ally and a support, instead of presuming you have all the answers. Because you may not.

Transplant Teacher Bulletin:

We interrupt your regularly scheduled programming for a note about sources of local knowledge. As you learn more about local history in your community, you may come across regional superstars. Our region certainly has them. These are people who have succeeded in multiple worlds. They are culturally competent in the ways of their heritage and formally educated in the way of outsiders. These people often speak and present at events, and their perspective is heard over and over.

While I value the contributions these people have made and what they offer our region, I love to focus on local sources of knowledge and information. If I have to choose between advice given by a regional superstar or someone in my village, I Will rely on the advice given by the local source.

Amazing sources of wisdom can be found in each community. They may not all be as prominent as the superstars or as formally educated, but they still offer valuable perspective and insight. Local will always trump regional for me. Don't just rely on regional superstars. *Build More and Stronger Connections* in your own community and let that be your primary source of information and insight.

Historical trauma

Now a word about historical trauma. Maybe not every community has experienced historical trauma, but it has certainly been a part of the communities of my teaching career. As you visit with people in your community, pay special attention to stories of colonization and loss. These events reverberate through generations.

White pastors came to Brevig Mission in the late 1800s and early 1900s to minister to the Saami reindeer herders that were teaching the Inupiaq people to raise reindeer as part of a government effort to help support Inupiaq families in Northwestern Alaska. The pastors' school was eventually taken over by the Bureau of Indian Affairs (BIA) and subject to its policies.

Early stories of Pastor Tollef Brevig (yup, Brevig Mission is named after him) tell of how he learned the Inupiaq language while working with the children and people in the area. Stories of Bureau of Indian Affairs teachers in subsequent decades aren't always so positive. Some Elders in Brevig Mission have fond memories of school and their teachers, but others remember being slapped with a ruler or put in a corner if they spoke Inupiaq. This promoted fear and shame toward their Indigenous language and generally resulted in raising the next generation in English so they would be prepared for school.

Most people in Brevig Mission mourn the destruction of their language and crave a revival, but there are mixed views on how to move forward. Brevig Mission only has a handful of proficient Inupiaq speakers. When people in town talk about the language situation, they will sometimes express that they wish the church had never come. When we discuss Alaska History in class, sometimes my students say (mostly in jest), "You destroyed our language!"

My knee-jerk reaction is to want to disassociate myself from the white people who first came. "It wasn't me! I wasn't there! I wasn't even born yet!"

Another reaction is to justify what happened. "Well, white people coming here wasn't all bad. You're glad you have snow machines, right? You're glad you have a clinic, right?"

A third reaction is to excuse the people who came and did the destroying. "The teachers were just following BIA policy," or "That's what people believed at the time," or "They thought they were being helpful." This reaction often goes hand in hand with shifting some blame to the people in your community. "Well, they got in trouble for speaking Inupiaq at school, but they still could have spoken it at home. Your parents could just teach you now."

None of these reactions is very helpful or healthy. The situation is certainly more nuanced than I've stated here, but the sentiments are real. It's easy to slip into a defensive role if you're the same race as those who colonized the area, or to try to prove you're not like the teachers of the past. Rein in that instinct and listen instead. This is an opportunity to learn and understand. This is a time to use *Humility*. A time to look inward and examine any preconceptions or defensiveness. A time to reach outward, to hear and understand.

My stomach tightens up every time somebody blames a current problem on the white people who came to Brevig Mission. I am also a white person who came to Brevig Mission, and it hurts to think people might view me in the same way. But, this isn't about me. It's about getting to know my community and understanding their perspective about what happened in the past and how that affects them, right here and now.

Historical and cultural trauma is real, and I look forward to being an ally in the effort to bring healing and affect change. But effective allies don't try to take things over. That suggests that the local people are incapable of leading efforts for change themselves. Effective allies listen, encourage, and comfort those who are leading the charge. They show up, but they shut up. They listen more than they talk. They honor the expertise and experience of the people working for change.

In his book *Yuuyaruk*, Alaska Native author Harold Napoleon outlines some tangible efforts members of historically traumatized communities can take to heal. These efforts are best led from within the community, but his book is a great resource for understanding some of the dynamics that exist in traumatized communities. I recommend it to anyone teaching in Alaska Native villages and anywhere else where colonization has had a deep impact.

Even after fifteen years, I'm not sure what being an ally in this work looks like entirely. Right now I just try to love as many people as possible and honor the knowledge and experience they bring to the world.

Bad things happen. Unjust things happen, and they can have consequences for generations. The role of the Transplant Teacher is to learn about these things in *Humility* and be sensitive to and nonjudgmental about the effects in your classroom and community. Above all, remember that it's not about your feelings or need to prove or defend yourself. It's about the people who carry the trauma.

A complex set of forces is at play in every community in the world. The forces aren't always apparent right away, and it's possible to go through your daily life without being aware of what's going on below the surface. Transplant Teachers who stick around for a while are in a position to open their minds and hearts to deeper understanding. They can learn more and judge less. They can offer acceptance. They can respond in a way that enhances their impact.

CHAPTER 22

Removing the Weeds of Negativity

Inconveniences, annoyances, and irritations happen in your Transplant Life, and they may be legitimately inconvenient, annoying, and irritating. How you deal with them is important. Complaining about your teacher housing may seem harmless. You make little jokes, share some "can you believe this?" stories or pictures, and feel clever and witty because of your pithy commentary. Parody or the low key mocking of your co-workers or students can work the same way. You make some jokes, do some impersonations, and people chuckle. You portray everything they do as ridiculous and get some more laughs.

It's nice when someone says, "Yeah, that's rough!" and we feel reassured that we're not hyper-sensitive or over-reactive. But constantly looking for and telling people about everything that's wrong with your classroom, your students, your house, and your life will choke out positive growth.

Weeds are like that too. In a garden, weeds are plants that grow where they're not wanted and that take resources from the plants that are. In a Transplant Teacher's life, weeds are attitudes and behaviors that drain your energy and keep you from thriving. Weeds are obnoxious, but they're opportunities to use the strategies *Stay Positive* and *Focus on What You Can Control*.

It's a good idea to take care of weeds as soon as possible. The best time to pull weeds is when they first pop up. They're easier to remove when they're beginning to grow; otherwise, the weeds get stronger and bigger as time goes by. What might have been a quick fix early in the life of a weed can turn into a massive pull requiring a shovel or hoe.

So it is with negative habits. The first time you gossip about a coworker may seem like no big deal. Just a small comment to blow off some steam. But, it can become a habit, and soon gossiping is your default conversation mode. Sometimes we may not recognize a weed right away. What looks like a cute little plant with flowers may turn out to be a predatory weed that will take over your garden. You might be tempted to ignore the weeds. You might convince yourself they're inconsequential or hope they'll go away on their own. That's not how weeds work. Left unchecked, they can choke out everything good.

Weeds don't mean you're a bad Transplant Teacher. They don't mean you didn't prepare the soil. They're not a sign that you've failed. No gardener says, "If I just do everything right, I won't have to weed." Weeds are part of the growing experience. They're an opportunity to dig in and improve your environment, and it's an ongoing process. You don't weed just once! You weed continually as new weeds crop up.

You can't be expected to anticipate every possible weed, but once you notice the weed, it's your responsibility to do something about it. As you put down deep roots, some things you will want to weed out are extreme thinking, gossip, and deficit thinking.

Extreme thinking is extremely unhelpful

When I think I've been carrying an unfair share of the load or dealing with the aftermath of a colleague's poor decisions and actions, I find myself prone to the weed of extreme thinking. Extreme thinking is marked by only seeing extremes. It's when you think things are either one way or another, there's no in between. Things are either black or white, there are no shades of grey. Earlier we talked about how things are rarely as clear cut as they might seem, and real life is full of nuanced situations of grey.

Extreme thinking is an extreme (see what I did there?) inward battle. To help myself deal with extreme thinking, I do a little exercise in my journal that helps temper the extremeness. I might find myself thinking: he always lets kids knock on my classroom door to borrow things.

I make a chart with two columns in my journal and write my thought in the left column[2].

HE ALWAYS LETS KIDS KNOCK ON MY CLASSROOM DOOR TO BORROW THINGS.	

[2] This idea is inspired by *Feeling Good: the New Mood Therapy* by Dr. David D. Burns. Check it out for other useful journaling ideas!

Then I try to identify what part of it is extreme.

HE (ALWAYS) LETS KIDS KNOCK ON MY CLASSROOM DOOR TO BORROW THINGS.	

Here I've circled the word *always*. A*lways* suggests that every single time he deals with students, he lets them knock on my classroom door.

I use the right column to write a more balanced thought. I'm going to zone in on *always* because it's not as if he allows every single student in every single one of his classes to knock on my door to borrow things. I might change it to: he habitually lets students knock on my door to borrow things.

HE (ALWAYS) LETS KIDS KNOCK ON MY CLASSROOM DOOR TO BORROW THINGS.	HE HABITUALLY LETS STUDENTS KNOCK ON MY DOOR TO BORROW THINGS.

It seems like a small change, and it is. But it's an important shift. Thinking that Neil Never Prepared's students are at my door interrupting all the time can stoke a fire of negativity and cause my attitude to spiral downward. The revised statement acknowledges the problem and how annoying it is. It doesn't try to make the problem into a nonissue, but it takes the edge off, which can make a big difference to your mental state.

Here's another thought for the left column: "All his students use Facebook during class."

ALL HIS STUDENTS USE FACEBOOK DURING CLASS.	

Next is identifying the extreme part: All.

ALL HIS STUDENTS USE FACEBOOK DURING CLASS.	

Now it's time to write a more balanced thought. Is every single one of his students really on Facebook during class? Consider the information on which you're basing the statement. Have you observed every student on Facebook during his class? Have you only heard about it? Are you making any assumptions?

Possible balance: I've seen multiple students on Facebook during his class.

ALL HIS STUDENTS USE FACEBOOK DURING CLASS.	I'VE SEEN MULTIPLE STUDENTS ON FACEBOOK DURING HIS CLASS.

Again, the difference between the extreme thought and the more balanced thought is just a matter of a few words, but the shift is important. Stating the facts objectively is less extreme. It acknowledges what is happening without exaggerating. When you slip into extreme thinking, it taints your perception. You're more likely to notice the irritating, incompetent, or ridiculous because you're looking for it. You might even fail to notice the good things when you're wrapped up in finding the bad. Turning extreme thoughts into more balanced ones can help you avoid that negative fixation.

The column method of writing more balanced thoughts also

works for thinking that isn't as extreme as the above examples. Take a look at this thought: he lets his class make so much noise in the hall.

HE LETS HIS CLASS MAKE SO MUCH NOISE IN THE HALL.	

There isn't a clear indicator of extreme thinking as in the examples above, so I'm not going to try to change it. Instead, I will focus on supportive thoughts that help me adjust my thinking about the situation. "He struggles to keep his class quiet in the hall."

HE LETS HIS CLASS MAKE SO MUCH NOISE IN THE HALL.	HE STRUGGLES TO KEEP HIS CLASS QUIET IN THE HALL.

The use of *struggles* indicates the teacher is making some effort to control the volume level in the hall. Just acknowledging that the teacher is trying might help my attitude.

Maybe the teacher is not trying. Maybe Calvin Chaos has given up and lets his students walk down the hall doing whatever they want. Then I have to focus on things I can control. Supporting thoughts I could write in this instance are, "I could tell him his class behavior in the hall is disrupting my students," or "I could offer to share my hallway routines with him."

HE LETS HIS CLASS MAKE SO MUCH NOISE IN THE HALL.	HE STRUGGLES TO KEEP HIS CLASS QUIET IN THE HALL. - I COULD TELL HIM HIS CLASS BEHAVIOR IN THE HALL IS DISRUPTING MY STUDENTS - I COULD OFFER TO SHARE MY HALLWAY ROUTINES WITH HIM.

Of course, I may decide against these options. Unsolicited advice is not always well received, and offering advice when people are not ready to receive it can be a futile effort. At least I've taken the time to acknowledge that I could do something to contribute to the solution, and the choice to do it is up to me.

There must be one thing that's at least sort of positive

Another technique is to look for very basic good things about your coworkers. To use this technique I usually start by thinking of how bad a teacher (or staff member) could possibly be. I might start with "at least he doesn't punch the kids" or "he has never once come to school drunk" or "he doesn't embezzle money from the school concession stand (that I know of)."

Thinking of these kinds of ridiculous situations makes me laugh and lightens my mood. It also reminds me that most people have a certain level of decency and things could truly be worse. After I've thought of a few outrageous ones (he doesn't make meth in his classroom), I'm ready to move on to things that are less outrageous. "He doesn't yell at kids" or "he's never sworn out loud in a staff meeting."

The hope is that I can work my way up to things that are genuinely good about this person. "He splits hallway duty with all of us, so there's one less time I have to do it" or "he is polite to parents" or "he seems to care about most kids."

Of course, it might be an entirely different story if any of the outrageous statements are true about a colleague. I've never worked with anyone quite that bad, so I'm fresh out of advice for how to handle those situations. But most of the time, I'm able to find at least some moderately redeeming qualities about my colleagues. I repeat those in my head when I'm frustrated by their less than appealing attributes.

A similar technique works for students. I can start by thinking of outrageous situations that illustrate how bad it could be. "She has never stacked my tables on top of each other and jumped off" or "she's never stolen my credit cards and booked airline tickets to Fiji."

Once I've chuckled over the outrageous ideas, the next step involves slightly less ridiculous scenarios like "she doesn't try to eat pancakes and syrup during second hour" or "she tells me I look fat in my pants only once a week."

Then I work my way up to more serious positive (or neutral qualities), even if it requires some creative thinking. I've worked with kids with the attention span of a lively little puppy during academic work, but who would jump at the chance to unjam my stapler or fix the collapsed shelves on my bookcase. Fidgety uncooperative students have offered to vacuum my classroom after an art project. Even kids who come to school exhausted and sleep through class can be polite when I wake them up for lunch.

It also helps to remember that people are multi-faceted. One bad habit or trait doesn't make anyone a bad person any more than one good habit or trait makes someone a good person. People can be a mix of good, bad, and every shade in between. A regularly disruptive student who often swears during class can be a loyal son and brother. An argumentative student might be willing to help anyone haul boxes and freight. A complainer might bring you fresh salmon (or does that only happen to teachers in Alaska?).

I try to fight the tendency to categorize people based on one trait or incident. When I take time to look for a more complete view of who a person is (whether student or colleague), I generally come away with a more understanding heart. I find it easier to be patient with that student or colleague, and I'm happier overall just noticing the good inside them.

One exercise that encourages this practice is Gratitude Time at our staff meetings. The principal sets out a box of small pieces of paper and pens, and we all write quick notes to someone who's helped us during the past week. We put the completed notes back in the box, and she delivers them to mailboxes in the staff room after the meeting. It's simple. It's easy. It doesn't take much time, but it forces us to spend a few minutes looking for the good in people. It's fun to get the happy notes in our boxes, and it feels good to be on sending end too.

Finding the negative can turn into a habit, and if you're always looking for the bad it can poison your whole Transplant Experience. Luckily, the opposite habit is possible too. You can inwardly train yourself to focus on uplifting things or positive ways to deal with difficult things. Allow your roots to go deeper by not siphoning most of your energy into finding the negative.

Weed out gossiping

Another weed that can crop up is gossiping. Gossiping combines finding the negative in a person and complaining to other people. It's like a double strength weed that's focusing on negative things and making sure other people know about them.

I worked with someone that would start gossiping about coworkers as soon as they walked out of a meeting. It would take literally two seconds before Giselda Gossiper would start telling us why the others should be discredited and have their opinions discounted. Sometimes I agreed with the gossiper, but the behavior contributed to an ugly dynamic. I constantly wondered what Giselda said about me when I wasn't around. I hesitated to share or be open with the gossiper because I didn't know when or to whom the comments would be repeated.

Transplant Teachers need friends. They need support, and they need to meaningfully connect with people in their Transplant Home. An atmosphere of gossip isn't conducive to forming those connections. You may be able to bond with a person over your mutual disgust for other people, but if you're known for gossiping, then that's what people will go to you for. They won't come to be vulnerable or share struggles or celebrate little victories. They'll come to you for gossip, and that will not help you put down deep roots.

If you're involved in chronic gossiping, you risk limiting your opportunities to form authentic relationships built on something besides snide comments and mockery. I'm not saying that gossiping and having friends are mutually exclusive; I'm just suggesting that you give yourself every opportunity to make good friends.

The gossip weed is so insidious, it's possible to be a complacent gossiper. Maybe you don't start the gossipy conversations, but you participate in them or just stay silent and listen. It can be awkward to know what to do. You may not want to damage your relationships with the gossipers. You may not want to appear self-righteous or holier-than-thou. Here are some suggestions to help when gossiping starts.

Walk away. This is a classic behavior for when you just don't want to be part of something. You don't need to stomp. Leave graciously.

"Well, I'll let you go" or "I'm going to slip out and make these copies" or "I need to hit the restroom quickly" all work to remove yourself from a gossiping conversation.

If you can't walk away, for example during meetings, you might be able to remind the gossipers about the importance of facts versus rumors. I'm not suggesting you whip out a PowerPoint of the definitions. That's likely to be inconvenient. Be a gentle and polite fact checker. You might say, "I've never experienced it personally, so I really can't say" or "I haven't witnessed it myself, so I can't verify." These types of comments could steer the conversation to more productive territory if participants realize that they, too, have no direct experience or eyewitness status to verify what they're talking about.

If the facts vs. rumors technique is too subtle, try reminding the group of the universality of imperfection. Again, forego the PowerPoint or interpretive dance. A comment such as "That's definitely unprofessional. I guess we all have our flaws. I certainly have mine" should suffice. Once I was speaking with a teacher from another school about administrators. It wasn't an overly negative conversation, but one thing he said stuck in my mind. After mentioning something about his principal, the teacher said, "You know, he's not a perfect principal, but I'm not a perfect teacher." I thought that was a healthy recognition that we all have room for improvement. Other variations that convey that same idea are "We're not all good at everything" or "It's tough dealing with imperfect people."

Another technique is encouraging the gossipers to find a solution to deal with the situation. Sitting around gossiping about a coworker and having everyone agree with you feels good! It reinforces the idea that you're right, and the other person is wrong. But, it rarely does anything to solve the problem.

In an earlier chapter, I recommended going straight to the source when dealing with a conflict and helping others do the same. This technique works with gossiping too. Consider suggesting things like "Go talk to him. You might be able to work it out" or "Have you asked her about it? She may not even realize it's happening." Comments like these may prompt the gossipers to pause and think. It may shift some responsibility back on them for working things out. It's also a good way to help yourself and others *Focus on What You Can Control*. You can always control whether you talk directly to people and what you say when you do.

One of my coworkers was really frustrated with the teacher whose class had recess right before hers because that teacher would still be lining up her class when the second class came in, cutting into their recess time. Even when the second class was five minutes late to recess, the first class still wasn't out of the gym.

After listening to the teacher's frustrations, I said something to the effect of, "That's a bummer. Go talk to her. Maybe she can tighten up her transition time." I validated the coworker's concern and frustration. Then I redirected her to a more productive course of action because gossiping about the offending teacher would not solve the problem.

It's not your job to be the Gossip Police. You don't have to run around and fix all the negative conversations in your school. Other people's negative comments are not your responsibility. But, you can contribute to a more positive work environment that will contribute to your personal happiness. As your colleagues come to see you as one who avoids gossip, they will probably feel more comfortable with you. *Staying Positive* might pay off in the form of more meaningful relationships, which helps you put down deep roots.

What might your gossiping be trying to tell you?

If you're frequently having to weed out gossiping, take a moment to reflect on why that tendency keeps cropping up. Maybe it's a social thing. Gossiping may offer you a way to start a conversation. It gives you something interesting to offer to the conversation and makes people want to listen to you. You might find connection as you bond with other people while commiserating together. Gossiping can also give a sense of inclusion. If you're with the group gossiping, you're part of "us" not "them."

If that's what the tendency to gossip is offering you, consider alternative ways to make connections. Start up a conversation with an idea from a book or article you've read. Ask about how a colleague does something in her/his classroom. "How would you teach the battles of the Civil War?" "What kind of experience have you had using games to teach phonics?" "Do you have any good introduction and conclusion sentence activities?" People generally love to talk about themselves and their classrooms, so start a conversation with something that allows them to do exactly that.

Connections also come from experiences outside of the school day. Invite someone over for dinner. Ask someone to go on a walk with you during lunch. Ask a veteran teacher for restaurant recommendations (if restaurants are a thing where you live. They're not up here!). There's always the old standbys of movie night, game night, etc. Interacting with your colleagues in a variety of situations will give you more to talk about, and you won't have to rely on gossip to start the conversation.

Gossiping might signal that you're feeling insecure. Putting others down is a way of making yourself look better by comparison. It's kind of a "at least I don't do that!" sort of thing. Hearing those around you agree with how bad/incompetent/rude/stupid the other person is temporarily insulates you from your insecurities. But, gossip doesn't make your insecurities go away.

Ask yourself what is it that you're trying so hard to prove by making someone else look bad (even if they are, well, bad)? If you can identify something, then you can take steps to address it in a healthier way. Maybe you're gossiping about a colleague's noisy class during hallway time ("And then a student bounced his foot off the wall and yelled 'hi-yah,' and she didn't even do anything!")

Expressing your disgust about the other class and hearing everyone else agree with how right you are might be masking your embarrassment about your own class's behavior during hallway time. Or, maybe your class's behavior in the hall is just fine. Maybe you're having trouble keeping your students focused while the other class is walking down the hallway. Hearing choruses of agreements and amens from other colleagues is just another way to feel good knowing it's not your fault.

Once you know that you're insecure about your class's behavior in the hall or your ability to keep them focused during outside distractions, you can start to work on that. You could practice the procedure for walking down the hallway. You might teach your students how to hold a bubble in their mouths (fill their cheeks with air and close their lips) and walk with their hands behind their backs. You might publicly praise the students who follow procedures. You might award bonus behavior points (or stars, or First Grade Bucks, or whatever you do) to students who walk quietly down the hall. Any of those efforts are better than tearing somebody else down verbally.

Gossiping might mask a multitude of insecurities, but gossiping itself isn't a productive solution.

You can find much better ways to meet your needs than gossiping. It may provide temporary connection and validation, but the side effects are harmful to the Transplant Life. You're better off making efforts to *Stay Positive* and *Focus on What You Can Control* instead of what's wrong with people around you. Your roots can go deeper if they don't have to push through the weed of gossiping.

Weed out deficit thinking

Another weed Transplant Teachers need to watch for is *deficit thinking*. I define this term the same way Richard Bishop and Mere Berryman do in *Scaling Up Educational Reform*. Deficit thinking is pointing to what's wrong with your students, your new community, their culture, the school, your coworkers, etc. as the cause of your difficulties. It's finding deficits in the people, places, and institutions around you.

The problem with deficit thinking is that it keeps you from focusing on yourself and what you can do to change or improve the situation. You fail to take responsibility for what you can control and blame other people instead.

When you're focused on the blame, you're not thinking about what you can control. It's much more productive to see what you can change about yourself or your teaching (inward) to better adapt to the environment and situation (outward).

Deficit thinking begets deficit thinking begets more deficit thinking. If you're not careful, negative thoughts can spiral out of control like a noxious weed spreading across a garden. One way to combat this weed and *Stay Positive* is to learn to reframe deficit thoughts when they pop up in your Transplant Life. The reframing requires looking inward to *Focus on What You Can Control*.

Deficit thoughts about students

Let's look at how I might reframe deficit thoughts about my students. Pretend that all of my students are obsessed with basketball. Every time I assign a computer assignment, the kids sneak onto YouTube to watch NBA highlights. When I teach a lesson on watercolors, they inevitably start painting orange circles and labeling them with their player numbers. I might say, "If the kids cared about anything besides basketball, they'd be interested in History." The deficit thought here is that there's something wrong with the kids and identifies the problem as their fondness for basketball.

Deficit thinking statements can have nuggets of truth in them. That's what makes them so easy to defend. I convince myself I can justify the entire thought because of that small truth. With the basketball example, the students might very well be super interested in basketball. They might not be very interested in History. Those are truth nuggets!

Truth nuggets can also come in the form of potentially accurate causes and effects. If the students were less interested in basketball, they really and truly might be more interested in History. Of course, we can't know that for sure because we're just speculating, but it's potentially true, so the entire deficit thought seems justifiable.

Even with those nuggets of truth, the deficit thought still places the blame for the situation on something that's "wrong" with my students. Instead of persisting with the deficit thought, I can reframe it.

The first step to reframing a deficit thought is to acknowledge the reality without the judgment that something is wrong with somebody or something. In the basketball example, it's acknowledging that my students care about basketball without suggesting that something is wrong with my students because they like basketball more than history. Reframing the deficit thought isn't about ignoring reality or pretending it doesn't exist. The reframing clearly acknowledges the situation, as difficult or undesirable as it might be.

The second step is deciding what I can do to deal with the reality. It's taking responsibility for what I can do to affect the situation. Blaming someone else lets me off the hook. It suggests I don't have to take action because it's someone else's fault. That's not helpful because I can't change anybody else. I can change me.

The reframed thought in the basketball/history situation could be "The students care about basketball. How can I connect that to my lessons?" That's a question that could prompt useful answers. Rather than waiting around for the kids to stop being interested in basketball (or whatever it is they can't get enough of), I look for ways to harness that interest.

Let's break down another deficit thinking situation. Senior (in high school) Stanley might love hunting. He regularly goes out with his dad and uncles whenever the weather is good, even during school. When Stanley returns to class after being gone for a day or two, he's frequently confused. He doesn't understand what's going on and how to get caught up. I might say, "If the kids didn't hunt and fish as much, they wouldn't be behind."

The deficit thought is that there's something wrong with the kids or the culture that encourages them to hunt and fish. It might be true that the kids hunt and fish. It might be true that they miss school when they hunt and fish. If they didn't miss school to hunt and fish, they might have more time to complete their classwork. But, hunting and fishing are important to my students and their families. That's the reality, and I need to acknowledge it without judgment.

Reframing the thought might look like "Some students miss school when they hunt and fish. How can I give these students the opportunity to make up the work and still learn after their absences?"

Then I might decide to keep extra copies of assignments and accept the late work or come up with another solution.

Looking inward to reframe deficit thoughts about my students helps keep the focus on me and my locus of control. I can control myself, so it's empowering to think of what I can do in each situation rather than give up control by focusing on what's "wrong" with my students.

You can deficit think your colleagues (though I don't recommend it)

Deficit Thinking isn't limited to beliefs about students. It's an equal opportunity mental process. Let's look at how it can be applied to colleagues as well.

Assume I'm frustrated about inconsistent rules and policies. Maybe students aren't marked tardy if they can convince the principal they had a good reason. Maybe there's a policy against running in the halls, but five staff members don't enforce the policy during breaks when students race down the halls.

I might say, "If the rules were actually enforced around here, the students wouldn't behave so badly." The deficit thought related to colleagues here is that there's something wrong with the school or administration or other staff members because they don't enforce rules. Consistency may be a problem. Students may make poor choices. Consistency may help teach desired behaviors. But, you can't control how your co-workers or the administration enforces rules and policies. That's the reality.

It can be tempting to argue with the administration that they're not doing the right thing. It can be tempting to tell coworkers that they *should* follow the policy. That might blow off some steam, but it's unlikely to change minds and likely to cause hostility. It's also likely to put you in a foul mood.

A better choice is to refocus and reframe the thought (inward). Just like with the students, reframing starts by dropping the interpretation that something is wrong with somebody (here, the administration or your coworkers) and acknowledging the reality. In this case, "Some rules and policies aren't enforced consistently." The reframe might sound like this: "How can I handle infractions and misbehavior in my classroom where I can control the consistency?"

You might still choose to discuss the issue with the administrator or coworker (outward) when you're in a better frame of mind. Any discussion is sure to go better if you've shifted out of blaming mode.

It's important to note that reframing deficit thoughts isn't necessarily signaling that the undesirable situation or conditions are okay. It's not condoning bad or irresponsible behavior. It's about choosing to focus on what you can control in a productive manner (inward). It's about emphasizing your actions and responses because that's what you can control. It's recognizing that you can choose your reaction in any situation.

Here's another example: I might say, "If Ted Tedium weren't so boring, my fifth hour students wouldn't be zombies when they get to me." The fifth hour teacher might be boring. He or she might lecture nonstop for forty-five minutes while the kids slouch in their chairs with their eyes glazed over. Your fifth hour students might be exhausted and bored when they arrive for your class. And they might be less sleepy if fourth hour was more interactive. But, that's not something you can control.

You can't control how the other teacher teaches. Reframing the deficit thinking could look like "Fifth hour is lethargic when they come to my class. How can I get them moving and invigorated when I start my lesson?" I might try a completely unique formation when they come in the room. I could move the tables and chairs to completely new places or stack them against the wall. That might provide enough intrigue to keep the students wondering what's coming next. Maybe I teach them a mnemonic device that requires full body gestures. I have a set of hand gestures for the Bill of Rights, but I could probably turn them into full body gestures. That would get the students moving and giggling right at the beginning. We could even do the mnemonic gestures at the beginning of class for a few days in a row. I could also instruct the students to toss a ball or soft object around as they each give a simple response to a prompt.

Coworkers (like most human beings) can be annoying, irresponsible, and incompetent, but you don't have to let them sap your of your strength. Coworkers can also be trying their best, having their own struggles, and learning and growing while making mistakes. In all situations, you can control your inward and outward responses in a way that copes with the reality and preserves your energy for more fruitful pursuits..

Get deficit thinking out of your way so you can find resources

Deficit thinking is often born out of frustration. It can be frustration with your physical environment, school or district policies, coworkers, student behaviors, or any related situation. Deficit thinking can be a way of avoiding responsibility. If it's somebody else's fault, and you can't do anything about it, then you're not responsible for making any changes. Deficit thinking justifies what you're doing (or not doing).

Shifting the blame outside of yourself might also indicate that you're not feeling brave enough to tackle the problem yourself. Maybe you don't know how to adapt your teaching or rearrange your room or design a system of consequences. When you admit that, you can start looking for resources. This can be part of *Focusing on What You Can Control*. You might research your problem and find options for dealing with it. You might get some kind of training in specific methods. You could ask other teachers for advice and ideas.

One year we had room in our schedule for a high school art elective, and I took on the challenge. I had virtually nothing to work with besides a draft of the Alaska State Art Standards. Our district had an outlined Visual Arts Curriculum, but it was designed for K-8. I could have used deficit thinking about my district and principal. I could have blamed the district for not providing a course outline. I could have said the principal was unreasonable to expect me to teach a class with no curriculum support. But those were things I had no control over and wouldn't have changed the reality.

Instead, I googled "designing an art curriculum." I found a series of articles and blog posts with useful information. Then I found a graduate class from the Art of Ed entitled exactly "Designing an Art Curriculum." I enrolled in the class, learned from some amazing resources, and submitted a final project of a year-long curriculum map (all while earning three credits!). The tuition was even eligible for our district reimbursement program.

The result wasn't a flawless art class, but it provided a workable structure within which I could explore and experiment. We worked with watercolor, collage, hand lettering, art journals, and poster design. We even started a class Instagram account. It was fun for all of us, and it became a class that was offered for several years.

Taking a graduate class isn't the only option in a situation like this. It may not even be a feasible option, but the point is that resources are available. You might find a treasure trove of examples and ideas if you only look for them. Training, advice, and ideas can go a long way to helping you improve your skills and increase your confidence. Deficit thinking might keep you from discovering the resources in the first place. Don't let that happen!

Resisting deficit thinking is the ultimate exercise in *Focusing on What You Can Control*. Instead of insisting that the people, places, and institutions around you are deficient, you see what you can change about yourself, your tools, or your approach to solve the problem. You are the only thing you can really control, and if you've cleared out the weed of looking around for what's wrong with everyone and everything, you'll be in a better place to put down deep roots.

CHAPTER 23

Meeting Your Needs

Once the dust settles from the whirlwind that is the first few months after arriving in your Transplant Home, you can take some time to reevaluate what you need and how to get it. *Focusing on What You Can Control* and *Being Flexible and Adaptive* can help you continue to meet your needs in a place that might be very different than where you came from.

For example, I'd never thought very much about daylight before, but as the hours of daylight in Shishmaref dwindled to around two per day, it became apparent that I get crabby in the middle of winter. Steve had subtly suggested this was the case, but I dismissed his suggestions until the light returned and I felt like I was fully awake for the first time in months. We researched lights and bought some that simulate daylight. Now I have one that acts as an alarm clock by gradually getting brighter and one that sits on my desk. I also try to get outside as often as possible when there is daylight, and the fresh air and movement improve my mood.

Identifying that need and finding a way to meet it helped me move toward thriving in my Transplant Home. I don't need the light lamps when I'm in other places, but I need them in Alaska. Transplant Teachers can go through the same process to help them be happier and nourish those deeper roots.

Homesickness might mean you need something!

Most people who travel for a long time, leave for college, or move far away from existing friends and family, become homesick at one point or another. Homesickness is especially likely if you're experiencing culture shock in your Transplant Home. Different customs, social dynamics, scenery, and manners might overwhelm you, even if you find the differences interesting and exciting. Longing for home might mean you're craving the familiar. Just like kids might need a favorite blanket or stuffed animal, Transplant Teachers might need some comforts from their previous home.

Think about how you might incorporate familiar routines into your Transplant Life, even if you have to *Adapt*. Maybe you always drank a cup of tea in the mornings and savored the moments as you gently woke up. If it's possible to order the same kind of tea, do it, and reintegrate that routine. If getting the same kind of tea isn't possible, try the same routine with a different beverage. Did you always make a certain brunch dish on the weekends? Try it in your new home too, even if you have to make some creative ingredient substitutions.

Familiar routines can be especially important around holidays and special events. My family of origin always had a Cheese and Cracker Party on Christmas Eve. We prepared a variety of appetizers (including cheese and crackers) to eat for dinner. It's a tradition I've carried to Shishmaref and Brevig Mission. I order as many cheeses, crackers, and treats as I can online and print cute little decorations for the table. Then we invite some people over and share the good food. We don't usually schedule the party on Christmas Eve because that's when the local church service is, but we plan it for some time around Christmas. It's not exactly the same as when I was growing up, but it is a familiar activity, and I feel connected to my traditions and my family, even though they're far away.

Homesickness can also signal a need to connect with family and friends. Even successful Transplant Teachers maintain ties to far away family and friends. Possibilities for connecting across long distances are endless these days. Phone calls, FaceTime, Skype, Facebook Messenger. Unreliable Internet can make things trickier, but there's always good old-fashioned letters.

I started calling my parents every Sunday after Steve and I moved to Shishmaref. It started as a way to share all the new things I was experiencing and get support for the hard stuff. Now it's a way to touch base and tell them silly stories about my kids. Kaitlyn and Levi have relationships with Steve's parents and mine, and I credit that in part to the phone calls.

Your need for connection can also be met with people in your Transplant Home. Your faraway friends and family are not the only sources of support and love in your life. The relationships you build locally can offer acceptance and understanding in person if you've done the work to cultivate those connections.

Relationships, relationships, relationships

Use your homesickness as an impetus to build on the relationships you already have (if you don't have any local relationships, go back to the Nurturing the Seedling section and review how to seek out people and to initiate conversations). Call a coworker and set up a time to have lunch together or play board games. Ask the neighbor you've visited with at the mailbox to go on a walk. Invite people over again. Follow up with the person who said you could come over sometime.

Deepening relationships requires persistence. Not the stalking kind of persistence, but the kind where you interact over and over. A meaningful connection that sustains you through your Transplant

Journey won't happen after one activity or event. Create opportunities to connect and then create them again. Without persistence, you'll remain on the surface and never get to meaningful.

Almost any topic can turn into a meaningful conversation. Take family. Discussing the number of siblings you have is more superficial. Discussing favorite memories of childhood is more meaningful. Or jobs. Discussing what someone does for a living is more superficial. Discussing what's most challenging or rewarding at a job is more meaningful. Even current events can be meaningful if you move beyond the headlines and discuss how they might affect the community and what they mean for the future.

Don't think I'm saying that all superficial interaction is bad. It's not. Small talk greases the social wheels and can be a good first step in getting to know someone. However, if you're trying to deepen your relationships, you'll want to move your conversations over to the meaningful side as often as possible.

And remember, you don't have to be best buddies with everybody. Focus your efforts on the people you click with or find most interesting.

As you navigate and strengthen relationships, try to find your Transplant Family. Just because you're far away from where you grew up or where your blood relatives live doesn't mean you can't find family. You may be lucky enough to find a Transplant Family. Remember that you don't always choose your family. Sometimes your family chooses you! Family is patient, loving, forgiving, and imperfect. We don't abandon our family because of their faults; we buoy them up and support them through their faults.

I had a friend in Shishmaref who later became a coworker in Brevig Mission. He helped me out in a pinch, and when I expressed my gratitude, he said, "We're a family. That's what families do, they take care of each other."

Those words touched me. Seeing my coworkers as family was new to me, but it can change everything. For example, instead of a bloviating colleague, someone becomes a crazy uncle who always tells stories at Thanksgiving. Instead of a nitpicky hallway neighbor, someone becomes a Type-A grandmother. You find ways to cope and love your family for who they are. Thinking of tolerating each other's quirks and valuing each other's strengths is healthier than continual frustration and anger. People are imperfect. We can choose to love them anyway.

Meeting our needs with food

Try not to judge me with thoughts about the ills of emotional eating, but food became an important part of how we coped in Alaska. Our food life didn't get off to a great start because I didn't have many cooking skills. I survived in college by making stir fry, spaghetti, and homemade chicken noodle soup. In Shishmaref I made a few things, and we ate them over and over. But being thrust into an environment with limited shopping options, I was determined to learn new skills. Dry beans seemed like a practical thing to use. We could ship them up dry, rehydrate them, and use them in cooking. Seems easy, right? Well, my first foray into this realm didn't go as planned.

I can't even remember now what I was trying to make. I only remember it involved beans. I put the dried beans in a pot of water and left them on the stove with the burner on low (which is kind of dangerous, now that I think about it). When I came home for lunch, they had made little progress, so I turned the burner up to high intending to turn it back to low when I headed back to my classroom. I forgot. The beans cooked on high for hours, turning them into chunks of charcoal, filling our house with smoke, and making the smoke detectors go crazy. (I heard that the smoke was so bad that they closed the store next door to us, but I was too embarrassed to investigate that rumor.)

It smelled so bad in our house that we couldn't sleep there. We spent the night on the floor of our friend's house, sleeping on top of a bedsheet. When I told my mom the story she said, "Why didn't you use your crockpot?" I almost slapped myself in the forehead. I had a crockpot. I even had my trusty cookbook *101 To Do With a Crockpot*. I had a lot to learn.

What started out as a way to avoid food boredom and not repeat the Great Bean Incident of 2005 became a hobby when I discovered food blogs. I read blogs of people I knew, and I think one of them linked to a food blog. The new recipes and ingredients seemed exotic and adventurous. The step-by-step pictures included in the blog posts made the recipes feel doable.

A culinary world of possibilities opened for me at this point. I could learn how to make almost anything I wanted via the pictorial guides on food blogs. The first blog post I wrote about food was my attempt at the Amateur Gourmet's bacon, egg, and cheese tart and is a hilarious (if I say so myself) account of me scouring the village for nutmeg, not having the right ingredients, and ultimately having to put off making the tart until the store opened the next day. Despite all the obstacles, the end result was still infinitely better than the pot of burned beans. I started exploring specialty websites that sold things like Orange Blossom Water, Ras el Hanout, and kits to make Vietnamese pho. I found a surprising number of sites that ship to rural Alaska.

Cooking also became a welcome diversion from my teaching life. The first couple of years I would obsessively prepare lessons or obsessively avoid preparing lessons by oversleeping and reading. Cooking gave me something to think about and look forward to outside of my classroom.

But it wasn't until I had settled into my Transplant Home that I was ready to pick up a hobby. I definitely could have started cooking earlier, but everything was so overwhelming at first that I'm not sure it would have unfolded the same way. The Putting-Down-Deep-Roots phase is a great time to expand your interests and hobbies. Think back to the hobbies you planned for back in Preparing the Soil. It might be time to dust off the equipment or reinvigorate the idea of what you want to learn.

Hobbies can equal friends (unless you're playing solitaire)

My cooking hobby soon turned into a Sunday baking date with one of my favorite students. Every week we picked out a recipe online and tried it together at my house. We made beautiful cupcakes, cookies, and dessert bars. She even brought over her grandmother's recipe for donuts, and I got to learn how to make Shishmaref-style donuts like the ones I'd been eating at birthday parties for years. I bought her a baking cookbook for Christmas one year, and we started working our way through it based on the recipes that interested us most.

The hours we spent baking gave us a chance to talk and laugh. She asked questions about my life and experiences, and I asked questions about hers. I loved it. Her family really opened up to me as I developed a relationship with their daughter. They invited me to go on drives with them to go beach combing. I received invitations to family events and birthday parties. When my mom came to visit, they fed her reindeer, whale, and other local delicacies. They were one of the last visits I made before flying out of Shishmaref when we moved, and my student's dad let me pick out a pair of ivory earrings he had made.

The baking wasn't just about the food (although that was nice).

It was also about developing relationships. My student and her family became quite special to me. I felt very comfortable with them, and she remains a friend to this very day, even as a bona fide adult.

Taking hobby baking to the next level

It won't surprise you to learn that Shishmaref doesn't have a bakery. Families can order sheet cakes from a grocery store in Nome, but a tiered cake wouldn't stand a chance during the plane ride. Well, after a couple years of baking with my favorite student, we were asked to make a wedding cake.

I was terrified. Weddings are a big deal, and I didn't want to disappoint anybody with a sloppy or ugly cake. My first grade teacher used to make me stay inside during recess to practice coloring in the lines, and since that moment, I had abandoned the idea of being a creator of cute or pretty things. My younger brother, who I know for a FACT adores me, responded to the news about the wedding cake with, "Wow, that person must have been desperate."

Leaning on a recipe recommendation from my sister (who inherited far more than her fair share of domestic ability) and the expertise of our heroes Bakerella and Pioneer Woman, we experimented with marshmallow fondant. We produced little figures and decorations and shared them with people who admired by oohing and aahing.

We moved on to covering full cake layers with fondant and increasing the size of our fondant figures, but we weren't sure what to do to elevate our decorations from cute to elegant.

In a beautiful moment of serendipity, a teacher from the regional vocational center visited Shishmaref. She was the Family and Consumer Sciences teacher and happened to have minored in food garnishing. I'm not sure what the odds of that happening were, but it was the equivalent of us winning the lottery. She heard about our wedding cake project and showed us how to make fondant roses.

She found a tiny circle cookie cutter in the home economics room at school. We used it to cut perfect circles out of fondant. Then we overlapped an odd number (never even) of circles and used a little bit of water to stick the petals together. Not surprisingly, my student was far better than me at creating sugary flora. I tended to use too much water and end up with a gooey mess. It was at this point that I officially became her assistant.

We started on the actual cake two days before the wedding by making the cake layers and the fondant. The next day we made several fondant roses of various sizes. (When I say "we," I actually mean my favorite student. I did apprentice level tasks like roll out the fondant, cut out the circles, and fetch beverages for her.)

We used a shiny frosting recipe from my Better Homes and Gardens Cookbook. (Pro tip #1: when you quadruple a frosting recipe, you need to consider that, even with a Kitchen Aid, you will not be able to beat that much frosting. Even if you tackle it in two batches. Be prepared to beat the frosting to the appropriate stiffness in multiple batches using your friend's hand mixer. Pro tip #2: quadrupling the Better Homes and Gardens Shiny Frosting recipe results in way too much frosting.)

We made the cake at my friend's house, across the street from the church, so the location couldn't have been better. She also owned a set of wedding cake pans and cake decorating tools purchased for her sister's wedding.

We worked on the cake until about fifteen minutes before the wedding, and then we had to get the cake to the church through the wind and snow. My friend's husband saved the day by loading the cake into a microwave box on its side and taping a garbage bag over the open side before carrying it to the church. I had just enough time to change into my friend's clothes before the wedding started (she refused to let me attend wearing my jeans and t-shirt covered in powdered sugar).

I had no expectation of ever making a wedding cake, and it's certainly not what I had in mind when I started my cooking hobby. The opportunity just sprang naturally out of my experimentation. I got to spend a couple of days baking with friends, and I took part in a local wedding in a meaningful way.

Who knows what experiences await Transplant Teachers on their own journeys of hobby-ness? Who knows what kindred spirits you'll find as you sew or box or fish or do Zumba together? If you can put down deep roots while enjoying yourself, learning something new, and making friends, do it!

Don't forget your spiritual needs

If you had told me before we moved to Alaska that one day I would attend church in my pajamas while arm wrestling children to stay still, I wouldn't have believed you. Turns out, that became a regular part of our spiritual journey in Alaska.

Meeting your spiritual needs can mean a lot of different things. It can mean going to an organized church or not. It can mean practicing meditation or not. It can mean getting out into nature or not. Whatever you decide to do, don't neglect your spiritual side. It can help you feel more grounded and focused and provides a nice release from the daily stresses of teaching.

(Note to readers: this section will be heavy on the church side of things because that's our particular flavor of spirituality. If you want ideas about spirituality through other avenues, you might want to supplement your reading with some other resources.)

If you decide to do the church thing, you'll have some choices to make. One option is to attend local worship services in your new community. This is a good choice if you're not attached to a particular denomination and enjoy the fellowship of communal worship.

You can also research distance options for attending church. This is a good choice if you have a specific denomination or congregation that you want to participate with. Like many areas of life in your Transplant Home, you may have to *Be Flexible* to take part in church services. Many churches broadcast their services on the Internet. You can also coordinate with someone from your hometown congregation to get audio or video recordings. A little bit of effort can help you get what you need spiritually.

Steve and I do a mixture of the local and distance methods. We are attached to our denomination, so we participate in regular meetings via telephone every Sunday morning. Local Lutheran church services happen at 7:30 pm in Brevig Mission, and we'll occasionally go to those if there's a baptism or the choir's singing or if I just happen to feel like going.

I sing with the Brevig Mission Church Choir and sometimes go to their midweek practices. During regional church conferences, I stand up and sing with the choir, just like I do when the choir sings at local funerals.

I like attending local church meetings, even if I don't agree with all the doctrine. For one thing, I enjoy singing out loud, so the congregational hymns are fun for me. It's also another chance for community members to see a different side of me. They can see me as a fellow worshipper and singer instead of just a teacher. The more facets of me the community gets to see, the more real I am to them.

It also lets me see another side of my students and coworkers who attend. They become more real to me as I see their different facets too. I see normally squirrely boys sit and listen to the sermon. I see girls who have been rude to me all week singing hymns in Inupiaq. I remember that there's more to my students than the behaviors I see at school.

Steve and I also participate in worship services over the phone so we can stay connected to the denomination we grew up with. Our congregation includes all villages in western Alaska that don't have a local congregation. The members are scattered across hundreds of miles, and most of us have never met face to face. Most of the members are teachers or principals (or married to teachers or principals). Our branch president (our version of a pastor), his first counselor, and the clerk/executive secretary live in Anchorage. The rest of the leadership positions are filled by members living in villages. Our branch has a conference line that we call for all of our meetings, with about ninety people taking part on Sundays.

We have to deal with the typical problems of people not muting their phones or leaving themselves on mute when they try to talk. There's also the problem of several people speaking simultaneously and trying to figure out who should talk first. Despite the often awkward communication, we've been able to develop some good relationships with members in our branch. After talking to them every week for years, Steve and I consider some of them good friends. The meetings are often very spiritual with a positive vibe.

Besides semi-awkward phone conversations, long distance worship requires other adaptations. When the son of one of my friends turned eight, he was baptized. Like most little kids in our church, his dad baptized him. Unlike most little kids, church leaders flew to his baptism. A wading pool in his living room doubled as a baptismal font, as a way for my friend to keep her son from being baptized in the nearby river (which would have required breaking through ice).

Church by phone has its challenges. Our kids sometimes have trouble understanding why they have to sit still and be quiet when they're in our living room or at the kitchen table, but we enjoy participating and feeling connected through common faith. It's important to us to maintain those ties to feel grounded.

Our occasional participation in local church services allows us to express our faith slightly differently but still connect in fellowship with the people around us. Singing over the phone will never be the same as singing in person. On the phone I get to sing familiar hymns that I grew up with. At local services, I sing less familiar hymns, but I get to join my voice with the surrounding voices in mutual praise, which is more difficult over the phone. I enjoy both.

Like most things in a Transplant Teacher's life, your spiritual life may look radically different from what you're used to. It's still worth making the effort to meet your spiritual needs. *Be Flexible* and find a way to practice in whatever way feels right. Things may not look or sound the same, but they still contribute to your overall well-being and strengthen your roots.

Transplant Teachers do a lot of work figuring out how to meet their needs when they first arrive in their Transplant Homes, but it's important to revisit as you're putting down deep roots too. Sometimes you can handle living without something for a while, but it takes its toll after a long period of time. When unmet needs languish, it's easy for those negative weeds to creep in and start sapping your energy. Keep them at bay by periodically reevaluating what you need and how to get it. Meeting your needs will allow your roots to be nourished and strong.

Plant Health Checklist

Putting Down Deep Roots is a great time for a Transplant Teacher to take stock of how things are going. Here's another checklist to help you reflect on your growth.

Signs that I am Sending my Roots Deeper:

- ☐ I deepen my relationships by moving beyond superficial interactions.

- ☐ I reflect on the deep culture of my Transplant Home and how to operate within it, even if I disagree with some of the cultural norms.

- ☐ I seek out stories of local history from local sources.

- ☐ I seek out stories about the school system in the past.

- ☐ I keep my mouth shut and listen to the stories, perspectives, and people of my Transplant Home.

- ☐ I seek for understanding before offering possible solutions.

- ☐ I am sensitive to the effects of historical trauma and reach outward to hear and understand.

- ☐ I redirect negative conversations toward possible solutions.

- ☐ I reframe extreme thoughts.

- ☐ I reframe deficit thinking.

- ☐ I look for positive qualities in my coworkers.

- ☐ I intentionally look for things to be grateful for.

- ☐ I find ways to connect with people other than gossiping.

- ☐ I identify my significant needs and take steps to meet them.

- ☐ I fight homesickness with familiar routines and long-distance and local relationships.

- ☐ I allow my hobbies to connect me to people.

- ☐ I meet my spiritual needs.

Like all the other checklists, perfection isn't required for progress! The lists are designed to prompt you to look inward, to decide what you can do to move forward and grow stronger as a Transplant Teacher. If you're able to check off a lot of things on the list, you're probably on your way to putting down Deep Roots. Use the rest of the list for more ideas on what else you can do.

Warning Signs that Might Indicate Root Blockage:

- ☐ My local relationships are mostly superficial.

- ☐ I dismiss cultural norms as misguided or unnecessary when I disagree with them.

- ☐ I constantly talk about myself, my upbringing, and my own stories.

- ☐ I assume I already know enough about local or educational history and don't need to ask about it.

- ☐ I dismiss the effects of historical trauma as exaggerated or irrelevant.

- ☐ I tell people how things *should* be.

- ☐ I blame my difficulties on what's wrong with my students, my school, my coworkers and/or my Transplant Community.

- ☐ I complain a lot.

- ☐ I gossip a lot.

- ☐ I ignore or don't take steps to meet my needs.

If you recognize yourself in any of the warning signs, there's still time! You can still do the inward work to adjust your mindset and perceptions. You can still seek after and strengthen connections that will yield more understanding.

Part V

How To Know If It's Time To Go

At some point in the Transplant Journey, Transplant Teachers may need to decide if they stay or go.

Sometimes a Transplant Teacher chooses to go. Around contract season 2010, Steve and I found out about two openings in Shishmaref's neighboring village Brevig Mission. I had been to Brevig Mission several times to visit a teacher friend, and the idea of teaching with her regularly was really exciting. Brevig Mission also had homes with indoor plumbing, which meant no more distilling drinking water and houses without toilets in the living room.

Brevig Mission's teaching staff was smaller than Shishmaref's, so the job openings included more responsibilities. Instead of teaching Social Studies all day long, I would teach Social Studies and English Language Arts to all the secondary students. Instead of teaching only third grade, Steve would teach fifth and sixth grade (with some seventh graders thrown in).

Coming to Brevig Mission also meant starting over in the professional relationships department. We knew some school staff members in Brevig Mission, but we didn't have years of inside jokes and conversations and gratitude to build on.

In Shishmaref, I was comfortable in my classroom, and my students were making progress. Five years with the same students allowed me to build on each year's experience, and I was pretty satisfied with where most of my students were. Five years of teaching Social Studies allowed me to create a more cohesive Social Studies program. Life in the classroom wasn't perfect, but it was pretty good.

We loved Shishmaref. We loved the people of Shishmaref. Some of our colleagues were outstanding teachers. We were comfortable in our teaching routines.

I spent three years advising an adorable class that had just finished their freshman year. We worked on extra projects after school together. We had our own gift exchanges at Christmas. We had been fundraising like crazy, and we were all looking forward to their senior trip. I had planned on staying in Shishmaref at least until the class graduated.

We didn't love our housing and the multitude of voles that inhabited our tiny house. I didn't love hearing the voles scream as Steve put them out of their misery when the traps didn't quite finish the job. I didn't love hearing the scratching of little feet under our bed as we drifted off to sleep. I didn't love paying kids one dollar for each vole they killed inside our house with a baseball bat or a broom.

We had been good sports for five years of distilling water every day, hauling our laundry over to the school once a week, and setting mouse traps for the voles. We handled water shortages and not washing our hair for days at a time.

The idea of plentiful running water and new housing, plus an instant friend sounded so attractive. We evaluated our situation and determined that Brevig Mission would be a good fit for what we wanted out of life for the next few years. Moving felt like the right decision for us. So we took the plunge and resigned our positions in Shishmaref to sign contracts in Brevig Mission

With our sights set on the move we began preparing. I took the necessary tests to qualify me to teach Language Arts. We packed everything up, and the school district's plane carried two plane loads full of our stuff to our new home. We mailed the rest in boxes and tubs before showing up in Brevig Mission in August 2010.

Confident in our decision, I thought I was ready for the first day of school. Things had been going so well in Shishmaref that I expected to slip into that same level of familiarity and camaraderie in the classroom.

I was wrong.

The kids complained that the activities I had planned were boring. I had no control of the classroom, and the junior high kids ran around the room chasing each other.

It was devastating. I came home and cried. I cried because I felt like a failure as a teacher. I cried because I had left a place where I felt comfortable, welcome, and loved to come to a place where I had to start all over. I was a New Transplant again. That meant going through the same process I did the first time to get to know people and establish trust.

I wanted to skip that part. I wanted to go straight to the rewarding part of the Transplant Experience without the uncomfortable part, but that's not possible. Going through the discomfort and awkwardness is the only way to reap the reward. I had learned it once. Now I had the opportunity to learn it again.

Moving to a new location didn't take away the struggles of a Transplant Teacher. Things didn't become magically easier or better. Sure, the water coming out of my faucet wasn't orange, and I had a washer and dryer in my duplex, but it wasn't all smooth sailing. I started out as a seedling and had to nurture connections and relationships so I could put down roots in Brevig Mission.

I encourage you to be as thoughtful in your decisions about whether to stay or go. You don't want to give up before you get to the reward that comes after struggling through the discomfort and awkwardness, but nobody benefits if you stay while you're unhappy. I've seen lots of teachers come and go, and I'm grateful to the ones who left when they knew Brevig Mission or Shishmaref wasn't a good fit for them or their lifestyle. No location suits every Transplant Teacher, and that's okay. Certain plants do better in specific areas. Some plants require more shade or more direct sunshine. Others require an entirely different climate.

There are different schools of thought about when to stay and when to leave a Transplant Home. I've worked with people who insist that two years/five years/any arbitrary number of years is the longest you should stay in any one location. Other people suggest staying as long as possible in one location to deepen and strengthen relationships and magnify your impact.

Deciding to stay or go is a very personal decision. The decision that others make does not have to be the same one that you make. Each Transplant Teacher has different needs and abilities. How long would you keep trying to grow a plant that failed to thrive in a certain climate? Would you continue to spend time and energy hoping to raise the first lemon tree in Alaska? Probably not. But, would you yank out a seedling at the first sign of trouble? Would you insist that the location was the problem if you hadn't tried fertilizer or a new watering schedule? Probably not.

Steve and I reevaluate every year when contracts come out. We examine how well our children are doing academically and socially. We consider who their teachers will be in the coming year. We think about our personal and financial goals and whether being in Brevig Mission is helping us meet those goals.

Steve and I also consider how happy we are. We wonder if moving would change our level of happiness. We discuss changes we could make in our lives to improve our happiness locally. We try to make a decision that's best for our family. So far, that decision has meant we stay in the Alaska Bush.

But, that may not be the same decision you make. There are valid reasons to leave a Transplant Home. Here are some things to consider as you make that decision.

Consideration: Would changing your expectations make it better?

If things aren't working out in your Transplant Home, you may think about adjustments before you uproot yourself.

An example in my parenting life illustrates this perfectly. I like to go to the gym and watch basketball games. I enjoy seeing my students play and cheering for the home team. I even attend community tournaments if my students are playing on the tournament teams.

My children also like to go to the gym for ball games. However, they mostly like eating concessions and playing with their friends. When we arrive at the school, we stand in line for fifteen minutes to buy slushies and popcorn. Then we stand in another line for ten minutes to get pizza. Then we sit at the cafeteria tables for at least half an hour while my kids nibble their food and talk and laugh with their friends. By the time this whole routine is complete, halftime is already over. I've missed most of the game.

This used to frustrate me. I would scold my kids to get them to hurry, and I'd desperately look toward the clock to see how much of the game I was missing. I dreaded game nights because I didn't get to do what I wanted.

Then I experienced a shift. I realized what I *really* wanted was for my kids to get out of the house and have fun. I liked watching my students play too, but that was less important to me than the experience for my kids.

Now when I go to ball games, I don't even try to watch the game. I buy my kids some snacks. I sit with them while they eat. I visit with other parents and community members. I wave at babies and little kids. When my son takes a break from eating pizza to run around outside, I let him and continue visiting with the people around me. When my daughter practices cheerleading moves with her friends, I watch and clap and compliment.

Sometimes we leave the school without setting foot in the gym. Kaitlyn and Levi get to be part of the excitement and have fun, and once I gave up the expectation of watching the games, I enjoyed myself too.

Why am I telling you about basketball and snacks when you're wondering whether to stay or go? Because if you're dreading something because you don't get to do what you want to do, you might need to change your expectations. If you're miserable from fighting with your students or colleagues to do something a certain way, a better choice might be to let go and make the best of the current situation. You can look for new expectations based on different contexts, needs, and goals.

It's like how I had really looked forward to debating constitutional law with my high school student but then they were completely uninterested and shied away from combative discussions. Instead, we talked about a few Supreme Court cases that were especially relevant to high school students and spent our class time doing other things that were more engaging to them (like make a *Law and Order* video). It was still a rewarding experience, and by changing my expectations I didn't feel like I was being robbed of something I wanted.

I could have pushed for those constitutional law debates. I could have tried to force them. I could have threatened to take away points if my students didn't participate, but it wouldn't have worked. Even if I managed to coerce perfunctory discussion, it wouldn't have been enjoyable for the students or me or resulted in meaningful learning.

Another dream I had for my teaching life was to introduce drama and perform plays. I assumed it would be fun for everyone! My students are completely uninterested in learning lines and performing in front of the community. But, they are willing to film themselves when they can try something over and over and choose the best take.

They are also willing to perform silly routines at the school Christmas Program in a slightly anonymous way. If the lights are out and they have glow sticks taped on their bodies, they will dance. If their faces are hidden behind a screen and just their arms are showing behind a classmate's face, they would animatedly gesture. If they are wearing sunglasses, they feel better about lip syncing. The silliness factor lowers the pressure. If they mess up, it doesn't really matter because everybody is already laughing anyway. The darkness or screen or glasses allow them to feel slightly protected.

Our performances haven't been spectacular Broadway numbers or sophisticated choreographed dance routines, but they have been fun. The students get a rush from performing, and the community is always eager to see what we have planned for the next show.

I could have pushed the musical theater thing. I could have demanded after school practices. I could have expected the same focus as I put into my college productions. And, I could have shown up on performance night with absolutely no students to perform. Letting go of doing things a certain way opened me up to other possibilities. Changing my expectations was the key to making things enjoyable.

Of course, this strategy doesn't work for things you aren't willing to compromise on. Giving up on watching basketball games and changing how my classes perform for the Christmas Concert are not earth-shatteringly important and wouldn't be deal breakers when deciding whether I should remain in my Transplant Home. Those situations simply required a shift in expectations. There may be times when shifting expectations is not enough. It's up to you to carefully decide if a shift in expectations can make the difference.

Consideration: You're not happy.

If you're consistently unhappy in your Transplant Home, you need to examine why. We've talked about a lot of potential sources of unhappiness in the book so far.

Maybe you're frustrated with student behavior and achievement. If you're unsure how to change your teaching so students can be successful, try going back to chapters 18 and 19 and reexamine the things you can control in your classroom.

Maybe you're lonely or lacking local relationships. If you're not sure how to reach out and initiate relationships, go back to chapters 9 and 10 for suggestions on how to look for and take advantage of opportunities to interact and build connections.

Maybe you're regularly cranky, angry, critical. If you don't know how to shift your mindset to the positive and things you can control, try rereading chapter 22 about weeding out negative tendencies..

Maybe you are finding no joy or fulfillment in your work. If you don't know how to lift yourself out of that cycle of despair, try the things in chapters 5 and 20 to adjust your expectations and reach out to take advantage of the resources in your Transplant Home.

If you've tried all the suggestions (or are uninterested in trying the suggestions), and you're still unhappy in your Transplant Home, go get your happy on! If you need a social scene of dinner parties and dancing and nights out, find a place where that's possible. If you need art exhibits and Broadway musicals and lectures by the historical society, go where those happen. If you need full-service grocery stores or farmers markets or restaurants, there are places that have them. If you need access to an airport hub that allows easy connections to foreign destinations, find it. Nobody can decide that for you. You get to determine what you want out of life, and it's your responsibility to go after it. Life is about trade-offs. Decide what you're willing to trade and what you're not.

Note to Readers: If a Transplant Teacher truly feels like there is nothing worthwhile about their Transplant Home, it's probably better to leave. Your potential as a Transplant Teacher is intertwined with your attitude toward your community and surroundings. Choose to stay positively, or choose to go.

Consideration: Your needs aren't being met

We discussed meeting your needs in chapters 2, 13 and 23 and how generally you can meet those needs if you're willing to be flexible. But, there are some things you have less control over.

An obvious reason to leave would be if things are unsafe for you or your family. Maybe it's the living conditions. Maybe it's the neighborhood where you live. Maybe you've been threatened. You are responsible for making the decisions that are best for you and your family. Just like living anywhere, if it takes leaving to protect your family, then leave! It doesn't mean you've failed as a Transplant Teacher. It may mean that you need another environment to thrive.

Some teachers leave for medical reasons. They may not have access to the professionals and regular care they need to take care of themselves. They may have to travel often to medical facilities, something that's both expensive and a burden on their schools and classrooms.

You might also choose to relocate your family, even if physical safety and medical needs aren't a problem. Maybe your children haven't been well-received by their peers. Sometimes the dynamic in certain classes isn't conducive to newcomers. In a small school, there may be no other classes to switch into, and the same combination of kids is together year after year. Rather than struggle through it, you might choose to leave.

We monitor the dynamic in Kaitlyn and Levi's classes throughout the year. The classes aren't perfect. The kids aren't perfect. But, there's a generally good feeling in the class and a nice core of kids who like to learn and work hard. That's what we want. We are less concerned about little habits they pick up at school (annoying phrases, naughty words, etc.). Those can happen anywhere (I picked up swearing in third grade because the boys thought it was cool when we played tetherball). We correct the annoying or inappropriate behaviors at home and reinforce the words and behaviors we want to see.

But what if your kids aren't thriving academically? Maybe there aren't enough opportunities for support or enrichment. Maybe there's a discrepancy in ability levels. Maybe Little Jeremy and his/her teacher didn't have good chemistry, or maybe you expect the same problem with Jeremy and his future teacher (when there's only one teacher per grade, it's pretty easy to guess who the teacher will be next year…).

As long as Kaitlyn and Levi are making progress toward reading independently, acquiring grade-appropriate math skills, and improving their writing skills, we feel good. We also keep in mind that we can supplement instruction at home. It's not a problem for us to read books in the afternoons and evenings and push our kids to be more independent. We have handwriting books that they work on before they can play games in the mornings. Steve has a graduate degree in math education, so it wouldn't be a stretch for him to help our kids work on their math skills.

Like with the previous section on being happy, it's your responsibility to determine what you need and act accordingly. Some needs outrank others, and it's up to you to prioritize and meet them in your Transplant Home or somewhere else.

Consideration: Administration.

One of the oft-cited reasons for leaving a school is problems with the administration. Dealing with conflicting views of education, criticism that seems mean and unnecessary, and sometimes even incompetence can be rough. If you're considering relocating because of the school's administration, consider the following things.

Watch out for deficit thinking, shoulds, and extremes

Remember all the work we did around deficit thinking your students or coworkers? It's also true when dealing with administrators. Watch your thinking. If you're blaming your administrator's deficits for all of your problems, you might overlook more productive ways to deal with the situation. Your mindset might not fix the problem externally, but it can help you cope with the situation without draining your energy and poisoning your life. Reframe the deficit thoughts about your administrator the same way you reframe other deficit thoughts: acknowledge the reality without judgment and turn inward to focus on what you can do to deal with the reality.

Rein in your *shoulds*. Thinking, "My administrator *should* do this" can signal that you consider your way to be the *right* way. Just like when dealing with coworkers or students, replacing *should* with *I prefer* can soften things and remove some of the adversarial atmosphere.

Also look out for extreme thinking. Those keywords *always*, *never*, *none*, *every*, *nothing*, and *all* can mean you've slipped into exaggerated thinking. You don't want to make a difficult situation worse, or create a situation in the first place, by thinking in extremes. Take a minute to reflect on whether it really is *always*, *never*, etc.

Deficit thinking, *shoulds*, and extreme thinking can contribute to trouble with administrators. Consider if any of your reactions fall into this category when you're considering how your administration affects your Transplant Life.

Coping

Also remember that you can still be an effective teacher if the administration is dysfunctional. You can sit through staff meeting lectures on principles you disagree with and return to doing your job. You can shut your classroom door and control the world of your classroom.

You can respond to poor policies by working things out in a different way. If your principal sends misbehaving students back to class with fistfuls of licorice, you can start using classroom consequences instead of sending students to the office.

You can also look for other sources of support. Connect with likeminded colleagues and work together to reach kids and keep your classrooms or departments functioning, despite external forces.

You might be able to find another administrator, perhaps at a different level, that you can trust and talk to. Keep in mind that it's usually better to stay factual when discussing what's going on. "The principal gives teachers negative feedback in front of students" cannot be as easily dismissed as "The principal is mean and a jerk." "Quarter grades are changed after we submit them to raise athletes' GPAs" is more objective than "The principal's blatantly favoristic." Reduce the risk of your concerns coming across as an emotional overreaction.

Whether an administrator *should* be doing all the things they're doing is not the question. The question is, how you can be a professional and effective teacher regardless of what the administration is doing? Your administrator does not control how you act. You control how you act. Of course, if it gets to the point where you believe the administration is truly inhibiting your ability to be an effective teacher, even after your adaptations and mindset-shifting, it might be time to consider leaving.

I should also mention that you could encounter potential deal-breakers that might be reasons to relocate. Unreasonable expectations of added duty responsibilities could be a reason to leave. If administrators demand or require hours of unpaid recess, hallway, or detention duty that violates the terms of your contract or interferes with your life and family responsibilities, that deserves consideration. If you are regularly required to use your allotted preparation time to substitute for other staff members or do clerical work, that is worth serious consideration.

Don't mistake this as counsel to avoid doing anything outside the letter of your contract. There are worthy activities that benefit students and schools that require extra effort, but it's reasonable to set boundaries based on your contract commitments and your life outside of teaching. If you can't maintain your boundaries, you might consider leaving.

Of course, an administrator involved in illegal or unethical activities would be a very clear reason to leave, especially if you're pressured to support those activities.

By all means, consider the behavior of your administrator when deciding whether to stay or go, but also consider what you can control in how you react to those behaviors.

Consideration: Responsibilities, opportunities, and dreams

There are countless other factors to consider. Some teachers leave because of personal relationships. Teachers get married or engaged to someone from outside Alaska or someone who has no interest in living in a village. Some teachers have babies and want to be closer to their extended families. Some teachers can't find a compatible match in the limited dating pool, so they move somewhere with more options. We had a single teacher leave Brevig Mission to teach somewhere else. After she found her honey, she brought him back to Brevig Mission!

Other teachers have family responsibilities. A parent dies and they move back to take care of the other parent. A tragedy happens and they're needed for support. Grandchildren are born.

Some teachers leave for professional opportunities. Some get their administration licenses, and without an administration vacancy in their Transplant Home, they move somewhere else to be a principal or assistant principal. Some teachers relocate for an opportunity for their spouse that isn't a teacher. Some teachers relocate for a job opening that is more ideal than the grade or subject of their current position.

Some teachers leave to pursue a dream. They might get accepted to a PhD program. They might decide it's time to own some property and a home (something that's almost impossible in Brevig Mission). They might decide they want to open a board game store.

All of these things are worth considering when deciding to stay or go. It's up to Transplant Teachers to assess their goals and what they and their families need and to decide how their current work and community measures up.

There are many reasons a Transplant Teacher might choose to leave. It's kind of a complicated decision with lots of things to consider. I'm not suggesting that you jump ship the first time things get hard. If I had done that, I would have missed out on fifteen memorable years. Remember that days or weeks might be hard sometimes, but you have control of what you do.

It might be hard to tell the difference between things being hard and things being hard enough to consider moving on. I recommend taking time to make up your mind. Don't decide to leave after a bad day or horrific staff meeting. Think about the decision and what that would mean for your life. I still have days when I'm ready to throw in the towel and start over somewhere new, but after some time has passed and I get in a better rhythm, I remember why we've decided to stay.

Some teachers always seem to be on a quest for the next great school. They sign a contract in a new place and can't stop talking about how much better the new school will be because they do this or they have that. Maybe they have found the Shangri-La of teaching. Or maybe they'll settle into their new positions, discover the new school is just a place too and has its own set of problems.

Wherever you go as a teacher, you take yourself with you. Even halfway across the globe, you'll still have your attitudes, expectations, and classroom management skills. The same goes for struggles with infidelity, substance abuse, and unresolved mental health issues. A dramatic change in scenery does not make those go away. So include some introspection as you make your decision to see if what you're running away from is within.

The Alaska Bush isn't for everybody, and we want teachers that stay to be happy and satisfied with their work and their lives. That's true for locations across the world too. Make a thoughtful choice that's right for you.

Conclusion

When we came to Alaska in 2005, it took eight years to become vested in the retirement system (it's different now, so make sure you do some research about current benefits if you're thinking of making the move to Alaska. I don't want to accidentally misinform anybody). After surviving the first year, our goal became to put in eight years. It took a little longer than eight straight years because we each took a couple years off (not at the same time) when our kids were born. But, we eventually reached the point when both of us had put in our eight full years.

The contract season of 2016 was an important one for us. Every year prior we had evaluated if we wanted to stay or go, but this was the first time we made the decision after having met our retirement vesting goal. Do we stay or do we go? We had our eight years. No matter what we chose to do, we would qualify for a state retirement when we turned sixty-five. We'd gotten what we came for. So, was it time for us to leave?

These turning points are often an opportunity to take stock of everything that has happened leading up to that point. Looking back on our Transplant Life gave us a chance to reflect on all we'd done and been through. As much as it felt like we were in uncharted territory, our experiences were kind of typical. We were going through the phases of a Transplant Teacher.

Phases of a Transplant Teacher

Just like on any journey, there are waypoints on the Transplant Teacher Life. Alaska teachers go through a typical sequence of phases during their first year in the bush, a life cycle of sorts. It roughly follows similar models of the first year of teaching or the first year of marriage, but there are some Alaska Bush specific adaptations. (You may not be transplanting to the Alaska Bush, but the principles can apply to locations across the world.)

There are patterns and phases common to almost everyone on the same journey. The patterns and phases are not always obvious while you're in the middle of it all but become clear over time. If you don't know what the plant is supposed to look like at different stages, you don't know what's normal or what might turn into a big problem later on. Recognizing the phases can also be helpful as you realize you're not the first and only person to pass through what is sometimes awkward and uncomfortable.

The inward and outward approach will help you navigate the phases. Looking inward to change yourself and reaching outward to connect with others helps you emerge, not necessarily unscathed, but stronger and closer to thriving.

Let's look at how the phases can play out for Transplant Teachers in the Alaska Bush.

My Great Alaskan Adventure Phase

This is the initial excitement phase. Some teachers have always wanted to teach in Alaska. Others came up on a whim because it sounds exciting. Everything is new and different and seems so exotic. This phase is full of enthusiastic blog posts and Instagram pictures (or e-mails home if you arrived in Alaska in 2005 before Instagram was a thing) about their fascinating Transplant Home.

This fun phase started for me before we left for Shishmaref. Steve and I got married a few short months before we headed to Alaska. The receiving line at our wedding reception was full of people to tell the story to when they asked us what was next in life. I was excited to tell anyone and everyone about where we were headed. I describe the isolation and remoteness of Shishmaref, the living conditions, and everything I thought I knew about my future home.

When we landed in Shishmaref everything fascinated me. The whole island was covered in sand! The kids were adorable! There was a dead walrus on the beach outside our house! Everything was picture worthy and added to the collection of new stories.

The Transplant Teacher seedling is sprouting in the Adventure Phase. It's growing! There's so much to nourish it! You can't believe it popped up out of the soil from a tiny seed. It all seems miraculous. Your natural excitement and enthusiasm carry you through this phase.

What the Heck Did I Do? Phase

The wonder and amazement of the Great Adventure give way as reality sets in. The newness of the place is starting to wear off, and the challenges of the environment and classroom appear. The onset of this phase generally coincides with the first day of school. This phase can also be known as "I miss my Starbucks….." "Where did Target go?" or "I just want to eat out. One. More. Time."

In Shishmaref, the honeymoon wore off after a few weeks, and everything that seemed so interesting became irritating. The sand tracked across my floors and somehow ended up in my bed sheets. The adorably curious kids didn't respond the way I expected in class. The stench of the dead walrus assaulted my nostrils every time I walked outside.

I was lonely. I was homesick. I was realizing that teaching would be more of an adjustment than I anticipated.

The seedling has grown into the awkward teenage phase. It's still fragile at this point, and the roots aren't very deep. It needs tender care, so it doesn't get crushed from the strain of culture shock or homesickness.

Getting through this phase involves the outward strategy *Explore and Find Out More.* Instead of focusing on what is missing, you can find out what your new home offers. Armed with knowledge, you can go out and *Get Involved, Try Things, and Participate!* Don't assume you won't like any of the things available to do. Try new things and add new activities to your routine. This will put you in a position to reach out and *Make Connections a Little at a Time* (you know, using the tips from the Nurture the Seedling chapter. How convenient!).

Transplant Teachers probably won't find replacements for everything they miss about their lives before arriving, but they can find enough to combat the shock and homesickness that are typical of this phase.

This Place is Purgatory and Will Never Get Better Phase

What the Heck Did I Do can turn into Purgatory. This is the overwhelm phase. The multitude of challenges is now apparent and teachers realize that simple solutions won't solve complicated problems. Teachers can start to blame their Transplant Home for their difficulties, challenges, and maybe even misery.

They convince themselves that anybody would be miserable in their Transplant Home and that the problem is with everyone and everything else. Shock grows into the realization that this is a long-term situation (at least until the end of the school year), and the Transplant Teacher feels stuck (get it? stuck in purgatory?) with no escape and little hope.

This stage can be brought on by things going horribly wrong in the classroom. For me, this was my junior high students running outside in the middle of class to slide down the slide on the playground. Nothing in my teacher preparation coursework or student teaching prepared me for that. I was dumbfounded without any idea of what to do.

Transplant Teachers will know they are in this phase when their instinct is to blame everything around them for the difficulties they face. Things would be different if "the students would only _____" or "the parents did _____" or "the community stopped_____," etc. This phase can also be marked by lots of "shoulds." "The principal should…" "The other teachers should…" "The staff should…" "My students should…"

Some Transplant Teachers get stuck in the Purgatory Phase. Those teachers are negative for the rest of the year and are critical of their students, the school, and the community. When you go out looking for everything bad, that's what you find. I think they call it confirmation bias in the academic world. You pick out everything that confirms your opinion and ignore anything that challenges it.

Transplant Teachers stuck in the Purgatory Phase don't send their roots out to get nutrients. They essentially cut themselves off from the good available in their Transplant Home. They gradually become toxic. They constantly complain and blame everything and everyone else for their problems.

Purgatory is a great time to practice *Considering Different Perspectives*. The things that drive you crazy about your Transplant Home and everything you think the people around you should do is based on your perspective. Hopefully, by this point in the book this doesn't come as a newsflash to you, but there are different perspectives in the world. *Humility* will help you inwardly *Withhold Judgment* and avoid further entrenching yourself in Purgatory.

One way to pull yourself out of the Purgatory Phase is to *Stay Positive*, like the suggestion in the Nurture the Seedling and Deep Roots chapters. Not to sound like a stereotypical self-help blog or anything, but focusing on things to be grateful for is a powerful process because it helps you intentionally focus on the positive.

Two things I was continually grateful for in Shishmaref were sunrises and sunsets. They were beautiful, especially over the water. I haven't always been a morning person, so the number of sunrises I'd seen in my life was pretty small. Because there were sometimes only two hours of daylight during the winter, occasionally I could see the sunrise and the sunset on the same day in Shishmaref! Even tiny things like noticing beautiful sunrises and sunsets can be enough to lift the Purgatory Phase.

Another strategy is *Focus on What You Can Control.* Find something fun to do! Lesson planning and grading student work can take over your life. Getting up, working, coming home, working, and sleeping before doing it all over again can contribute to a feeling of being trapped in Purgatory. Carve out some time to do something that brings you joy. I like to paint and collage, and when I spend some time in my Art Journal, I feel better about everything.

You could try new recipes, take pictures, sew, play board games, read new books, learn a language, create silly videos to post online, or eat at new restaurants (that's not an option for me, but it might be in your Transplant Location). You might find hobbies specific to your Transplant Home. Look in chapter 7 for more inspiration.

Another strategy to deal with feeling stuck is to get outside. This might be more applicable to me since I live in a place surrounded by wide open spaces, but it might work in a crowded urban area too. If all you do is plan lessons and grade, you likely spend a lot of time inside. You go from your classroom to your house and back again. Breathing fresh air and taking time to enjoy outside gives you a break.

Things seem dark in Purgatory. Relief seems nowhere in sight. Sometimes it's a case of things getting worse before they get better or it's always darkest just before the dawn kind of thing. It might be normal to go through this phase for a while, but it doesn't have to last forever.

Survival Phase

The overwhelm and discouragement of the Purgatory Phase can give rise to the Survival Phase. Things aren't quite as dark as they were in Purgatory, but the Transplant Teacher is still a long way away from thriving. At this point, teachers try to hang on day by day. They've given up hope of success and fulfillment, and just put their heads down and try to get through it. During this phase I was consumed with what I would do the next day. Because of my lack of success in the classroom, it didn't seem to matter what I did. I just wanted activities to fill the time and minimize behavior problems.

You'll know you've reached the Survival Phase when you are consumed with getting through the day. You might have accepted that many things are outside of your control, you've grown tired of fighting against them, and you're just trying to survive.

You can level out of the Survival Phase by using some of the strategies offered throughout this book. Remember all that talk about Flexibility and Adaptation? Remember the pleas to *Focus on What You Can Control?* This is when it really matters. It can make the difference between slowly giving up and withering or pushing through toward vitality.

Try to make things work within your new reality. Use your energy on things you can control. *Ask for Help* when you need it. *Accept any Feedback* that comes your way and act on it. *Keep Making Connections* (with people, places, etc.) that might nourish you.

The Survival Phase is also the time to make sure your needs are being met. Not in an everyone-else-should-cater-to-me-and-what-I-want kind of way, but in an I'm-going-to-be-proactive-and-take-care-of-myself kind of way. It might take *Planning Ahead*. It might take asking around to find resources, but it's worth it to do more than just survive.

Transplant Teachers stuck in Survival Phase are in danger of withering away. Without roots deep enough to provide strength and nourishment, they won't be able to withstand the challenges of their Transplant Lives. They never reach a turning point where things start to get better, and it's exhausting to constantly fight for survival. Often these teachers don't stay for another year.

Okay, This Place Isn't So Bad Phase

Teachers who make it out of the survival phase generally move into the Okay, This Place Isn't So Bad Phase. My personal turning point was Christmas. I had hit rock bottom, but things looked up for a moment, which grew into more moments. The unexpectedly successful classroom experience I mentioned before (involving me and a broken broom) combined with the amazing cultural experiences over Christmas Break kept me from staying permanently stuck in negativity. As my trajectory changed, I started to look around me and notice that my Transplant Home was actually quite beautiful.

This phase is also marked by the Transplant Teacher's increasing acceptance that things are not the same as where they came from, and they might not understand how or why these things exist. Beyond just noticing the differences, Transplant Teachers start to realize that different is not necessarily bad, and they consider how they might operate in this environment. The acceptance and realizations happen inwardly as Transplant Teachers shift focus from what seems wrong and hard to what's interesting and possible.

Reaching outward is also important in this phase. Relationships can move beyond the surface and into deeper levels of trust. Teachers begin to feel comfortable seeking advice and open to receiving it and move beyond the instinct to run away and never come back.

Transplant Teachers that move into the This Place Isn't So Bad phase open themselves up to the sources of nourishment around them. They continue to *Make and Build on Connections a Little at a Time*. They continue to *Try Things* and *Participate* in events and activities. Their roots go deeper with every interaction. The deeper the roots go, the greater the chance for nourishment and support.

How Could I Make That Work? Phase

The next phase is How Could I Make That Work? This represents an upswing and movement toward positive possibilities. Armed with a better understanding of their communities and their students, Transplant Teachers start to act on the advice and examples of community members and veteran teachers (and learn to avoid the ones that are toxic). Their mindsets shift as they move past assumptions and adapt their approach in a manner more compatible with local norms. This might mean inviting local guest speakers into the classroom, making connections between the curriculum and life in the community, or even speaking with a gentler cadence the students are used to hearing.

As teachers experience more classroom success, they can reflect on possible reasons for the change. They might discover things that work really well in their classroom and do more of it. They might try things that spectacularly flop, but those can be instructive too as teachers find the commonalities and patterns that don't work.

The highlight of my journey through this phase was my involvement with Inupiaq Days. A few staff members got together in Spring 2006 to organize a week of cultural activities for the Kindergarteners through high schoolers at Shishmaref School. We wanted the kids to have fun learning and trying things with community members.

There were a million reasons it might not have worked. Imagine thousands of fuse beads, boxes of yarn skeins, and fabric everywhere. Imagine frozen seals in the locker rooms. Imagine countless schedules to coordinate, connections to make, and supplies to secure. We dealt with miscommunications and last-minute cancellations. But, we made it work.

That's how you know you're navigating through the How Could I Make That Work? Phase. You don't give up before you start. You don't offer a million reasons something won't work with your kids in your classroom at your school. You try something and adapt it.

The Transplant Teacher is stronger at this point. The deeper roots allow for growth. Things may not be easy. There are still difficulties and weeds to deal with, but the Transplant Teacher isn't as likely to be stunted by them.

Ready for More Phase

Transplant Teachers who fuel success with reflection and adaptation are Ready for More. They're starting to feel comfortable in their classrooms and communities. Things might not be perfect, but there's definitely less misery and more satisfaction than in earlier phases. They crave more success with their students, more connection with the community, and more understanding of everything. This is where we hope teachers arrive so that they want to return for another year.

I realized I was in this phase when I started thinking about what I could do the next year. I thought about how I could better organize Social Studies units. I thought about new activities I could try or old ones I could refine when I taught them again. I thought about what kind of presents I could bring up from the Lower 48 to put in people's bags during Christmas Week. I was ready for more.

This phase is when the Transplant Teacher blooms. All of their hard work and connections and adaptations start to pay off. Ready for More is a springboard for Thriving. You've made it through the shock and the awkwardness and the hopelessness and into a place of possibility and promise, and it's a time to renew your efforts as a Transplant Teacher and grow stronger.

Thriving Phase

The target for Transplant Teachers is the Thriving Phase. Thriving is feeling comfortable in and enjoying your Transplant Home. It's knowing you're effective in the classroom. It's being a part of things and learning more and more through relationships and experiences.

Reality check: thriving is not the start of an enlightened teaching existence in which you transcend all difficulties. It's not a final destination, and it can be something you move in and out of. I still have to put in serious work to cultivate my Transplant Life every day, even though it's a pretty good one.

Tastes of thriving are possible, even when you're wading through the other phases. I remember walking Steve's students home after a class party at our house in the fall of our first year. The night was dark and tiny ice crystals were falling down on us as we ran from house to house. The kids were laughing and didn't want to go home. Neither did I. In that moment, I knew I was right where I needed to be. I was enjoying our students. I was having fun. I was experiencing some of the fullness of my Transplant Home.

Remember, I was still in the crying-on-the-couch stage at this point, but this beautiful moment happened in the midst of it. Steve and I made an effort to engage with his students and build connections outside of school and got a tiny little payoff. Even without perfection the strategies can yield satisfaction and joy.

The truth is, thriving takes investment. I didn't frolic through the ice crystals on day one (it wouldn't have been ice crystals then anyway, it would have been grains of sand). The experience was born out of shared experience and relationship building with the kids in school. Similarly, you can't walk into a house, pick up a baby, and start visiting if it's the first time you're there. You won't get invited to go berry picking if your neighbors don't even know your name. You can't share with your friends if you haven't planned ahead to have enough food and supplies. You can't laugh at an inside joke if there's no joke to begin with.

Even if one hundred percent thriving isn't possible one hundred percent of the time, Transplant Teachers can apply the strategies in this book to experience it as often as possible. You get better results when doing the inward and outward work that connects you to your Transplant Home.

No matter where you are in the life cycle of a Transplant Teacher, if you look inward and outward, you'll move closer to the Thriving Phase. The advice is the same no matter where you are in the world: look inward to adapt and focus on what you control and reach outward to form meaningful connections and relationships.

Back to contract season 2016. We're solidly in the Ready for More Phase. The couple making the decision to stay or go were very different from the bright-eyed and bushy-tailed kids who came up to Alaska in 2005. We'd been teaching for almost a decade. We'd added two children to our family. We'd cycled through all of the Phases of a Transplant Teacher (and even came back and hit a few for a second round).

Sure, we were vested in the state retirement system, but there were a lot more things to think about. What about our kids and their extended families? What about the work we were doing in our classrooms? What about the grant I was working on? What about the community that had embraced us? What about all of the blessings that had nothing to do with our original financial goals, the kind of things you can't put a price tag on? Somehow, imperceptibly, the question had shifted from why would we stay to why would we go?

The lure of a retirement wasn't there anymore, but we didn't need it. We decided to stay on our own.

Don't get me wrong, our life in 2016 (or now, for that matter) wasn't an endless parade of blissful experiences. Brevig Mission isn't a perfect place, and we don't always rise perfectly to the challenges of living here. But, we decided to stay. After thinking long and hard, we decided the rewards of living here were worth the challenges.

When Kaitlyn's Inupiaq grandfather died unexpectedly in 2018, his funeral was a whirlwind of activity. There was the eulogy to write, the slideshow to edit, and the program to design and assemble. I helped the family with the preparations and was asked to do the scripture reading at the service.

I sang with the Brevig Mission Church Choir when songs were requested. Four members of the choir invited me to sing a hymn in Inupiaq with them as a small musical number during the service. It was a blessed moment. I was singing my heart out for my daughter's attaata (Inupiaq for grandfather), in a different language, and I felt comfortable. I knew the words, and I mostly knew the pronunciations. The fact that the choir members invited me indicated that they felt comfortable with me and my use of Inupiaq too. I felt integrated and unified with the community as we sang to honor this great man.

What a change from when I first attempted to perform an Inupiaq dance in Shishmaref. Those first attempts were awkward and had to be corrected. This time I knew what to do. I knew how to stand. I knew how to sing. I knew how to blend my voice with the voices of the other members. I knew how to perform appropriately in the Inupiaq manner.

I started off in Shishmaref as a young eager teacher, ready to share all of my knowledge and change the world. Instead, I allowed Shishmaref and Brevig Mission to teach and change me. I now know how to filet a halibut (even if I'm not very good at it). I feel more comfortable showing up at a house unannounced, taking my shoes off, and settling on the couch for a visit. I can adapt my teaching on the fly to account for snowstorms, Internet outages, and overwhelmingly sleepy students.

Over time, looking inward helped me examine my assumptions and consider alternate viewpoints. It helped me move past blame and focus on what I could control. It helped me accept the reality of my Transplant Home without knee-jerk judgment. I looked inward to change myself and was rewarded with an appreciation for all the beautiful traditions and people around me.

Looking outward helped reach out to those people and get to know them better. It prompted me to try things and participate even when I felt awkward or nervous. It expanded my opportunities to experience my Transplant Home and gain more understanding about how life works up here.

These strategies helped me put down roots that connected me to my family, my community, and my work. I grew into something quite different than I had originally imagined for myself, and it turns out that the journey has been about my growth all along. Your journey can be the same. A bountiful world awaits the Transplant Teacher willing to look inward and reach outward.

Acknowledgements

Thank you to Leslie Watts for the endless guidance and validation. This book is infinitely better because of you. Thank you to Ginger Crockett for the gentle feedback and inspiration. Important sections of this book grew out of conversations with you, and I'm grateful for your wisdom.

Thank you to Steve, Kaitlyn, Levi, and Ella for putting up with me hunched over my laptop and loving me anyway. You guys are my favorite. I love you more than this book, just in case there was any doubt.

About the Author

Angie Busch Alston is a teacher in Brevig Mission, Alaska. She writes about life, learning, and teaching in her Transplant Home. She is constantly humbled by the things she doesn't know how to do (like sew, butcher a moose, and pluck a goose in under forty-five minutes). She enjoys herding her three children through life and occasionally consents to play board games with her husband. Her online home is theAlaskaTeacher.com.

Made in the USA
Monee, IL
20 June 2024

60247211R00177